A DESTINY IN THE MAKING:

From Wall Street to Unicef in Africa

Boudewijn Mohr

Foreword by Sir Richard Jolly

Grosvenor House
Publishing Limited

All rights reserved
Copyright © Boudewijn Mohr, 2018

The right of Boudewijn Mohr to be identified as the author of this
work has been asserted in accordance with Section 78
of the Copyright, Designs and Patents Act 1988

Book cover illustration by George Butler
www.georgebutler.org
Book cover illustration is copyright to Boudewijn Mohr

This book is published by
Grosvenor House Publishing Ltd
Link House
140 The Broadway, Tolworth, Surrey, KT6 7HT.
www.grosvenorhousepublishing.co.uk

This book is sold subject to the conditions that it shall not, by way of
trade or otherwise, be lent, resold, hired out or otherwise circulated
without the author's or publisher's prior consent in any form of binding or
cover other than that in which it is published and
without a similar condition including this condition being imposed
on the subsequent purchaser.

A CIP record for this book
is available from the British Library

ISBN 978-1-78623-148-2

Part of the proceeds from every book go to the British charity
'Hands Up Foundation' (registered charity number 1156491).
The Foundation focuses on funding sustainable projects in health and
education, where possible inside Syria and run by Syrians. This includes
medical salaries and procuring prosthetic limbs.

"A singular figure in the two worlds of banking and then of the United Nations system, Boudewijn Mohr bracingly recalls his love affair with UNICEF. His engaging family weaves in and out of the narrative as do several iconic personalities about whom we come to care. We miss them all at the book's end. His powers of description are strong. This hard driven, lean and elegantly written volume will capture and maintain the attention of virtually any reader throughout."

David M. Malone
Rector of the United Nations University
Under Secretary-General of the United Nations
Tokyo, Japan

"A groundbreaking, inspirational book that will hook anyone working or thinking of working in the humanitarian sector, as well as those who love Africa. Using a personal, poetic and readable style that pays extraordinary attention to detail, Mohr candidly gives us an informative insight into the challenges and dilemmas faced in humanitarian work and the way top UN management decisions are taken within the context of momentous world events of that time. We meet people from all walks of life, from presidents to those working in remote communities, such as the sappers clearing landmines in Mozambique. We come to know his adventurous family, colleagues and friends. I loved the book and was sorry when I finished reading it!"

Ruth Ayisi
Former UNICEF staff member and journalist/consultant

"From Wall Street to remote villages in Africa is a human adventure and true UNICEF story. A must-read for business people interested in a humanitarian challenge, newcomers to the United Nations and all others who care about Africa."

J. Denis Bélisle
Former Executive Director
International Trade Center (UNCTAD-WTO)
and Assistant Secretary General of the United Nations

This book is dedicated to my parents
who made this life's journey possible -
through thick and thin
and unconditional love

"I want very much to set down my thoughts and my experiences of life. I want to do so now that I have come to middle age and now that my attitudes are all defined and my personal drama worked out. I feel that the toil of writing and reconsideration may help to clear and fix many things that remain a little uncertain in my thoughts because they have never been fully stated, and I want to discover any lurking inconsistencies and unsuspected gaps. And I have a story".

H.G. Wells,
'The Passionate Friends', 1913

Table of Contents

Foreword		xi
Introduction		xv
Chapter 1:	Take-off on assignment	1
Chapter 2:	Preparing a quantum leap	10
Chapter 3:	Retracing a banker's journey	27
Chapter 4:	First steps in Unicef	47
Chapter 5:	A glimpse of Unicef in the "field"	61
Chapter 6:	Sport Aid and the Race Against Time	85
Chapter 7:	Rise of the Unicef National Committees	102
Chapter 8:	Ghostbusters of West and Central Africa	150
Chapter 9:	"A luta continua"	206
Chapter 10:	De-mining: preparing the ground for development	249
Chapter 11:	Two pearls in the ocean	265
Chapter 12:	Towards an African Movement for Children	307
Epilogue		325
Annex:	References of sources	327
About the Author		329

Foreword by Sir Richard Jolly
Deputy Executive Director, Unicef (1982-1995)

What is it like to work for the United Nations?

Many probably imagine little more than an almost endless round of boring speeches, bureaucrats and governments discussing and disagreeing over long-standing conflicts with stalemate and few results. After all, this is so often what one reads about the UN in the newspapers. And it is true that this is a part of what takes place in the UN buildings in New York or Geneva.

However, such activities are only a small fraction of what the UN does. In contrast to debate in the Security Council and the General Assembly, most of the UN's work and most of the UN's staff - 80% or more – are engaged in things more practical, more positive and much less fraught. These include health, agriculture, education, culture, employment, technology, economic development with a focus on children, women and human concerns – and a multitude of other issues which countries want to pursue and which make up the agenda of what the UN calls development. In some of the worst trouble spots of the world, UN activities have to be more basic, providing immediate support for children, women and vulnerable communities caught up in the tragic consequences of violence and destruction. For all its difficulties, even this for the UN has its positive and humane side.

This honest and forthright memoir tells what working for the UN is like on the frontlines, in a range of different situations and different countries, large and small, poor and rich, many in Africa. Most unusually, the perspective is that of a banker, who after some 17 years of banking in money making Wall Street and later at the French Bank Société Générale decides to try something different and gets taken on by UNICEF, the UN Children's Fund.

Initially, there is caution on both sides, the banker wondering whether this is a good career move, UNICEF wondering what skills the banker can bring which would really be useful. But with emerging experience on both sides, the story becomes a love affair, the banker realizing that he now has the best job in his life, his wife, son and daughter discovering roles for themselves and UNICEF promoting the banker to ever more responsible positions.

There are bits in this fascinating story for everyone. Those wondering about what the UN actually does when working in Africa will find fascinating examples, with frustrations and failures as well as struggles and successes - and uplifting accounts of creativity and commitment by staff, national and international. Those who have worked for the UN, past and present, may recognize some of the names and situations as well as enjoying the well-told experiences. Everyone will find memorable anecdotes. Even some bankers, I hope, may be led to reconsider their daily preoccupations with money-making and wonder whether it is time for a change.

Boudewijn illuminates his story with colour and detail, enlivened by accounts from his diaries written at the time. Fortunately, he has not edited out frank comments and reactions about some of the less helpful colleagues or officials he has encountered on the way. All this makes for lively reading.

It is also a family memoir, with detail of how Annette, Boudewijn's wife, developed her own parallel interests and activities, with her anthropologist's eye for what also was going on and what local people were thinking and feeling. And their son, Nadim, when not away in school, joined in with his own activities which are recorded. Their daughter Vanessa followed her own multicultural track that included acting in the First All Children's Theatre of Manhattan and then sociology with study and research in London, Paris and Hanghzou, China.

At a time when it is in vogue to urge governments and non-profits to learn from international business and banking, Boudewijn

Mohr's insightful book offers a different lesson. It shows how much international business and the banking sector have to learn from the UN and NGOs – about motivation and commitment, about goals focused on human welfare rather than profit, and about broader approaches to efficiency and effectiveness.

The book is a great read –for a wide variety of readers, NGO workers in development, in the UN, people young and old, possibly even some bankers!

Introduction

This is first and foremost the story of a personal transformation in search of greater fulfilment in life. I am forever grateful to my mother who from 1971 kept our correspondence for almost 25 years. Without her, this book would never have been written. The story benefited also from the correspondence with my wife and children, who were often separated from me as a result of extensive travel. The impact that this transformation has had on them is extensively covered here through adventures they mostly created for themselves wherever they were. Finally, the story is set against the background of major historic events of the time.

The book paints the extremes of my two-hatted career. It gives an insight into life in banking in the downtown Manhattan of the seventies, the patriarchal style of David Rockefeller's Chase Manhattan Bank; sharply contrasted by a French-style banking environment of the 1980s. The other extreme was my transformation into an aid and development official of the United Nations. Once in Africa, I buried my former banker's hat fast, only towards the end to admit to unbelieving ears that, at one time, I had been a corporate banker in New York. My destiny developed slowly until it reached its full circle on that memorable day in New York in May 2002, when I left Unicef House on 44th Street for the last time.

The book identifies the triggers that readied me to take the leap into the unknown. First of all, there is no doubt in my mind that my MBA year at multicultural INSEAD[1] has been instrumental in seeking a world much larger than my own.[2] That was the first

---

[1] Promotion 1969.
[2] In my time courses were conducted in French, English or German, depending on the nationality of the professor; for example, Anglosaxon marketing, a subject rich in English words, was taught in German.

trigger (1969). When the INSEAD faculty invited me in 1999 to serve on a panel of "unusual careers" of INSEAD alumni, it was the right time to look back on that sea change in my professional life. I was close to retirement; and several friends began to urge me to write this book. They wanted to know why I had left an increasingly lucrative banking sector for aid and development.

Then as a corporate banker in New York, the sovereign debt crisis of Mexico in 1982 turned me away from the banking world for good – even before the idea of joining an international organisation came to mind. In feature articles for the renowned Dutch newspaper *NRC-Handelsblad* I gradually moved over to the side of the defaulting nations. That was the second trigger (1982).

Finally, after a six-week orientation trip through sub-Saharan Africa and Asia for Unicef to familiarise myself with its programmes in the field, I was bent on working one day for Unicef in West Africa. That was the third trigger (1986).

These then were the three hinges on my door to "a destiny in the making". Each hinge bears a name: INSEAD, Mexico and Unicef.

How was it that I had turned from pragmatist and realist into sentimental dreamer and idealist? If so, how did I survive that transformation? And why did it succeed? Were there lessons to be learned for others? Should the vast sums pumped into Africa not have achieved more for children? What was Unicef's take on that? And in general, was there any hope for Africa?

Even before joining Unicef, I realised that sub-Saharan Africa had made significant gains in health and education since independence. In fact, since 1960, child mortality rates had been dropping fast. In West Africa alone, U5MR dropped from 292 deaths per 1,000 live births to 183 by 1990. At independence very few Africans had formal education. The first national development policies began to prioritise programmes to significantly expand schooling. In the euphoria of independence, the literate volunteered to teach in adult literacy programmes in Mozambique and Tanzania. By 1980, millions of eligible children went to primary school. The question was whether this was sustainable, once donor funds would decline. At the same time, there was still a long way to go to realise the goal of "education for all".

There were also other, not so positive signs on the wall. By 1980, commodity prices in world markets were declining fast. Excessive population growth continued to undermine health and education targets, in spite of efforts of promoting birth spacing and other controls. War and civil conflict destroyed the little that had been achieved. Poverty was on the rise.

I was seduced by the grand initiatives of Unicef of that time. So much was going on all at once. It seemed that Unicef had woken up from another age. Jim Grant's Global Revolution on Child Survival seemed a way to force a breakthrough towards Alma Ata's goal of *"Health for All"* by the year 2000. Low-cost interventions in growth monitoring of under five year olds, oral rehydration therapy to fight diarrhoea, and breastfeeding to build up a baby's immune system, could potentially save millions of lives. Its tangible goal of immunisation for all children against communicable diseases by 1990 could well become the cutting edge for better health care all around.

An issue with which I felt a particular affinity was Sir Richard Jolly's crusade for structural adjustment programmes *with a human face*, to ease its heavy burden on the poor through social safety nets, while in no way denying the importance of economic growth. *AWHF* mirrored my own feelings about the injustice of excessive sovereign debt extended to developing nations by Western governments and banks, as promoted by the International Monetary Fund at the time.

Well, without further ado, off we go on our voyage. Are you coming with us?

Chapter 1: Take-off on assignment

At the heliport at 63rd Street the 'copter was already roaring its engines. Rotor blades were spinning ever faster for the 6 pm departure to JFK, just as we were running to make it. It was a clear day in early September 1985, such as only New York can give them. Blown away by the strong headwinds, four Unicef staff trailed this tall, rather fit and sprightly 63-year-old man. That was our Executive Director of Unicef, James P. Grant, sprinting right along with carry-on luggage slung over his left shoulder, as was his custom. I was one of them, on a mission to Warsaw for a meeting with the Unicef National Committees. I was thrilled: one of my law study electives in Leiden had been *The Political Process of Eastern Europe Going Communist*, but I had yet to set foot behind the Iron Curtain. I had taken this elective with an eye to taking the Foreign Service exam after getting my law degree. Although a new dawn seemed to be coming to the East, this was still the Cold War era. It was a most unusual beginning at Unicef for me, to be the new kid on the block, having been a Vice President of a major French bank in New York barely six weeks before.

At midday I had closed the door of our apartment at 111 East 80th Street for the last time. Before leaving the now empty place, I took my time to look the place over one more time. I imagined all the ghosts of those having passed through here during the past eight years and who were now going to enjoy their own farewell party after my departure, perhaps with some of them lingering on for the some hundred years more. I was utterly moved to leave New York and rather scared of the risk I had taken. I knew there was no return to the banking world possible. Banking stood at the dawn of rapid change. In two years' time I would be completely outdated and no one would hire me back. But at the same time I had no plans to return to that kind of life. It was a deliberate leap into the unknown.

This day was my fourth day at the United Nations Children's Fund. The first three had been devoted to attending a high-level strategic Retreat in the context of the Child Survival Revolution and social mobilization. I had been introduced as the new staff member who represented Geneva; no one else had come from that office. There were some 40 people, mostly top-level managers from Headquarters with several field staff from Africa, Asia and Latin America. As Unicef stood on the brink of a major leap forward, this Retreat was of extreme importance. The atmosphere seemed lively, youngish (even though several staff had already some 20, 30 years of service behind them) and people struck me as extremely motivated and engaged. After three days I had met and talked with almost everyone. To be locked up in a retreat where nobody could go home was a golden opportunity. In this way there were the relaxed and funny evenings, when socializing took the upper hand. I could not wish for a better introduction. I soon came to realize that it was Jim Grant who had swept them up from NGO type approaches to more global thinking, of which the Child Survival Revolution as he called it was to be the cutting edge. Unicef after all had been appointed as the United Nations lead agency for children on the occasion of the International Year of the Child, and so the idea was that we'd better live up to it and take this mandate very seriously. This was still the era of the pioneers, a time of unusual management without strict rules and regulations, but times were changing fast here too.

The venue for the Retreat was the Maurice Pate Center of Human Development in Danbury, Connecticut, a sprawling 100-acre property that the Pate family had donated to Unicef. Maurice Pate was the first Executive Director of Unicef. All the top brass of Unicef New York were there with several field people attending. The meeting was partially organised as a workshop, with working groups deliberating strategies for themes such as health, education and emergencies. I had of course nothing to offer in the discussions in my working group on health led by Fouad Kronfol, an affable Lebanese. Our group had been assigned a place in the garden, so I had ample time to stealthily take in the beauty of the

CHAPTER 1: TAKE-OFF ON ASSIGNMENT

rolling green hills of this magnificent property. At the end of the Retreat at the suggestion of Tarzi Vitachi, Deputy Executive Director for External Relations, Jim Grant and his deputies agreed that Mohr, as a former banker, should make a six-week round the world orientation trip to familiarize himself with Unicef Programmes. I felt that all eyes were upon me. This had never happened with a newcomer in Unicef. But as I was about to join the Programme Funding Office's arm in Geneva, this was considered a *sine qua non* for understanding Unicef's work and promoting it in order to raise funds. Now on my fourth day, other surprises were in store.

On take-off the 'copter first turned back to Manhattan before aiming for JKF. Nostalgia had already taken the better of me and I felt rather miserable to leave New York behind after 14 years. As a family, we had gotten the best from life in Manhattan. Here we had skied cross-country after big snow storms down Park Avenue, up Madison and crossing over into Central Park; here I walked our son Nadim to the French Lycée every day, playing football in the winter with a block of ice that functioned as ball until it was no more, once in a while stopping to look for quarters left behind in phone booths; this was where I fetched our daughter Vanessa from theatre class on the Upper West Side; and there, at the Children's Centre of the Metropolitan Museum, right around the corner from our apartment, Annette – A. for short in our little family – was doing art with children, including our Vanessa and her little brother Nadim.

Far in the distance I spotted the ferry to Staten Island and the Statue of Liberty, thinking how many times had I made the crossing with Chase Manhattan colleagues during the one-hour lunch break. While still circling above my old town this was too much to take. Allegra Morelli, Unicef focal point for non-governmental organizations, must have seen or felt something: "you'll be back," she consoled me. But no longer would we live at "one-eleven" as we called our home at 111 East 80th Street. If ever we did come back things would never be the same. With a sharp curve the 'copter suddenly swung sideways turning in the direction of JFK, crossing Long Island Sound, Queens and Brooklyn. Not too many memories here. Meanwhile, the colleagues of the Greeting Cards division were asking themselves what we are going to do in Warsaw. They decided on sightseeing first thing Monday. Then, one of them adding mockingly: "the rest of the meeting is to brief Boudewijn Mohr".

We are fetched from Warsaw airport by a Polish government official plus some staff from the committee. In the bus the discussion is about the weather, a convenient topic given the oppressive circumstances here. It is the first of September, a Sunday and everyone is out on this splendid sunny day. I take a stroll through the old centre. Cars seem to be mostly Ladas and Trabants, the latter a highly polluting midget car with a two-stroke engine like a motorbike and going by the affectionate nickname of "Trabbi". Young well-dressed people in casual jeans with a Western look, wanting to be seen. At Castle Square the statue of King Sigismund III, still revered as a hero by many Poles, a favourite gathering place for young Poles. It was this king who briefly invaded Russia and held Moscow during 1610–12. Sitting on the steps of the monument is strictly forbidden but the people still do it as some kind of a still protest. I witnessed two young men being shoved into a police car that then speeds off into the distance as if they had had the catch of the day. A nearby church was packed with people of all ages praying, even without a service going on.

For all that week, this was the nearest I would come to real Poles. The next day was opening day with official speeches by Jim Grant and government officials. Clearly the Unicef Committee plays a minor role here, I thought. One Pole insisted that in its immunization drive Unicef should not lose track of a country's culture. How little could we foresee then the resistance of some of the traditional leaders in northern Nigeria against polio vaccination that threatened losing the goal of polio elimination.

Meanwhile I begin to wonder about the strength or influence of the Polish Committee in the context of Poland itself. Little or no mention is made of its work and aspirations. In the evening we attend a performance of the Children's Theatre *Gaweda*[3]. I cannot help thinking back to Meridee Stein's First All Children's Theatre in New York where Vanessa performed in many a musical from when she was eight. Here the musical performance is *Les enfants modèles*, based on the book of Paul Thorez, son of the long-time communist leader of France, Maurice Thorez. The story is about the model summer holiday camp in Artek (Crimea) for the young communist elite from all over the world, where young Thorez spent several educational holidays. Good for youth re-education and global networking. Here in Poland, communist propaganda is all around us. Two hundred children are dancing and running on the stage, with mouths moving to imitate the pre-recorded music blaring out of gigantic speakers as if to make sure we hear it all right. Such hard work just to get to this level of performance with perhaps little time left to be a child. There is some very good professional dancing indeed: the Slavic dance between a boy and a girl; the "carousel" dance (a boy in the middle tied to eight girls moving in a circle); and the "Charleston" are exquisitely performed.

The following day we listen to the daughter of Dr Ludwik Rajhman, the Polish doctor, who tells the history of Unicef and the role her father had played to make it all happen. Dr Rajhman, a former senior health official at the League of Nations, was a pioneer for children's well-being, in particular health and nutrition. Although the expression does not seem to have been used at that time, he was the first to realize that children have special needs; and that, as such, children should be a special target group in public health, which a United Nations Fund for children could best address. Rajhman was executive secretary of a committee defining Unicef's mandate; diligently allied himself with and made use of the long experience of the US Federal Agency the Children's Bureau founded in 1912; and lobbied to obtain credible funding from left over UNRRA funds and the US government to start operating from the ground running.

---

[3] Tale.

On 19 December 1946, eight days after the birth of Unicef, Dr Rahjman was appointed chairman of the Board. Shortly afterwards UN Secretary-General Trygve Lie appointed Rahjman's friend Maurice Pate Executive Director. Maggie Black, in *The Children and the Nations* vividly recalls these heady days around the birth and first weeks in the life of Unicef and Pate's years at the helm. When the Norwegian Committee for Unicef proposed the Executive Director in 1960 for the Nobel Peace prize, Pate suggested in true fashion that Unicef be nominated instead. Unicef received the prize in 1965, but Pate did not live to see it.

During coffee breaks I move around among the delegates as if I am at a diplomatic cocktail reception trying to meet as many people as I possibly could. Then back to plenary, speech after speech again, truly a training session in listening. I meet Canon Joseph Moerman, a Belgian, who is credited with the idea of the UN International Year of the Child (realised in 1979). Moerman lends me a gramophone record of the *Gaweda* group to record at home for my children. I tell him it could be weeks before he sees this record again. He does not seem to mind. At least he does not have to carry the vinyl record all the way back to Geneva. The Canon is all smiles: yesterday he received the "Order of the Smile", a Unicef award for services to children. Somehow our conversation moves to my family background. Moerman knows Bremen and says the town hall of Bremen has a wine cellar hundreds of years old. My great-great grandfather Carl Friedrich Gottfried Mohr, who was mayor of the *Hansestadt* from 1864 to 1867 and again in 1871, must surely have made good use of it!

Finally the Committees are getting the floor. The Polish and Portuguese delegates give an exposé on the situation of children in their countries. Street children are a problem in Portugal and Italy, the latter suffering earthquake related emergencies. The French Committee has provided some direct funding to poor Portuguese children, which it is not supposed to do, as all funds raised by Committees must transit through Unicef New York. Lucjan Wolniewicz, Executive Secretary of the Polish Committee looks and speaks like a Parisian. He regrets not having stayed in France after finishing his studies. In private, Lucien is fiercely anti-communist. A film is shown narrating now almost 40 years of Unicef history. At the coffee break I meet John Charnow, who knew Dr Rahjman during his time at the US State Department and joined Unicef as a young staffer at its creation. Charnow is in charge of researching the history of Unicef that will be published in 1986.

The next day is excursion day. We are going to a monument for children fallen in the Second World War and to a children's hospital. In the minibus I settle down next to the Bulgarian delegate. This entire trip I seek out colleagues from East Europe, as I am keenly interested to know how people live under communism. As the driver burns a red light, I remark that he drives like a Frenchman. I ask him, *"si les Bulgares respectent un feu rouge"*. And he answers: *"Bien sûr, nous respectons tout ce qui est rouge"*... wry humour which you can expect a lot of in a communist country. I read enough Kundera to know that. The hospital is a fifteen minute ride out of town, giving us a glimpse of the other Warsaw: Soviet style drab grey blocks of flats, food stores looking like shacks, with long, long lines of people waiting patiently. Everything is grey now, people, buildings, and sky. Even the mood is a little sombre. In the hospital we visit the cardiology department. The all-important computer without which *rien ne va plus* has broken down, no date given. "American equipment", the guide explains with some glee. But the truth is, I am told, that Poland has trouble procuring spare parts from America because of suffocating foreign exchange controls. Just this morning the Polish news agency PAP reports that relations with the United States are excessively bad.

The Unicef visit has some good press coverage, not in the least as a result of a brilliant exposé by Dr Stephen Joseph, Unicef senior health adviser. Suave and urbane American, Joseph makes the full immunization pitch, explaining with the help of mortality and morbidity charts why all children should be immunized against preventable communicable diseases. "Keeping children alive who later will die anyway," retorts Christopher Cooper, the young West German delegate, insisting Unicef must concentrate on programmes that will last for those who will live. A crash immunization programme, if not sustained, would lead to catastrophic epidemics. I thought of A. who had already warned of this in a discussion this summer at our farm in Upstate New York. Not for nothing do I call her sometimes our wise old owl. After the plenary, Uffe König, Director of the Geneva office, calls a meeting of his staff. König, a rather scruffy Dane and one of Grant's "boys", strikes me as nervous and insecure. This meeting seems more like a free-for-all rather than a structured approach to deciding on a division of tasks, daily assessment of the meeting so far and strategies for running this meeting the next day.

In the hallway the newly acquired friend from the Rumanian Committee, Mihai, invites a couple of us to come and have a glass of *tuica*[4] in his room. Most leave after one glass but the French delegate and I linger on to know more. Mihai knows Artek, a resort on the Black Sea; he has spent summer holidays there. "Too politicized," he says. I look around if the Rumanian government official, who follows Mihai around like a dog, is around to hear this. We are in luck, he is not. Then I mention Paul Thorez and the musical show based on his book *"les enfants modèles"* we saw the night before. I put forward that the son of communist leader Maurice Thorez also had doubts about this camp. No reaction from Mihai, who refused to be drawn out into risky territory. Mihai shows us photos of a similar children's camp in his country. It seems definitely more fun there than at the Soviet-style Artek camp. The doctor from Bulgaria tells me he has been waiting to get a Lada for eight years now. He has the money ready but has been told to wait some more. He clearly does not belong to what Milovan Djilas has labelled the "New Class".

On the last day I am invited to attend a luncheon with the Cuban Vice Minister of Health. Cuba has sent doctors and nurses to

---

[4] The Rumanian version of slivovitch.

CHAPTER 1: TAKE-OFF ON ASSIGNMENT

some 23 countries as their contribution to development. Later in Africa I would encounter several of them, very committed but more often than not having to face broken equipment and long lasting stock-outs of vaccines and medicines. In the evening the Committee offers a farewell dinner. Although Poles are known for their hospitality, I am not looking forward to yet another meal of potatoes, salty dried out salmon and tough meat. Naturally this points to food shortages the country is facing. I am told that sometimes Unicef picks up the bill. I am not surprised given the circumstances here. The hotel bar that could have helped us to wash away the food is closing on us just as the dinner ends. On saying our goodbyes some delegates say they are interested in A.'s work with children at the Metropolitan Museum and hope that she will once come and talk about it.

Early in the morning, the Swiss Air plane takes off in a hurried ascent. I am thinking, after the culinary experience in Warsaw, the sooner they serve a Swiss breakfast the better. Suddenly the green manicured hills dotted with little villages appear under a clear sky. Switzerland, home sweet new home, my first and who knows perhaps my last duty station at Unicef.

I had no clue what to expect, no plan to base myself on. It all sounded good but was it? Was I going to fit in, make the transition from New York banker to development specialist? This was a hard call indeed.

Chapter 2: Preparing a quantum leap

On a clear day in May 1985, I had slipped out of Société Générale's Rockefeller Plaza branch, well before my lunch break, half running as if I had to catch a train, destination the United Nations sculpture garden. I had been there many times for a stealthy brown-bag lunch with friends and colleagues – eating and drinking was strictly forbidden in the gardens. But this time I needed enough time to go over my notes, to reduce my points to just a few and then learn them by heart. Adriana Vink, senior secretary at Unicef, had phoned me that morning to say that my interview was allotted 30 minutes – she had gotten hold of Grant's programme of the day. I knew I needed to be brief and to the point. Armed with a Fanta and sandwiches from *Au Bon Pain* in my pockets I settled down on a wooden bench near a statue given by one of the member states. I had chosen the spot carefully days before: away from the beaten track, under a pine tree and with a view of the East River for a Zen mindset and mysterious calm. For almost two hours I remained there, sometimes stretching my legs and strolling to the edge of the river to watch the boats gliding by. The hours passed in no time at all. Finally I started walking very slowly to 48th Street and First Avenue where Unicef had its offices at the time. Taking the elevator to the sixth floor, I settled down on a simple sofa in a sparsely furnished reception area, rehearsing my answer to the one question I thoroughly expected Grant to ask: Why Unicef?

Just weeks before I had called Geb Ringnalda at the Ministry of Foreign Affairs in The Hague, who I had befriended in New York, when he was *"gevolmachtigd minister"* (minister plenipotentiary) at the Dutch Permanent Mission at the United Nations. Geb had been trying for a while to get me a senior post at an international organisation. Now he was number three at the Ministry and still focal point for relations with the UN. I said, "Geb, I think I will

CHAPTER 2: PREPARING A QUANTUM LEAP

not pursue this Unicef idea anymore, it's been nine months now; my banking career has recently taken off again, so maybe I should just stay with that," but he retorted: "no, no, I will call Jim Grant and I get you an interview with him," and adding, after a brief pause, as if selling this idea to me: "you both will hit it off very well".

Geb knew Grant well from Unicef Board meetings when the latter was doing a hard sell of a Global Child Survival Revolution, got into a fair amount of trouble for it, but pursued this idea against all odds. Among Unicef colleagues there was a great amount of scepticism and success was not possible without winning over the naysayers. In hindsight I now believe that the two men had something in common: none of them taking no for an answer. A few days later Geb called back with the news: "22nd of May at half past two". Only two weeks left to prepare!

Geb Ringnalda was a rather unconventional diplomat. A Frisian, he was a straightforward man. He struck me as a bon vivant, someone who loves life. He had been one of the founders of D66, at first a centrist political grouping with innovative ideas for a better and more just society in Holland. It had been the subject of intense debate inside D66 whether the movement should become a political party, which in the end it did. Ringnalda told me that he had been one of those against this idea, thinking that more could be achieved by staying outside the political system itself.

D66 was not alone in rethinking Dutch society. The sixties were a time of huge social change. The radical Provo's, anarchists provoked against established socio-cultural values, in particular the strong "pillarization" of Dutch society and the monarchy. A. and I had started our married life in Amsterdam in 1966, moving into a house on the Eglantiersgracht in the Jordaan neighbourhood. With much shuffling of chairs and the sound of voices above us, we found out that the Provo's held their late night meetings right above our heads! The Provo's were best known for their "white bicycle plan", white bikes that one would find in Amsterdam without a lock and free for everyone to use and then leave somewhere after usage. One of the goals was to rid the inner centre of carbon dioxide pollution. They already warned against the health risks of cigarette smoking. Although little talked about in France, the Provo's were way ahead of the May 1968 student movement. The Provo's dissolved themselves soon after having concluded that they had made their point.

In 1985 the Netherlands was vastly under-represented in international organisations in comparison with the level of its contributions. Other major donor countries were in effect far more vocal on this than my own country and Ringnalda wanted to correct that. At first he sent me to the OECD in Paris. I passed the first hurdle, was put on a roster and asked to apply after six months for a post in its banking department, which tracks the well-being of member banks and the banking environment in member states. Next came an interview with the United Nations Commission on Transnational Corporations. UNCTC's mandate was to offer advisory services, technical assistance and capacity building to developing countries, to harness investment by transnational corporations and thus accelerate development. The interview resulted in an instant offer, which was to be for only one year because of a lack of funding. Red lights flashed and I declined. Many years later UNCTC was absorbed within the United Nations Conference on Trade and Development (UNCTAD) in Geneva, a forum on international trade issues whose objective was to make developing countries and countries in transition equitably integrated into the global economy through capacity building. There must surely have been some duplication of mandate here, so the merger seemed logical.

Geb Ringnalda was tenacious and simply did not give up. In 1984, he put forward my candidacy at Unicef for the post of Deputy Director of its Programme Funding Office, responsible for funding relations with governments and private sector. Geb said that Grant wanted to attract some candidates from the private sector to help professionalize management and operations. Grant wanted the National Committees for Unicef to expand beyond just greeting cards and direct mail, and raise funds with corporations.

CHAPTER 2: PREPARING A QUANTUM LEAP

Although an inside candidate was selected for that post, it triggered a series of interviews with the Division of Personnel that lasted many months. I met three times with Steve Jarrett, a young, affable and soft-spoken Englishman. Jarrett was the only Human Resources Officer I got to see. In hindsight I now think that that was just as well! Would there have been the same chemistry with someone else? Although these meetings did not identify any posts, they helped me enormously in understanding the mandate, the issues and the organisation of Unicef.

As soon as I learned of the interview with Grant I called Adriana Vink. I had met her at a buffet dinner at the home of Henk Gajentaan, who had succeeded Geb as the number two of the Mission. Gajentaan was another co-founder of D66. Since that dinner, Adriana and I regularly had lunch together in a self-service cafeteria near the UN when she would be telling me what was going on in Unicef. She also thought that I would hit it off well with Grant. That made two, and although I was rather reassured by this I certainly did not stare myself blind on it. Another regular luncheon companion was Dirk Salomons, an old-fashioned looking type straight out of a 19th century novel, who briefed me on political and legal issues he dealt with at the UN Secretariat. This time around, these briefings had to be stepped up, coupled with extensive homework.

I began to read up on all the hot issues of Unicef, and there was a bunch going on: Jim Grant's "Child Survival Revolution", with its focus on immunisation; Richard Jolly's Structural Adjustment Programmes *"with a human face"*, the trend towards advocacy and mobilisation of societies for child survival which Unicef called "social mobilisation"; the growing importance of National Committees in fundraising, development education and collaboration with the private sector; and the all-important drive for far more reliable data on children. An important step in that direction was Unicef's flagship publication the *State of the World's Children Report*, the brainchild of Peter Adamson and Jim Grant. Its 1982–83 publication reported on the Child Survival Revolution and how this could prevent millions child deaths per year through simple interventions: it was now increasingly feasible to immunise all children against measles, diphtheria, tetanus, whooping cough, poliomyelitis, and tuberculosis, a WHO goal to be achieved by 1990. These six diseases killed an estimated five million children a year in the developing world and accounted for approximately one third of all child deaths. Tetanus alone was responsible for a million child deaths a year. Whooping cough for another 600,000.

Adriana explained that it was Jon Rohde, Grant's close friend and adviser on health issues, who convinced Grant that the goal of *Health for All by the year 2000* established at Alma Ata in 1978 was far too large to focus on. He advised to just focus on a few interventions. The Child Survival Revolution thus came to be pinned on "GOBI". I gaped: "On what? GOBY???" And I burst out in laughter. "No", she said, "with an I". I found it hard for any marketing pitch to go with such a rather strange acronym. Adriana laughed heartily with me. We simply cracked up at something extremely serious, and that made it even funnier! The acronym in effect stood for several low-cost interventions that could successfully combat child mortality. The sequence seemed wholly artificial to me as it seemed to accommodate the acronym and that, in my mind, seemed a totally wrong strategy. Adriana assured me that I was not alone in this. Some had joked it could confuse with Mongolia's desert. Others pointed out that GOBI meant cabbage in Hindi.

Adam Fifield[5] tells how this acronym was born. In September 1982 Grant called a weekend meeting at the Unicef offices at which several outside experts had been invited to discuss the global revolution for child survival. At one point a WHO colleague who had remained rather silent until then, scribbled GOBI on a piece of paper and passed it to Jim Grant, who jumped at the idea: Growth Monitoring, Oral Rehydration Therapy,

---

[5] *"A Mighty Purpose: how Jim Grant sold the world on saving its children"*, Adam Fifield, Other Press, New York.

CHAPTER 2: PREPARING A QUANTUM LEAP

Breastfeeding, Immunisation! Bingo! But by the time I was hired, the acronym had almost outlived its days: universal immunisation of children had become the "cutting edge" (Jim Grant's words I believe) of the GOBI strategy. Grant made ORT famous by pulling out of the side pocket of his jacket a tiny sachet containing salts to stop dehydration as an illustrative tool of a particularly low-cost intervention that saved lives of millions of children.

At this time Unicef programmes were beginning to focus on women's health without which the child of course had little chance to survive. Over time Grant was persuaded to add three low-cost interventions to GOBI: food supplementation, female education and family spacing making for an even more unwieldy acronym, GOBI-FFF. Now one staff member reportedly joked that the three F's stand for the four-letter word three times over. With the renewal of the commitment to reach universal immunisation of all children, the acronym was discreetly dropped. But all GOBI-FFF interventions remained very much an integral part of what became the Child Survival and Development Revolution.

Another hot topic for Unicef was the global economic trend towards structural adjustment of that time. The world was facing the deepest global recession since the 1930s and alarm bells were ringing in Unicef, as these SAP's did not at all build in measures to protect the well-being of vulnerable children. Unicef commissioned a study on *The Impact of World Recession on Children*, carried out under the leadership of Richard Jolly and Andrea Cornia and published in 1984. The study was a watershed in development circles. Although it acknowledged the need for economic structural adjustment, it makes the point that this should not be to the detriment of child survival. Through statistical data the study proved its point that vulnerability increases, if adjustment programmes do not have a strong component for protecting child health and survival, development and protection. As such, Unicef created yet another global movement, promoting *"Adjustment with a Human Face"* and Unicef was leading it, once again. Few could foresee its long-term effect in that today's poverty reduction strategies of governments the world over now include an ever stronger social protection pillar benefiting the most vulnerable children.

Another key development was the adoption, by WHO, of the code on marketing infant formula that bans the advertising of formula to health centres. The code was an excellent tool to promote breastfeeding, but there was a glitch, because Grant was walking a tightrope: on the one hand the code specifically targeted Nestlé, a powerful multinational company, and this could potentially upset other companies with which Grant wished to nurture ties. In Unicef proper, business had been a dirty word. Union Carbide with its Bhopal disaster was another case in point. At the same time WHO and Unicef were trying to pressure the drug companies to lower their prices of vaccines through joint procurement arrangements and aggressive advocacy. Jim Grant needed the private sector to fund his Child Survival Revolution, but not at all cost.

Armed with this knowledge acquired through Adriana's briefings I was led into Grant's office by Mary Cahill, his personal assistant. It was a corner office with a wide view on the East River, rather light, spacious but simply furnished – a far cry from the environment of a senior New York banker. There was a large round wooden table of a light natural colour at which two men were sitting opposite from each other. I recognised Grant from photos of course. The big man rose up from his seat on the left side at the table taking my hand in a firm grip. What struck me was Grant's sheer presence. Taller than my six feet, he seemed to tower over you. He was wearing a grey summer suit that hung a bit loosely on his big frame. His face was deeply lined with blue, intensely observing eyes. I could feel that here stood before me a man with a mission, intense, driven and in a hurry. A powerful presence radiating something big. Then I turned to the young man who was getting up from his position on the right. What a pleasant surprise to see Steve Jarrett back again! He and I were beginning to know each other rather well. Steve's soft British demeanour put me at ease at once. My place was in between these two men and the interview began.

CHAPTER 2: PREPARING A QUANTUM LEAP

I started to tell him about my life in the French-American business community as a Vice President of Société Générale. I was already well connected with French business since my days at Chase Manhattan Bank Headquarters in downtown Manhattan. In the late sixties and early seventies French direct investment in the United States was catching up fast with the Dutch and the British who were far out in front. My job was business development with French-owned businesses in the US, later expanded to developing relations with other European companies. Within six years, the branch had become a multi-billion dollar business. But life at the bank had become too routine for me.

After some 17 years in banking altogether spent between Amsterdam, London and New York, it was time for me to leave the profession. At around that time, the Dutch government had asked me to be one of their candidates for an international organisation where my profile could fit. The Ministry of Foreign Affairs had long been complaining that representation of their nationals at the UN was far below what it should be in relation to the Netherlands' contribution. I knew of course full well that Grant was aware of the Dutch complaining about this, pestered as he was by the Italian government to hire Italians in big numbers after a one hundred million dollars contribution for immunisation. I thought I heard Geb Ringnalda whisper, "well done". To top it all off I mentioned in passing that I had already had interviews with the OECD and the UNCTC.

And then the key question came: "Why Unicef?" And I replied: "it is the culmination of a life lived so far". From there I began to explain how my life had reached that decisive point at which total change, even a leap into the unknown, had become totally normal for me. To reach that point of culmination, certain influences and events had triggered this state of mind. I could relate three or four specific milestones that would remain with me forever. The first one was the sovereign debt collapse of Mexico. Although this was not my area of lending responsibility at all, I somehow began to be keenly interested. For me the most striking aspect was the patronising role of the International Monetary Fund that pressured commercial banks to lend ever more to countries that were effectively already in default. I also wondered out loud about the quality of oversight at Central Banking institutions of the industrialised countries. Dr Witteveen, a former IMF Director, had once argued that soon the world would need a "world central bank", a global oversight institution for all Central Banks. When Mexico defaulted in 1982, effectively suffocating on excessive debts, its ultimate demise should have been fairly straightforward to foresee. However, in spite of their dwindling net worth as a result of massive provisions, commercial banks were pushed into making more loans. This was quite in line with the opinion of the US Secretary of the Treasury who was on record saying that banks needed the higher profits to offset the increased provisions for defaults on loans. *Ergo*, more loans! Our branch already had built up considerable exposure to Latin America, when I began to follow things with great curiosity.

Then I felt that it would be just tantalisingly challenging to write about it; and that started with writing my first feature article that was published in the Dutch newspaper *NRC-Handelsblad*. It was called *"Sovereign lending: towards a new world order"*. Its main ideas I had outlined in a letter to the Editor of the *Economist*, who published it. More articles followed in rather quick succession. In the process I wondered out loud, how come that these banks did not realise that debtor nations could never have been expected to absorb these inordinate and unmanageable levels of debt. I went on to say that in these articles I suggested several possible solutions to solve the sovereign lending crisis – in particular in relation to Africa. Grant urged me on to give details. I could feel that *Adjustment with a Human Face* was already on his mind.

I told him that one proposal was to transfer all sovereign loans to the IMF after a phased in write-off of unrecoverable loans, with the IMF then becoming the sole lender of sovereign debt with access to international money markets. Naturally, the IMF staff would have to be beefed up with qualified international banking personnel from the major foreign banks. Commercial banks would return to what they do best: lend to commercial and industrial enterprises in the private sector. Another idea was to couple balance of payments debt servicing to a percentage surcharge on the price of imports of raw materials self-imposed by industrialised nations, the proceeds of which would go into a fund lodged at the respective Central Bank to repay outstanding debt owed by the exporting developing nations. The surcharge, a highly unusual measure I admitted, could perhaps be seen as recognition of the undeniable contribution by the developing world to the West's own industrialisation and development! These were the days of a million and one ideas and proposals made to increase liquidity in the developing world and thus accelerate their development. For example, two consultants at UNCTAD proposed that the gold holdings at the IMF, no longer used for transactions between member states since 1975, should become a fund for development, replenished by gradually selling off its gold holdings in the market.

I pointed out that in the Mexico debt restructuring the IMF and Western governments had a greater involvement than ever before in spite of the fact that the majority of debt was held by commercial banks. Rather than debt relief, it was suggested that Mexico should improve its balance of payments. But if there was going to be any debt relief, then as a quid pro quo, trade links with the West were to be strengthened, which would then have the effect of benefiting employment in the industrialised nations. Simultaneously, developing countries would never solve the balance of payment deficits! When the population of São Paolo took to the streets blaming the IMF for their misfortunes, it was a sign of how sociopolitical the international debt issue had become. At that point of the interview *Adjustment with a Human Face* crossed my mind in a flash, thinking how timely it had arrived on the scene. And I mentioned it in passing.

I said I was especially concerned by the sovereign debt on the African continent. In some countries debt service represented well over half of the national income. I maintained that these countries were unable to get a fair price for their commodities in a fast declining market, unable to service the debt, and certainly unable to get more loans. But some African nations had taken their fate in their own hands: social unrest had led Zambia to abandon an agreement with the IMF. Côte d'Ivoire had temporarily suspended all debt instalments. With Africa's foreign debt at over 100 billion dollars, which represented just 10% of the entire developing world's debt, I began to argue for substantial debt forgiveness. I pointed out to Grant that I began to realise that a profound change was taking place inside me: I was taking the side of the indebted developing countries. I had essentially moved away from banking to the "other side".

But there were more triggers than sovereign debt alone that changed me. It had to do with my family. They knew for a long time that banking was not for me. An avid reader of Ayn Rand, A. declared herself ready to stand behind me and whatever I wanted to do in life as long as I quit banking. She had been working for eight years at the Metropolitan Museum' Children's Centre as an assistant art teacher. Children between two and twelve, including our own, would come after school to paint and make sculptures inspired by their walks with the teachers through the galleries. The novelty of these art classes was that children were entirely free to mix their own colours and paint as they wished, undoubtedly inspired by their walks through the galleries with the teachers before getting to work. They received minimal guidance; imagination was what counted most; and some incredible paintings saw the light of day. Once a week A. would do similar work at the Harlem School of Arts. At this point in the interview I suddenly realised that Grant was taking notes with a red ball pen on a small notepad. I could not believe it, him taking notes as soon as I talked about my family, but on my own story nothing! I was fascinated by this man.

So I continued with another factor that influenced my thinking over time: the Meri Mini Players of the First All Children Theatre (First ACT for short) in Manhattan. The theatre was founded by Meridee Stein, its young and dynamic executive director. Its initial location was in the basement of a run-down transient hotel on Broadway and 76th Street, euphemistically called the "Continental Ballroom". First ACT became a family affair. We enrolled our eight-year-old daughter Vanessa with the 6–13 year olds. More than half of the kids came from deprived backgrounds in Harlem. Interestingly they did better in school since joining the Meri Mini Players. The kids felt important, and they were indeed important, because the theatre could never exist without their commitment. How they could sing, dance and act with an incredible energy after so many hours of rehearsals after school was not to be believed. Meridee certainly had touched a nerve there on my family and me.

One day I was allowed a peek in the dressing room and noticed a very large poster of a swan up in a blue sky with the very appropriate tagline: "Birds fly because they think they can". Some of the parents were actors themselves, like the comedian Jerry Stiller and his wife Anne Meara. Their son Ben Stiller went on to become a famous actor himself. Diane Paulus and Michael Greif became award-winning Broadway directors, for "Pippin" and "Rent" respectively. There were several performances on Saturdays and Sundays, constantly playing to a sold-out theatre. We as a family, often together with friends and parents themselves, trekked faithfully every Saturday to 65th Street with our three-year-old son Nadim in tow – he had to stand on my lap for better viewing – all of us enjoying seeing these very professional musical performances over and over again – and never getting bored.

Meridee asked me to become a member of the Board. For once I was going to do something for children other than my own. I was still at Chase Manhattan Bank, a most useful contact for her, what with David Rockefeller at the helm, a true mécène of the arts. He once invited the company to perform at the lighting of the Rockefeller Centre Christmas tree, and afterwards, he sent a donation on behalf of his Foundation. Donald Feuerstein, then partner and general counsel of Salomon Brothers, led our five members Board. With most of us coming from the business world, fundraising took off in the right direction. The theatre could now take the big step to move to a new much larger space in a former perfume factory at 37 West 65th Street occupying an entire floor that was turned into a 3/4-round, 150- seat theatre, if including the little ones seated on cushions on the floor. The move gave First Act far greater visibility and, through its proximity to Lincoln Centre, Meridee could now claim that First Act was effectively part of Broadway.

The interview was now moving rapidly towards its conclusion, with Grant directing Jarrett to organise at once an interview with his Deputy Richard Jolly, in charge of Programmes, and then Tarzie Vittachi, his Deputy for External Relations, in that order. And then as an afterthought, Jarrett asked: "perhaps Vianello-Chiodo too?" I was aware that Marco Vianello-Chiodo was Director of the Programme Funding Office, to whom the Dutch government had proposed my name for the Deputy post in 1984. Grant paused and replied, "no, no need". To get these top level interviews with no post in sight was in any case an immense step forward.

Only days after I had called the Hague to brief Geb Ringnalda, the day for interview with Richard Jolly had already been fixed. A development economist, Jolly had previously been Director of the Institute of Development Studies at the University of Sussex. In 1982 he joined Unicef as Deputy Executive Director with responsibilities for programmes that were focused on reducing child mortality and implementing the goals agreed at the 1990 World Summit for Children. Jolly was the absolute driving force in promoting that the special needs of children should be taken into account in each and every economic adjustment process, which he called *Adjustment with a Human Face*.

Adriana warned me that this interview was going to be crucial: As a former professor, Jolly would surely have his own ways of evaluating a candidate, searching coolly for what the candidate really knew, almost like at an exam. Reserved as a true Brit, his personality therefore was very different from Grant's. In any event I expected a rather substantial discussion on the sovereign debt

CHAPTER 2: PREPARING A QUANTUM LEAP

question as a factor in *Adjustment with a Human Face,* and I was ready for it. Of course I was not going to lose track of the fact that I was only a lawyer by training and not an economist like him. I felt it was not going to be an exam but a debate on facts, and especially ideas, but of course one could never tell beforehand. At some point, his *Adjustment with a Human Face* and my ideas for solving the sovereign debt problem of the developing world were bound to meet at the crossroads, eye to eye so to speak.

I remember now that the first few minutes were rather formal and reserved, the ice definitely needed to be broken. But I could feel that Jolly already knew certain things about me and that put me at ease. For example, this time I did not have to face the "Why Unicef" question. His approach was perhaps more about how I could possibly fit into Unicef, perhaps in his Programme Division, coming from the banking sector as I did. I was not an economist and considered myself not very useful for his *Adjustment with a Human Face* crusade. I was not a researcher by profession on development issues. But I had been published about this one aspect, sovereign debt, and that was very much on Jolly's mind in the context of structural adjustment. This time I went into far greater detail on the proposals I had made in the articles towards solving the debt problem. Our discussion became animated in the end, with Jolly unwittingly stimulating me to continue writing articles about this issue. It seemed at that point that Jolly was perhaps forgetting the next item on his undoubtedly busy schedule, because there was a quick tapping on the door. It was Jim Grant sticking his head in saying: "Ah, you are still going at it, I can see you two are hitting it off well," with Jolly replying something like: "We are just about finished, Jim, I'll pop in, in a minute". He then asked me to send him copies of all the articles and so the interview came to an end.

Barely a few days later I was called to come for an interview with Tarzie Vittachi. As I was waiting on the now familiar sofa, I saw Grant approaching and plopping down next to me. It was a rather tiny piece of furniture, two people could just about fit. With this big man so close, I tried imperceptibly to make myself a bit smaller moving further to the left. "I am looking for a Comptroller, can you do it?" I was flabbergasted! A D2 position! I was well aware that these were still the days of the pioneers in Unicef. Management and Operations were not yet fully cemented in rules and regulations to say the least. I for one could now certainly ascertain to some of that, being witness to the external recruitment process, with Grant as the head recruiter. I replied that although I knew a lot about figures and numbers I was really an external relations person, including in my present job, which was business development.

Grant dropped this idea at once and, putting his hand on my arm as if to console me, declared: "There's only one thing wrong with you, you're not a woman". I was well aware that women in Unicef were pushing hard for equal rights. It was the era of the Equal Rights Amendment to the American Constitution, which had yet to come into force. Unicef had commissioned a study on the status of women within Unicef. Initial findings indicated that the organisation was a long way off from reaching gender parity. As a first step in the process qualified women were systematically encouraged to apply. The preference was clearly for hiring women over men. But I was aware that Grant had had some reservations about some of the aspects of the gender study, in particular where the debate touched upon women in development. The risk was that the focus on children would diminish in the process.

I had only a split second to think about Grant's observation; and I thought it was now or never. The remark I had in mind was very, very risky, but then I replied, "Mr Grant, I would do almost anything for Unicef, but there's one thing I will not do," – pausing ever so briefly for greater effect – "and that is to change my sex". Two seconds can seem like an awfully long time, but then he burst out in laughter so loud that many on the sixth floor must have heard him. What a relief, I had taken the hurdle and it was still standing!

Tarzie Vittachi, a Sri Lankan journalist joined Unicef in 1980 as Grant's Deputy for External Relations, a new and crucial post no doubt to overhaul Unicef's communication machine in view of the social mobilisation drive for the Child Survival Revolution that was coming. The interview was relatively short but I remember it as very pleasant. Unbelievable as it may sound now, the interview with Vittachi was my first real discussion with someone from the developing world. I remember him telling me that each country has its North and its South, the former wealthy and the latter the poorest. He specifically mentioned India, but I could also think of a country closer to home: Italy.

For several weeks I heard nothing. An interview with Vianello-Chiodo was indeed never arranged. And then the call came from HR, and a voice said: "would you be against going to Geneva?" That was a strange question because most people in Unicef would jump at the proposal. I felt very different. I was very well aware of the tensions among staff there, several of whom had fallen out with its Director. Sheila Barry, the focal point for National Committees, was preparing to return to New York Headquarters after just a brief stint. Likewise Doris Bertrand, chief of the small Programme Funding Section for only two years, had just resigned and was about to return to her Ministry of Foreign Affairs in Vienna. The proposal was that I was to succeed her. I knew I was going into a very difficult situation, but it was a way to get into Unicef. But enthusiastic I was certainly not. Days later Jim Grant signed off on an Executive Order appointing me in Geneva, thus bypassing regular recruitment process. He did that often to speed things up or to avoid problems. I suspected that my candidacy might have been met with opposition from several quarters. Curiously in my whole career at Unicef, none of my appointments ever went through normal procedures!

Early one morning in July well before colleagues came to work, I walked into the office of Société Générale branch manager Monsieur Jean Sebire. It was around 8 am, the only time of the day he was sure to be alone. As I handed over my resignation letter I felt that this was not a perfunctory goodbye to a man for whom I had always a great amount of respect. I had been there with Sebire from the beginning.

Days after my resignation, he invited me to lunch at one of the finest French restaurants in town. I seem to remember that never once did he speak of banking matters. In a way I was sorry to leave this cultured, modest and elegant man behind. Sebire himself would soon leave the branch, retiring to his home in Deauville, Normandy to finally be able to read his collection of vintage books. It was the "end of an era"; and from now on it would be "a destiny in the making", with a leap into uncharted territory, its outcome totally unknown. But one thing was certain: I had left banking forever.

Chapter 3: A banker's journey

In November 1972 A. and I were invited to dinner at the home of Henri de Chergé in Brooklyn Heights, where he lived in a brownstone. Henri was desk officer at Chase Manhattan Bank for French companies based in the United States. I had befriended him during my credit analysis training and had done several jobs for him.

About that time I was finishing the credit course training and waiting for my first assignment, most likely in one of the Chase branches in Europe. Our credit department class consisted of about 30 trainees who came from Paris, London or Frankfurt to finish training at HQ. I myself had come from Chase's London branch. Our class often socialised together in small groups on Fridays after work. I remember vividly how we were always joking around. One day over a few drinks in the pub, Michael from Ireland, who bubbled over with Irish humour, broke the news to big Tom from Dallas: "You know Tom, you could never be a WASP". In spite of the multiple beers consumed we were all horrified, because Tom was black. Except Tom, he merely asked: "Why?" And Michael, "Because you are Catholic". And we all roared with laughter, Tom the loudest. The racist monster had passed!

In the late sixties and early seventies, companies such as Michelin, Pechiney, Rhône- Poulenc, Ciment Lafarge, Air Liquide, Elf, Total, Renault, Peugeot, Möet Hennessy, Librairie Hachette, Thomson-Brandt, began to invest heavily in the US. Medium sized companies, often family owned like Moulinex, Poclain, Rossignol Ski, Damart and Look Bindings came in this train of euphoria, and of course they also required financial arrangements, not to forget advice as to the American way of doing business.

Henri and I hit it off well. Of course my being fluent in French and conversant in French culture and politics helped a lot. Henri was a congenial fellow and a great lover of classical music, in particular Mozart. At dinner, with one of the Mozart piano concertos in the background, he broke the news that he was going to be transferred to Geneva; that the bank was having trouble finding a Frenchman to fill his post; and adding that not one of the young Chase colleagues in the branch at Rue Cambon was willing to do time in New York, preferring instead to enjoy Parisian life. Would I be interested in taking his job? Henri thought that I had *tous les atouts*[6], stating that I could almost pass for a Frenchman, what with fluency in French and an MBA from INSEAD in my pocket.

In January 1973 Henri began to brief me extensively on his job. I was sorry to lose a budding friendship so soon after arrival. Henri's leaving was to have an enormous impact on my career, and not only in banking, as we shall see. If young French people of that day had been more enterprising like they are today, I would never have had the type of career I did have. How times have changed!

Once or twice Henri's briefings spilled over into lunch at the corporate dining room on the 60th floor of the Chase Manhattan building, a spacious and modern setting which breathed the Rockefeller taste and was only accessible to officers of the Bank – a far cry from the ultra-tacky downtown cafeterias that I was used to. Chase's hallways and waiting areas were "littered" with modern art – Chase had an art department whose job it was to scout for paintings and sculptures often of up and coming artists. During my time, a spectacular Dubuffet sculpture representing a group of four trees was erected on Chase Manhattan Plaza, a gift of David Rockefeller, who was reportedly a friend and great admirer of the sculptor. It was the first order Dubuffet received for a monumental outdoor sculpture. What fun it was to walk under these "trees" during lunchtime. The sculpture gave a strange, but somehow very good feeling. Office furniture was by famous designers, with Mies van der Rohe chairs a common fixture throughout Headquarters. I can't say I knew much about modern art at the time, but through

---

[6] All the attributes.

CHAPTER 3: A BANKER'S JOURNEY

A.'s interest in the art scene I soon realised that Chase had a superb collection of it, and still counting.

One day after lunch at the 60th floor restaurant I happened to enter the elevator to return to my desk on the 14th floor, only to realise with a bit of a shock that David Rockefeller was one of its occupants. I remember that the elevator was rather congested but the Chairman gestured me in anyway, saying: "There's always room for more". With him was a group of Portuguese visitors. The time was barely a year after the Carnation revolution of 1974. Among them I recognised Mario Soares, the socialist leader who was already very much in the news, but not yet in power. Soares' activities in the anti-fascist movement had landed him frequently in jail. In 1968 he was exiled to São Tomé and Principe – two islands off the coast of South West Africa I myself was to come to know rather well as we shall see. Clearly, Rockefeller, who rubbed shoulders with many foreign leaders, was already preparing the bank for the changes in Portugal that were beginning to take shape. No doubt Soares had come to Wall Street and the world of high finance to prepare putting Portugal back on its feet after years of cruel and economically destructive Salazar dictatorship. Barely one year later Soares became prime minister.[7]

Great communicator as he was, Rockefeller would brief Chase staff after his foreign travels on rare Friday mornings when he was in town, reporting to staff on meetings with heads of state and prime ministers, opening of Chase branches abroad, acquiring participations in banks and other important deals. I remember one such Friday morning. Hundreds of us would rush to the basement room to get a good seat. This time he had just returned from Amman and reported enthusiastically on his meeting with King Hussein and the upcoming opening of a Chase branch there. There was a huge rivalry between Chase and Citibank for scoring "firsts". In fact Rockefeller reportedly met with some 200 heads of state over 40 years – opening the world for Chase. These were

---
[7] Soares served two terms as President, 1986–96.

fascinating times for a young banker like me to see power at work from up close. It is said that his foreign visits were motivated greatly by his desire to promote understanding between nations.[8] We loan officers, including those who had come from Europe to finish the credit training were sometimes called Rockefeller's blue-eyed boys and we were mighty proud of it too. My credit course counted only two women, but that changed rapidly in following years.

I integrated fast in the French-American business society, calling on French-owned companies all over the United States and proposing short and medium loans to them. Our French portfolio grew rapidly. Four years into the job I was promoted to Second Vice President. Over the years I befriended many senior representatives of French companies in the United States. One was Pierre Marion, lobbyist for Aerospatiale in North America since 1971, based in Washington DC. Marion was the focal point for advocating and obtaining landing rights for the supersonic Concorde obtained in 1972. Even more importantly, Aerospatiale was eying to sell the Concorde to airlines in the US, but this did not meet with success. The Americans thought that the plane, although admittedly a superior product, would be a loss-making proposition. It was never really clear to me what else Marion did in terms of generating business for his company, the office seemingly devoid of any visible activity. In any event, while I was in his office the phone never rang once, his desk was totally clean. And then, Marion always seemed to have time for me, even at short notice, inviting me invariably to lunch at his favourite restaurant in Georgetown, for which he took all his time. I made it a point to visit him consistently last on my schedule so as to spend as much time with this fascinating man. Marion certainly struck me as a bon vivant and a man of impeccable taste. For me he briefly became some kind of father figure, some 20 years my senior, who empowered me in a good many ways. Our discussions were

---

[8] "David Rockefeller Banker and Philanthropist", Obituary in the *Financial Times*, 20th of March 2017.

animated, about rampant protectionism in the US airline industry, but far more interestingly, on French politics and geopolitical issues.

After ten years in Washington, President Mitterrand appointed Marion to head up to the counter espionage agency *SDECE (Service de documentation extérieure et de contre-espionnage)*. But Marion did not last long in this post. His ardent and ambitious reform of the agency, in particular his efforts to reform counter-terrorism activities had rubbed the Elysée, the military and the staff of the agency up the wrong way. Pierre Marion was sacked, barely a year into the job. With many of his reform proposals having come apart, his principal legacy was the new name he had given the agency: *Direction Générale de Services Extérieurs* or *DGSE*.

I regularly called on French parent companies in Paris to brief them on our business relationship with their subsidiary and identify new business opportunities for the bank. I specifically recall with fondness my visit to Voiron near Grenoble, where the ski company Rossignol had its headquarters. I was very close to the management of Rossignol Ski Co Inc., a ski factory in Burlington, Vermont. Situated on the shores of Lake Champlain, Burlington was in serious decline in 1981 when Bernie Sanders became the first ever socialist mayor elected anywhere in the United States. None of the political pundits gave Sanders a chance to go further in politics than that, arguing that Vermont was "different" and "special". How wrong they were! In Voiron, President Directeur-Général Laurent Boix-Vives kicked off the meeting with a *tour d'horizon* of Rossignol's history. In 1954 he had bought the company from the Rossignol family. He said that Rossignol planned to diversify into tennis rackets, to mitigate the effects of snow-less winters. Afterwards I toured the plant, which I remember as well organised and spotlessly clean. There reigned some kind of easy-going family atmosphere.

Upon leaving, Boix-Vives invited me to dinner in Lyon the same evening, where I was staying. Lyon is some 100 km from Voiron so I considered this quite an extraordinary invitation. I did know that Boix-Vives had roots in Lyon: he had been in the *maquis* together with the great French resistance leader Jean Moulin. We dined in Lyon's *Vieille Ville*. He recalled his days in the French *resistance* with almost youthful fervour and passion. Jean Moulin was given away in June 1943, only to be liquidated by the Gestapo two weeks later. Afterwards, as a proud *Lyonnais* Boix-Vives took me on a tour of the old town through its cobblestone-covered streets and alleyways, showing me where to light up the inner courts of old buildings. What a surprise when pitch-dark courtyards suddenly lit up in all their age-old splendour on a cold and misty evening! Boix-Vives was visibly proud of his city. I will never forget this emblematic and passionate man.

My integration in the French American business community took on another dimension when I joined the new Société Générale branch in Rockefeller Plaza in early January 1979. I was now suddenly in the midst of a French business setting, even becoming a bit "French" myself. This was a huge contrast with Chase. The French are no workaholics, but work hard when it makes sense, and are in general far more concerned with the pleasures of life. I had always liked their style, elegance and interest in history, art and politics. In fact I remember many a business lunch where the real meat of the business was only broached toward the end. It was fascinating for me to "live French" and study how the French tick within their French enclave in the middle of Manhattan.

For example at the new branch one of the most urgent tasks at hand was to find a chef for the corporate dining room. Our General Manager took personally charge of this together with Deputy, Jean-Bernard Mas. The challenge of choosing a spot for wine cellar was a hard one. I still see Sebire, Mas and the chef fast-pacing single file through the branch, scouting for the best location. In the end the choice fell on a very low "creep-in" closet located practically adjacent to my desk. I honestly don't know what Sebire's criteria were because the space did not lend itself at all to becoming a wine cellar. Without fail the chef would crouch in there each morning – he was conveniently small to do that

– and come out with a handful of bottles while I might already be on a business call. Luckily these wines had no time to spoil, as turnover was fast. A small group was constituted by Sebire to come and test Bernard's culinary powers for about a week or two. When it came to food and wine, Sebire left nothing to chance. Every day Chef Bernard made a different dish. I partook in these delicious food-tasting exercises more than once. Each dish was evaluated in minute detail and the results communicated to him on the spot. The corporate dining room was made quite good use of. When there were no customers we would still have lunch amongst ourselves.

One morning I was called in by Sebire to discuss the menu and the wines for my customer Voya Peters, Executive Vice President of Michelin Corporation in New York. I knew his tastes very well. For example Voya was an *"amateur de magret de canard"*. Sebire, Mas, Bernard Gourlaouen and the chef were already waiting. Although Bernard headed up retail banking, Sebire at times asked him to join in on corporate lunches for his happy disposition and animated participation. In fact of all of us, I believe Sebire liked Bernard Gourlaouen the best. They were neighbours in France, one being from Normandy and the other from Brittany. The meeting did not dwell on the menu for too long. I believe that only the entrée was slightly adapted to better suit the main course, which was indeed going to be one of Voya's favourites. Selecting the wines was far more complex. On that subject the French can expand even more than on food itself.[9]

It began with the chef proposing a Côte du Ventoux, a very ordinary wine in those days. My heart sank for the poor man. It was like a credit analyst saying that the company was doing well, while danger signals for bankruptcy were there for everyone to see. It was Bernard Gourlaouen who spoke up first, a Mont Ventoux for our biggest French customer, we can't serve that! And

---

[9] The French manager of Thomson-Brandt New York once told me over lunch that a Bordeaux is for a business lunch; and a pinot noir Bourgogne one drinks with his *amoureuse*, because it makes you drowsy.

Sebire gently inquiring whether we had any St. Emilion by any chance? The chef said he was out of it but would buy some this morning. There was no talk about a specific *millésimé*, but that was understood: the wine had better be excellent. I thought I was witnessing a very French play at Odéon.

French banks and French Politics

French banks were never far from French domestic politics. It was Monday the 11th of May 1981 and I was greeted with "Bonjour Camarade" by Jean-Bernard Mas whose office was next to mine. François Mitterrand had just become president of France the day before. The wry humour was an apt illustration of how France was going to take a sharp turn to the left. It was a black day for the French business world. Throughout French history privatisation and nationalisation of the top banks and industries have played musical chairs. No doubt it was now the turn of renationalisation of major banks and companies. And that is what happened in the early days of the new administration. As one of the three largest banks Société Générale was going to be among them. How little did I realise that the new political landscape of France would affect me personally one day too! It eventually led to my leaving Société Générale, and even more importantly, the banking profession as a whole.

One morning Mas showed me with a big grin a copy of the satirical weekly *Le Canard Enchaîné* with the headline: *"Elf victime d'un escroquérie: avions rénifleurs qui ne réniflaient rien"*.[10] Back in 1979, an Italian scientist and a Belgian aristocrat pretended to have invented technology capable of detecting oil deposits from the air through some sort of radio detection device mounted on a plane. Such a plane was nicknamed *avion renifleur*, "sniff plane". The government supported Elf to go ahead. Credibility of the two inventors evaporated when oil drilling at a "promising" site in South Africa contained not one drop of oil. Elf lost hundreds of millions of French Francs in the process that were never accounted

---

[10] *Le Canard Enchaîné*, 22 December 1983.

for. The French have a very special humour and here is a good example: In the 1970s the saying went, *"France n'a pas de pétrole, mais on a des idées."*

And then in 1983 Jacques Chirac, now mayor of Paris, held a press conference at New York University organised by the Maison de France in Greenwich Village. A. joined me and a small group of French colleagues, including Danielle, my secretary, Patricia Luque and Nicole Ariano of retail banking, three close friends with whom I often banded together. All of them were highly politically motivated, in particular Patricia whose old father was a Spanish communist who had fled the Franco regime in the late thirties. The gathering was in an amphitheatre with a rather large stage. I will never forget Chirac, this huge man in a blue suit who seemed to relish in pacing all over the stage. At the outset he emphasised that he was here to talk in his capacity as mayor about his plans and projects for Paris. Nobody believed him. With these powers Chirac had now taken possession of this formidable national platform from where to conduct his campaign for the highest office.

Naturally many questions from the media centred on the changed political landscape in France and very little on Parisian issues. Chirac avoided these questions as best as he could which made this whole event slightly disappointing. Perhaps it is best remembered for a question a French woman journalist asked at the very end: *"Monsieur Chirac, quand vous étiez étudiant à Harvard, vous étiez apparemment amoureux d'une jeune femme américaine. Êtes vous toujours en contact avec elle?"* Instead of replying, "no comment," or something to that effect, Chirac said: *"Madame"*, pausing a few seconds for effect and, who knows, for a quick reflection, *"en effet j'étais passionnement amoureux d'une, ce que vous appelez ici 'southern belle', qui aujourd'hui, je peux vous le confirmer, mène une vie heureuse avec son mari et ses deux enfants quelque part dans le sud-est des États Unis"*. And that was all he had to say. Elegant, and at the same time putting the woman and her loaded but irrelevant question to shame. Wild clapping followed this brilliant response.

The Bank entertained

When it comes to entertaining the French have style. And so it was that one day in 1982 the Gardinier family, then at the height of power and position in the Florida phosphate industry, invited their New York banks and other business relations to get a firsthand view of Gardinier's production facilities, to be topped off with a visit to Disneyland in Orlando. Wives were to be in the party of course. For geographical reasons, Gardinier had been assigned to me in 1979, as the Eastern Seaboard all the way down to Florida was one of my territories. Gardinier was essentially a family business, 60% owned by the Gardinier family and 40% by a French banking consortium, which included Credit du Nord, Credit Lyonnais and Banque de Suez et des Mines. Gardinier was incorporated in Florida in 1973 in order to buy phosphate rock reserves from Cities Service Company, which held mines and lands in several counties.

The company had chartered a Fokker Friendship for the occasion. A conflict of interest? It never crossed our Francophile minds, *Vive la France*. Jean-Bernard Mas led our group with a whole French contingent in tow. The plane had not even taken off from La Guardia before we were already sipping a cool *Veuve Cliquot*. Bottles kept popping all around us, with corks sometimes flying out of control. Champagne flowed abundantly with the *amuses-bouche* soon making us thirsty for more. A tasty three-course meal was served in mid-air. The PR man of Gardinier welcomed everyone on board and handed out an information kit containing company profile and two-day programme. All was prepared with great professionalism. As we rolled off the plane, everyone was in a jolly good mood indeed, like children on a school trip. Gardinier staff, among whom my two counterparts from Finance, stood on the tarmac of Tampa International Airport as if receiving a group of foreign dignitaries. Having been stuffed on *foie gras* like geese, we took our rooms at one of the Gardinier resorts and turned in for the night having simply no stomach for more food and wine.

The following morning a bus took our party of some 60 people to the East Tampa plant. The PR man presented the history of

Gardinier in phosphate mining and fertilizer production in Florida. Gardinier was presented as one of the big players in the market. It claimed to possess one of the largest phosphate deposits in the world. The phosphate to fertilizer transformation was explained in detail. Since 1973, phosphate fertilizer prices had been rising steadily and Gardinier thus became a highly profitable business by 1977, leading *The New York Times* to state that the Gardinier family's investment in Florida phosphates was "probably the most successful French investment in American resources". Gardinier was on top of the world, but that was not going to last.

After touring the plant, the bus drove us down to a small-forested area for a Texan style barbecue. The fact that we could sit under a tree in burning heat was rather special in itself, because Southern Florida is not known for dense forests like in Eastern France. The Gardiniers boasted that the meat came from Texas, which has supposedly the best cattle for BBQ steaks[11]. The Gardinier family had imported the wines directly from France for the occasion. *Pommes frites*, which Americans call "French fries", were cut in French-style thinness. Thick Texan sausages and corn on the cob rounded out the *plat de resistance*. To our surprise well-frozen ice cream turned up in the suffocating humid heat. To coin a phrase that could apply to their mining activities, the Gardiniers left no stone unturned. Everything was thought through to impress. Even the guy flipping the steaks was presented as a native from Texas... as if only Texans knew how to flip a steak!

Gardinier was working in an extremely volatile market. In the early 1980s when American farmers were highly in debt, demand declined fast and so did prices. The company was ill prepared for this and in the end business folded under a debt of more than 375 million dollars. Looking back on it now, the glamorous entertainment in Florida barely three years before had been the beginning of Gardinier's swan song[12].

---

[11] The French make a similar claim with their "charolais".
[12] A song of great sweetness said to be sung by a dying swan (Webster, 1831).

The rush to make loans

One of our first major loans to the French textile group Agache-Willot for the acquisition of the landmark institution Korvette's. Korvette's was a popular fixture in New York retailing. Back in the 1960s it had been a leader in defining the new concept of a *discount* department store. In the process it pushed out the extremely popular five and dime retailers of another era. Our Headquarters in Paris had initiated the negotiations. I was chosen to run with the ball, with backstopping by Jean-Bernard Mas. Blinded by the objective to become a major player in the New York banking scene fast, Société Générale stepped into a most entangled situation.

Korvette's belonged to the Arlen Realty and Development Corporation, one of the largest real estate developers in Manhattan. In the 1970s the group was hit when the real estate bubble burst dealing a serious blow to its cash flow situation. Arlen began milking Korvette's fifty stores as a source of cash flow to cover loss-making units. Korvette's began to lose control over its destiny and was haemorrhaging fast. This practice of bleeding a subsidiary for the benefit of another is well known in France under the name of *"abus des biens publics"*, which is punishable by law. In fact in France the Willot brothers went by the nickname *les Daltons*[13] for their adventurous ways of doing business that resembled the Arlen practice[14].

When the crisis deepened, Arlen was looking to sell the Korvette's stores. Enter the brothers Willot, looking for an "affordable" deal to gain a foothold in the United States. And they could "afford" Korvette's; its worth had shrunk to a mere 55 million dollars. A consortium of commercial banks led by Citibank and Chase Manhattan invited the French banks to join by cutting the exposure of Citibank and Chase themselves in half. This is when some

---

[13] Named after the Dalton characters in the comic books who are constantly up against Lucky Luke, the cowboy known to shoot faster than his shadow.
[14] Later Jean-Pierre Willot was convicted on *abus de biens publics* with a fine and suspended jail sentence.

of us got apprehensive. Why would US banks wish to reduce exposure if the deal was so good? Clearly the US banks knew the insides of Korvette's much better than the French banks, all relative newcomers to this very New York type of deal. It was definitely not sound banking practice to step into this nest of wasps, but there were apparently other interests and forces at work that were beyond our control. It made me think for the first time that banking decisions are not always based on what you had learned from the credit analysis training.

The meetings took place at Sherman and Sterling, the law firm for Citibank. The legal work was enormous. I remember a rather opaque corporate structure of endless Arlen subsidiaries, many of who supposedly profited from draining Korvette's. I stuck closely to Pierre de St. Phalle, partner in the law firm Davis, Polk representing Lazard Frères, the investment bankers for Agache Willot. I had befriended Pierre during my days in Wall Street, where Davis Polk had its offices. Pierre had all the ins and outs on the Willots. Beyond two in the morning I could no longer hold out, but Pierre carried on as one of the last, swamped as he was in reading legal clauses and negotiating drafts. I would call him in the morning just before going to the office. Often he had just returned home for a couple of hours sleep, only to resume again after lunch. Such was the life of young lawyers aspiring to become partners in a New York law firm.

Barely a year had passed and we were all back in the same room. This time we were going to liquidate what we had helped to create just over a year ago. Korvette's, whose empire had been amputated to just 17 stores, had just filed for liquidation. Endless meetings of creditors with legal counsel to explain our rights. After months of haggling, Korvette's was declared bankrupt. A New York landmark institution, so endeared with ordinary New Yorkers, had needlessly disappeared.

These two cases, in which I was closely involved, added to my doubts about banking. Gardinier and Willot had several things in common. There were plenty of danger signals before they declared bankruptcy. In Gardinier's case it was the ambitious diversification in luxury resorts, which was not at all Gardinier's area of expertise. In both cases they were family businesses with patriarchal leadership and improvised management. The Willots thought naively they had done a splendid deal on entering the US market. And so did the French bankers mounting the financial package.

Another factor that was gradually building up my determination to leave banking was the killing of my career prospects by the French unions in France. This is what happened. In 1982 Sebire introduced me to Gilbert Audurier, a colleague from Paris who was in the process of setting up an international corporate unit servicing European multinationals. Audurier had inquired at the branch whether there were any non-French candidates who might qualify to join him.

Audurier struck me as a modern, dynamic banker, about my age and of a pleasant disposition. In terms of European business development and organisation of the unit, he had strategic vision. For him this new assignment was a key milestone in his career. And would I be interested to join? My answer was unequivocally yes. Sebire then threw his full weight behind this proposal, apparently giving me high marks in the department of Human Resources. Very soon thereafter my dossier was being prepared. Things were beginning to look well. Sebire felt so confident that A. could leave for Paris with the children ahead of me, in time to enrol them in school, the Ecole Bilingue in the 15th arrondissement.

From September, I stayed behind in New York continuing my job as before. It so happened that Dutchman Noud Ingenhousz was one of the in-house lawyers for Société Générale at Headquarters. I had known Noud during my student days in Leiden. He lived in Paris married to a French woman, having already many years behind him in Société Générale. Noud thus became my ears and eyes at Headquarters, often calling me to inform me how my file was moving up the ladder alright. It all seemed to be going well until a hitch developed.

CHAPTER 3: A BANKER'S JOURNEY

One of the trade unions maintained that the job for which I was proposed could very well be done by a Frenchman – conveniently leaving out that young French professionals were still quite poor in speaking foreign languages in those days. When my file arrived with that annotation, Marc Vienot, Deputy CEO of Société Générale, apparently did not have the guts to overrule trade unions and withheld final approval. In December my little family returned to New York, leaving old and newly made friends behind. It was all very traumatic and it hit me hard.

Not long after this mishap, Mitterrand threw the communists out of his government and hard red socialism began to move gradually to the centre. Two years later I said goodbye to banking. Meanwhile, in the changed political context of the day Société Générale's top management picked up the courage to do what they should have done three years earlier: to build up the unit with expatriate staff from other European branches. Three years had been wasted with an immeasurable business opportunity loss to boot. A disillusioned Audurier left the bank shortly thereafter to join a small private bank in Paris. I was bent to do the same, but not to another bank.

Several months later the French bank Indosuez announced plans to boost operations in the US. The call was not long in coming. Harmon Butler, a former Chase Manhattan Bank Vice President who knew me from my credit training, asked if I would join his new team. An interview was arranged with the visiting Chief of the Indosuez International Division. I got an offer that one usually would not be able to resist. I asked for time to discuss it with my family and then I declined. I thought it would be unfair, dishonest even, to join this bank only to quit as soon as I would get an offer through the Dutch ministry of Foreign Affairs. A shocked Harmon Butler asked me to reconsider there and then, but it was in vain.

It was Saturday the 16th of September 1984. A. walked all the way up to the cabin on the hill to bring me the sad news. My father had passed away after suffering a stroke several days before.

My mother told me he had no more will to live because he could no longer use his hands, with which he had created so much.

My father was an advertising man, a brilliant copywriter, but he made his mark as a graphic designer, often in his free time. I saw him making many a book cover on weekends. I watched him designing the logo of the liberal party VVD in the 1960s, which is still in use to this very day. As a 23-year old he made hundreds of book covers from 1933 onwards, including for famous Dutch authors of that time, such as Weremeus Buning, A. den Doolaard and Willem Elschot. My father told me once that when Churchill received the Dutch translation of his war memoirs at Chartwell, he noticed on the spine the Morse V (Victory) signal ..._ (da-da-da DAHH), and commented what a clever detail that was: The signal opened the daily BBC broadcast to occupied Europe on the opening notes of Beethoven's Fifth Symphony.

All along my banking career I was well aware that banking was not for me. I could play the part, just as I could pose for a journalist, but it was certainly not the real world for me. The excessive and overly expensive lunches in some of the best restaurants of New York turned me off. It is hard to believe now that I was a regular of Lutèce, a restaurant that TV culinary personality Julia Child once called the best restaurant in the world. With comfortable red velvet *banquettes* and the whitest tablecloth of damask linen with enormous napkins stretching from chin to lap, one could only guess the final bill. I have often noted that the taller the glass the more expensive the restaurant. Lutèce had the tallest of them all. I developed a complex as soon as I walked in: just by reaching an inch too far for the pepper and salt shakers or simply by gesticulating like a Frenchman to make a point the table cloth would spoil and become a deep red. From then on I would choose fish and white wine to be on the safe side. I still suffer from a complex seeing an excessively high wineglass, moving it as far away from me as politeness permits.

There were many interesting "extracurricular" moments during my time as a banker in New York such as the monthly lunches of the Dutch Financial Club, invariably with a speaker from the financial world, an initiative of Hans van den Houten and Toon Deiters. For Société Générale, Bill Venable once put me in charge of organising the annual Société Générale golf event at the Westchester Golf and Country Club, which Hans van den Houten facilitated as he was a member. Then I will never forget the party at LU Biscuits. That account was handled in retail banking, but the corporate officers had been invited too. The French make excellent parties, with lots of laughing, good food and sometimes dancing. In good French style the wives received upon leaving a present of one old-fashioned LU tin box filled with an assortment of their best biscuits. It was on this evening that I learned the roots of *bis-cuit*: twice cooked. Often the first in spotting a collector's item, several French women managed to take home more than the one box.

The Gourlaouens became very good friends right from the start. Whenever you needed a good laugh, you just went and spent some time with them. The name Gourlaouen cannot be more Breton. In fact Bernard was selected for the New York retail position to nurture business with the Breton community, many of whom worked in the restaurant business. The Bretons are faithful savers of their income and Société Générale was vying to get a good slice of it. Most came from Pont-Labbé and Quimper, and many intended to eventually return there to retire. We got to know a good many Breton-run restaurants. The bistro *La Bonne Soupe* on W55th Street became our *point de repère*.

It was Bernard Gourlaouen who persuaded me to invest in real estate, pointing out that we as employees paid only half of the current mortgage interest rate. So then we found an old farmhouse in the middle of nowhere where the Gourlaouens joined us from time to time. In summers, when the family was upstate and I sublet our Upper East Side apartment to summer interns of law firms such as Davis, Polk or Sherman and Sterling. That money we used each year to make home improvements upstate. Bernard invited me two summers in a row to come and camp out at his appartement near us for a couple of summers, while Christiane and young Carole were already in Bretagne. His *steak au poivre* mistakenly made with cassis will forever be remembered. I thoroughly enjoyed this life of a few weeks as two bachelors waiting to join their families in the waning days of summer.

Mexico and the sovereign debt explosion

As we have seen, I had begun to take a great interest in Latin America's sovereign debt when Mexico defaulted on its sovereign debt burden. Latin America was not my area of lending at all, but the situation there pointed to a serious lack of oversight by the Central Banks of the industrialized countries on their respective banking system, which continued to heap loans on essentially bankrupt nations. My first article: *"Sovereign Debt: towards a new world order"* was published in July 1983 in the Dutch newspaper *NRC-Handelsblad* proposing ideas for bringing some kind of order in the chaotic lending practices of the banks. For example I thought that all sovereign loans should be handled by the International Monetary Fund, whereas commercial banks were to go back to what they do best: servicing the private sector only.[15] An excerpt of these ideas appeared in my letter to the Editor of the *Economist*.

My ideas in the *NR-Handelsblad* began to draw the attention from an investigative journalist of the left wing newspaper *Vrij Nederland*. *VN* was founded as an underground newspaper during the German occupation. One day in 1984 I received a call from *VN* journalist Vincent Bakker who was on the story and wanted to know more. He had done extensive research for his newspaper and was now writing a book. He had the macro view of banking, something that I had only begun to do. When he said he was going to attend the annual meeting of the IMF and World Bank in Washington in September, I asked if *Vrij Nederland* could accredit me as a journalist. And so I passed for a journalist for two days. I moved around the delegates often following Bakker on the heels,

---

[15] See also pages 12 and 13.

CHAPTER 3: A BANKER'S JOURNEY

a bit anxious that someone might find out that I was just a banker posing as journalist. After the sessions had adjourned we sounded out some of the Dutch delegation of the Ministry of Finance at the bar, the minister himself probably locked up in a dinner somewhere. I sensed that they did not have too much time or respect for us journalists. In his book *De Krach van het Kapitaal*[16] Bakker describes me as *"a banker as they should look these days, slim and fit, a bit arrogant and charming"*. Apparently I was a good cast for the role of banker, but journalist? And he continues: *"self-assured, the young Vice President of Société Générale New York maintains that the banks are governed by the IMF which tells them to lend to dubious debtor nations; banks are no longer banks, but are castrated; they pee in their pants"*.

As the largest source of financing available to the developing world, the commercial banks were forced to restructure loans and simultaneously make new loans – all in the name of solidarity. In his book Bakker quotes me as predicting that the public at large will come to realize that banks are weakening themselves with this approach, will see their shares fall, their capital base shrink, with tax payers eventually picking up the slack to recapitalize them – with or without nationalization. It was known as the bubble that burst. [17]

Living a well organised and comfortable professional and private life is no reason not to think about changing direction and follow your dreams. After 14 years in New York my family and I were indeed settled very well. We lived on 111 E 80th Street in a two-bedroom apartment with a working fireplace that was about to go co-op, and all the main museums[18] and Central Park within easy reach. A. worked at the Metropolitan museum, which became

---

[16] Translates as "The Crash of Capital".
[17] And this is exactly what happened during the financial debacle of 2008 and beyond. The knowledge Vincent Bakker shared with me on the ins and outs of the world finance.
[18] Metropolitan Museum, Museum of Modern Art (MOMA), Whitney, Guggenheim and the Frick Collection.

somewhat of a second home for all of us. Central Park was there for picnics and biking, and even cross-country skiing with the children. We fully participated in the art scene, not in the least through the contacts of Hans van den Houten, who had been detached for a while from Chase to assist MOMA in financial matters. We had regular visitors from Europe, and sometimes arranged for painters to show their work in our apartment. On weekends we often drove upstate to our 200-year-old farmhouse in upstate New York that sat on a large tract of hilly land with a stream and forest. We lived the life of the land, with our neighbour hunting on our land and giving us venison steaks and sausages in the fall. So why change?

Gradually, in being so far away from one's roots there comes a point of no return. I am convinced that a few more years would probably have made us stay in the States forever. But the age of 44 was the right moment to still make a major and most likely last move, even at the expense of giving up this good life and starting from scratch in a totally different and alien field. Such was the spirit of my family. All three of them could pack up and easily move on. I am forever grateful to them for that. In fact A. herself had no deep roots anywhere, least of all in Holland where she had spent little time during her adolescent years. As to our children, they had grown up in a multitude of schools and moving to another country just meant an additional adventure. This gave me the "wind in the back" to act assuredly and definitively, never looking back.

It was all just behind me when I finally closed the door of my office for good, driving across the George Washington Bridge into a full red sunset on the way to a holiday at the farm to prepare the family for the dramatic change in our lives that was upon us.

Chapter 4: First steps in Unicef

The offices in Geneva were still in an ugly prefab building at Avenue Jean-Trembley, euphemistically going by the name of *Pavillons du Petit Saconnex*. In fact the offices looked more like a temporary school building or a makeshift medical facility. The hallways were covered with linoleum, offices were all the same size and that was very confusing for a person like me who gets lost even in an easy-to-get-to-know town.

I remember strolling through the hallways that first day stopping at a crossing, and looking for Doris Bertrand, whom I was going to replace as Chief of Programme Funding Section. The first person I came across was Fernando Cordero, a Chilean national, who was her assistant. Doris was leaving Unicef to return to the Austrian Ministry of Foreign Affairs after only two years in the job. For two months I had the luxury and pleasure to work with this intellectual woman. Doris told me about the problems of the office, which I had already heard about while still in New York. Not only she, but also the focal point for liaising with the National Committees had fallen out with the Director and was about to leave after only less than one year in that post. Doris introduced me to several National Committees who came to Geneva to visit. One was Christopher Cooper of the West German Committee, who became a very close friend.

Uffe König called a meeting with the Warsaw participants to review the event held the week before. I detected a sense of humour in him, which I had not seen in Warsaw. In Unicef an evaluation of a big meeting is called a "post-mortem", an expression I have always had a problem with, even though I could never think of a more appropriate word. Uffe said that the meeting had "gone well". Such judgements were often part and parcel of a "post-mortem" regardless of its actual outcome. A couple of weeks later he introduced the new colleagues in an all-staff meeting. He presented me as someone who "makes the impression of being already a Unicef person because of the homework he has done". I smiled secretly at Adriana, my guiding light, now far away in New York.

My first trip out of Geneva was a philanthropic conference with Italian NGOs in Venice. A. and Nadim had gone by car to spend the weekend there with me. I found them fast asleep at hotel Cavalletto just behind Piazza San Marco. It had taken them only 10 hours in the little Renault Five, which we had shipped from America. The venue of the meeting was a former psychiatric institution on one of the islands. I remember it as a very dilapidated place, with crumbling buildings, a totally neglected garden and some stray cats roaming around. The meeting was all about charity and was organised by Interphil, an international philanthropic organisation promoting private giving for community purposes. The conference was held under the unfortunate slogan: "philanthropy thrives where there is democracy; and democracy thrives when there is philanthropy". A highly charged political statement with which I disagreed. Canon Moerman who received an award for his philanthropic work with NGOs had based his acceptance speech wholly on this theme, realising later that the tag line of the conference in fact offended some 95% of the world's population. Indeed a lot of mutual help exists in non-democracies – just think of the often-quoted example of "African solidarity".

After a farewell reception at the town hall on the Grand Canal, I strolled with A. and Nadim through the back streets and alleyways and found a restaurant where mainly locals go. On scampi, calamari and spaghetti we befriended the waitress who upon leaving planted kisses on our happy cheeks. Oh sweet Italy! Back home we found Vanessa in good spirits after having attended the three-day art festival in Coppet.

Back in the office the speed was beginning to pick up. I wrote my first speech ever – for Uffe König to be delivered in Buenos Aires

CHAPTER 4: FIRST STEPS IN UNICEF

before the International Hotel Association. It was excellent teamwork, with secretary Jilly typing it up and Janet Nelson doing the final editing. The gist was to present the work and mandate of Unicef and to propose a major fundraising scheme based on a small charge per room reservation that would benefit Unicef. The proposal was very well received. Since then the *Check-Out for Children* programme, a partnership with Starwood Hotels and Resorts, has raised millions of dollars for Unicef.

Work and pleasure were often mixed. One Sunday UNHCR held a gala benefit for refugees, with Peter Ustinov as master of ceremonies. The whole family went but Vanessa was grumpy, as she had already had a benefit event at school for victims of the Mexico earthquake the night before and had been dancing until very late. The UNHCR gala was held at the Palais des Nations and was a glittery affair. Vanessa remarked that never once were refugees mentioned, not even Yul Brunner who had died just days before and who had done so much for refugees. The lottery of expensive watches shocked Vanessa the most. She simply did not listen to my argument that the manufacturer had donated them and that without a lottery it would be more difficult to get people to join the event.

Shortly afterwards I went to Italy again. Aldo Farina, the ebullient Executive Director of the Committee had invited René Latenstein of the Dutch Committee, Greeting Cards Division Director Bob Walwer and myself to discuss the agenda of the upcoming NatComs Fundraising workshop in Oslo. My diary noted: *"meeting got off on a tangent with Aldo reeling off all the fundraising campaigns his Committee has undertaken in the last couple of years. A long list with which we are already familiar, but in his enthusiasm the Sicilian is unstoppable. Aldo is a fanatic when it comes to his island. Almost all his colleagues are from Sicily. We all get a bottle of Amaro Siciliano. The drafting of the agenda for the Fundraising workshop has gone more or less to the backburner. I will now go to Oslo to tour potential venues."*

After five lessons of Assimil's *"l'Italien en 90 leçons"*, I was ready to face the Italians at the official dinner with the National Committee.

I was lucky to sit opposite Luigi Bucci, 63 years old, who had the face of a *bambino*. Bucci was in charge of the development education programme with schools. Trying some of my new Italian on him, he smiled (*ridere*, I said to myself). To my right there was Marisa, an actress who livened up the table.

With the following day reserved for some sightseeing in the morning, an animated discussion ensued between Farina and Bucci as to who should be guide for Marjorie Newman-Black and me, and who should take care of Bob Walwer. Bucci got to guide us and what a wonderful guide he was. Beginning the day with a cappuccino in Trastevere, he took us both by the arm with himself in the middle. He showed us St Peter and the Pietà and put us on the spot from where the columns on the square merge visually into one. Arm in arm, as friends do in Rome, we walked all the way to Piazza Navona with that rather pompous Bernini sculpture. Bucci was the only Roman of the Committee in the middle of a Sicilian "sea" and could now finally proudly show his city after two days of everything Sicilian. We walked many streets. He said, "Every street has a story to tell". Upon parting, Bucci gave us each a photo book of the *Castelli Romani*.

Barely home I was already on the next plane. From Latin Italy to Viking Norway, the cultural change was fast indeed. With Italian human warmth far behind me, I met the Executive Director of the Committee, Annie Sogaard. She was a rather reserved person, who needed the charm offensive rather badly. Driving over to the venue identified by her, Annie seemed to do a hard sell on me. I will never forget the horror I was coming face to face with. The Norgen Hotel was golden and glittery all over. Stone animals and stuffed reindeer and bears stared "extinctly" at you. I choked when we looked at a room whose telephone had a pink velvet cover. This was not the Nordic minimalism I was used to. But how to explain this to Annie – who had been so enthusiastic about this venue – without losing sight of my goal: breaking the ice with her. When we finally found a rustic place in the mountains near a ski jump, I had succeeded and we became good friends. In the evening

CHAPTER 4: FIRST STEPS IN UNICEF

I showed Britt, wife of Hans Petter Finne of my INSEAD promotion – he was in Mexico for business – the venue for the workshop, the Voksenåsen hotel. It turned out that the manager was a friend of hers. So that reassured me even more. Then Britt showed me her old school, the house where she was born, where they were married, all on the same hill! How good it is, I thought, to have roots on a hill and stick to them for life.

Get-to-know visits with other National Committees followed in quick succession. One day it was with the French Committee. I remember an older Committee member in charge of development education telling us that aid and development served a hidden purpose: *"on développe, si non ils vont venir bouffer chez nous"*. As crude and shocking as this sounded then, in hindsight I think he had a point. Make conditions of migrants and refugees in their home countries sustainable and prevent people from getting uprooted. How true does this sound today – and how little do we do about it with wars destroying the little that had been achieved.

Next was the Finnish committee with Jesper Morch. Only six months before I had been in Helsinki as a banker on a business development mission for Société Générale. Jesper was quite a bit younger than me and, with Marjorie Newman-Black, was definitely one of the more interesting colleagues in the Geneva office. He ran the development education section, which among other things developed educational materials for schools. I thought that A. could link up very well with him given her link to art education with children. Art might be an interesting dimension to introduce in development education. One day I was indeed able to tell Jim Grant that A. was working as a Unicef volunteer in DevEd, and he exclaimed: "Ah good! Two for the price of one".

On the tarmac waiting for the plane to return us to Geneva, I could not help thinking of the just ended Reagan-Gorbachev summit on disarmament held in a villa on Lake Geneva very near us. "Let's hope there's hope," reads the entry in my diary. The Summit led to a breakthrough in US–USSR disarmament thus ending a long period of instability caused by the Cold War.

I still see this stark image of Bob Walwer and myself walking with our suitcases from West to East Berlin. Checkpoint Charlie had a narrow pathway with high concrete walls on either side. So narrow that my suitcase kept banging against it. It was a misty dark day in December, with a cold drizzle to boot. We had landed at Tegel airport in West Berlin that obviously had better flight connections with the West. From there we took a very modern underground train straight to Checkpoint Charlie. Walking this symbolic but very real passage way from modern West Berlin into gloomy East Berlin changed my mood instantly. I thought of John Le Carre's first novel *The Spy who came in from the cold*, but most of all of John Kennedy's speech in 1961 shortly after the wall had gone up. Standing on a lookout tower he shouted to the imprisoned East Germans on the other side: *Ich bin ein Berliner*. But most of all I thought of the uprising of 1953. As a 13-year-old it made a deep impression on me. How could half of Europe be imprisoned like that? What began as a strike by construction workers escalated into a people's movement that called for East Germany to be free. The uprising was violently suppressed a day later by Soviet troops and tanks.

Werner Grimm, yes that was his name, stood waiting for us at the other end. He was the Executive Secretary of the GDR Committee. Grimm cut an excellent picture of your typical communist: grey, dull and yes, grim, without a smile, without a grain of charm or emotion. It was already dark but the Christmas trees and streetlights tried to cheer up the oppressed population. Meetings with government and Committee were very formal. There were long silences as nobody dared to open himself up to criticism. I was beginning to copy the *Ossies*. In such a situation one tends to hold back the real questions. Luckily the programme was filled up with sightseeing and cultural events. I looked forward to this as we might see or perhaps meet some real people.

On the way to the hotel, Grimm shows us the "border", which is the name for the Wall most people here use. A new economic theory has seen the light of day: Grimm says that since the Wall was built, the economy of the DDR has improved significantly. So then, let's surround struggling economies with a wall and all will be well. Walwer in the front seat and me in the back keep silent. I notice that the wall runs like a slithering serpent through the streets of this once thriving city. My maternal grandmother, who was born and raised here, had known its better days. We pass the Brandenburg Gate, its columns "cemented shut" by concrete. In the distance bright street lighting is trying to make the point that life is better in the West.

We get to meet with the entire Unicef Committee Board, all members of the party and representing various interest groups. One is the "Solidarity Movement" – not to be confused with the Polish trade union movement – in effect a Fund that gets contributions through "voluntary" salary reductions. Some of the proceeds go to aid for developing countries and to Unicef. I notice that the president's hands are trembling like a humming bird's wings. The meeting is very stiff and of no consequence whatsoever. Fundraising in non-convertible currency is only possible if the money is used for procurement in that country. But what could Unicef buy in the DDR? After the meeting the Board members loosen up a bit with beers and schnapps.

In the evening I go to see a play with Herr Rudolf Greiser from the Ministry of Culture, who had been assigned to take care of me. I am lucky. Greiser turns out to be a cultured and erudite man. He is a fan of Berthold Brecht, the playwright whose home was East Berlin. The play *"Die Rundköpfe und Spitzköpfe"* is set in a village surrounded by a wooden wall with fascist soldiers marching two and fro; serfs tilling the soil are routinely kicked and tortured for protesting against higher taxation from their lord; scared villagers try not to notice; and prostitutes provide lightness of being.

I am fascinated that such a play could be produced in such a way – surely offensive to the current DDR regime the way it was staged. The crowd of young well-dressed couples seems to thoroughly enjoy the acting even though it must remind them starkly of their own situation. At the intermission Greiser asks if I want to go home. He thinks the play too *"clownisch"*, referring to the make-up of some of the victims in the play who have white faces with black rings of fatigue under the eyes to accentuate their plight. I say I thoroughly enjoy the sets and the way the play is staged. It is my first honest statement of the day. And so we stay on. The play ends with a destitute peasant saying somewhat mysteriously: *"Vielleicht geht der Regen von unten nach oben"*. The next evening I want to go and see it once more. In checking the newspaper for times, I notice to my chagrin that the Volkstheater has taken it unexpectedly off the programme. Dutch actress Cox Habbema told me many years afterwards that this was nothing exceptional. In fact, actors in the DDR suffered that fate all the time.[19]

There is still more time for sightseeing as we had planned one day too many. Changing a plane reservation from East Berlin is of course out of the question. A young guide who had just graduated from Leipzig University takes Bob and me around to see the Soviet war memorial site in Treptow Park, which takes up a fair number of hectares. The central piece is a statue of a Soviet soldier crushing a swastika with his sword while holding a child on his arm. The National Museum is filled with post-war patriotic paintings. I spot though a magnificent 1967 Picasso, *Le Mousquetier* and a Frans Hals portrait painted with his trademark bold brushstrokes. Walwer reveals he has gone through art school and still paints in his free time.

The pub at the Pallast Hotel is the watering hole for young urban white-collar workers. I order frankfurters to go with the beers. But even that universal name is political: East Berliners call them just *würschtchen*. A couple in their thirties pull up two chairs to sit with us. The man announces for everyone to hear that he is ready to go with us to West Berlin. In fact he begs us to take him. His wife places her index finger on his lips as if to seal them. The poor soul does not stop; she is getting more and more nervous and in the end leads him out to go home.

---

[19] *Koffer in Berlijn,* Cox Habbema, 2003.

CHAPTER 4: FIRST STEPS IN UNICEF

The next day we fly to Warsaw to meet with the National Committee. Its Executive Director, Lucjan Wolniewicz is in a sombre mood. He is a Francophile at heart since his studies in Paris. He has this eternal regret of not having immigrated in France when he could have. Discussions about the Committee's work do not take up much time; the Committee is a weak organisation. With Lucjan any subject under discussion would always divert to the political situation. The big news now is the new rationing of meat; paper is scarce; schools and hospitals are overcrowded with the baby boom putting pressure on services; and the following day the country is to commemorate the fourth anniversary of the crackdown on the Solidarity movement. All efforts of *Solidarity* have been for nothing or so it seems. No wonder that people are depressed around such commemorative days. Wolniewicz is bitter that trade with the West has greatly diminished – even France had followed the Americans in this – making good products scarce. Poland is saddled with a foreign debt of some 30 billion dollars, but nobody can say with precision what this debt has financed.

The dinner hosted by the Committee cheers me up again. Lucjan had invited Professor Jan Szczepanski, a well-known sociologist, politician and former mediator between the government and the trade union movement *Solidarity*. Szczepanski is 73 years old and a personality in Poland. His works concentrates on the history of sociology, in particular the transformations of social structures. A member of the Polish Council of State at the time, he was the only one to vote against martial law that was declared on 13 December 1981. He says there is a huge revival of religion with some 700 churches under construction. He then adds ironically, "maybe one big church should be dedicated to Marx and Lenin for having revived Christianity".

The Professor has written a famous essay on *Individuality and Society* commissioned by the West Germans and the British. In it he makes a clear distinction between individuality and individualism. Individualism wants to be different just to be different. Individualism also tends to be greedy: Each individual strives to get as big a slice of the social pie as he or she can (generally with the result that others get less). Individuality, on the other hand, is the flourishing of a person's creativity. Each new idea is genuinely unique ("individual"), because nobody else has ever had it. Individuality is generous: A person wants to share his or her new idea with others. One person having a new idea takes nothing away from anyone else. Even better: each new idea increases the size of the social pie, so that there is more for everyone. Szczepanski sees capitalist America as a model of individualism, where everybody competes to get more for himself (the selfish attitude). He argues that a society based on individuality, i.e. on each individual's unique creativity, is the *third way*, in which *both* the individual *and* the group are winners. Such a society, he says, has existed long ago, but seems impossible to be achieved again.

He agrees with my analysis that tactically speaking Solidarity had gone too far too soon. The problem was, he explained, that *Solidarity* consisted of many diverse movements and interests. Every day there were long negotiations that paralysed the country. I ask him about our daughter Vanessa and where she should study anthropology. He says in the United States, emphasising that universities in California and the Mid-West usually have strong anthropology departments because of their proximity to the American Indian. Lucjan comes back on his regular depressions of which I have seen one this afternoon and how to suppress them. "I often go to an orphanage or a hospital to see the relativity of life, and then I feel a lot better." That pictures the mood in Poland, the tensions and pressures of daily life Poles have to face. How long still for them?

Back home I see Nadim perform at school in *The Emperor's Clothes*, a Hans Christian Andersen tale about two tailors, fooling the emperor in weaving an invisible cloak. Nadim as one of the tailors carries the play with engaged acting and even singing. Theatre and charade at the farm with Vanessa, Kyla, Husain and his younger brother Assad, plus the sessions Nadim and Vanessa had with famous actor Spalding Gray in New York, clearly paid off.

CHAPTER 4: FIRST STEPS IN UNICEF

The last mission of the year is to the Rumanian National Committee, together with Isabelle Austin of Development Education. Mihai Delcea is waiting for us on the tarmac along with the Chief of Protocol and an interpreter. Before I know it I am holding a bouquet of red carnations in my hands. Clumsily, I try to arrange it in a bearable position, like a mother with a baby in her arms. In those days I simply had no idea how to hold on to a huge bouquet in a proper way. We dine with Mihai and the Chief of Protocol on tender veal steaks, a stark illustration how privileged these government people are compared to the rest of the population for whom such luxury goods are rationed.

The meetings with government are extremely formal. The large conference room is not heated – with the onset of winter, fuel was rationed – and I feel the cold air slowly creeping up my legs. Isabelle Austin and I are sitting at an immensely long table with Unicef on one side and a handful of civil servants across from us. If a photo of our meeting had made it to the newspaper, the reader might have thought that an intense negotiation was being worked out here. The only bit of substance is with the ministry of Foreign Trade about the Lei account which is of course non-convertible, but which could be used for Unicef if we procure in Rumania. I propose to use a system of middlemen who could buy local products on behalf of Unicef. The problem with these mechanisms is that the products Unicef needs most are scarce, often not for export or simply not available.

After the meetings it is time for some propaganda. Mihai takes us on a tour of the Palace of Pioneers, a huge concrete building with classrooms for art, political affairs, electronics and so on. As in other "socialist" countries, the Rumanian Pioneer Organization was created for selected young people between the ages of nine and fourteen, to learn about the values of their leader Ceausescu and communism. The art room is a haven that seemed to be free of propaganda and indoctrination. It is the only place where his portrait is not on display. Children are making paper puppets (that day the assignment was Father Christmas). They are happy when you sit with them and admire their work. Upon leaving I receive my second bouquet of flowers. This time I am better prepared, holding it now like a seasoned party official. The pioneers give us an embroidered tablecloth made by them.

In the evening Mihai and Michaela, a lively young colleague of the Committee in a simple but stunning red sweater, take us to the oldest restaurant in town. The *Buchuresti* had opened in 1808. Almost every course in the tasty six-course dinner is based on pork one way or the other lavishly served with a Rumanian red, full-bodied wine. Mihai says that the Committee wants to invite Unicef next year to participate in a children's summer camp. I see the ghost of Paul Thorez and the summer camp in the Crimea, loaded with communist indoctrination. This would be somewhat of a political decision. I promise to submit the idea to our Director for consideration.

Bucharest strikes me as a pretty city even as some of the old buildings had to make room for Soviet style architecture like the Palace of Pioneers. With its roomy boulevards the city reminds me a bit of Paris – without the traffic. It even has an Arc de Triomphe in an Etoile-like setting. Almost devoid of cars, our driver takes to driving as in a Formula One race, honking incessantly as he chases poor pedestrians. Street lighting is very sparse to save energy. We see silhouettes of people hurrying home in the cold to their dark and cold houses. The driver seems to relish the power he exercises over these struggling people. I feel disgusted at this scene. It is hard to believe that in this day and age, this too is Europe.

The model school is in a very poor neighbourhood school on the outskirts of Bucharest. On the way we see long lines of cars waiting for a fill-up of a few litres. And this country used to be self-sufficient in oil… The welcoming is the usual ceremony with bouquets of flowers, this time presented by little girls and a kiss. Mihai is already there, and so is Michaela. A young boy called Claudiu, perhaps seven years old or so, speaks fluent English. Isabelle adopts him instantaneously. This art class impresses me very much. The children are painting after a famous painting and use the colours with flair. At lunchtime the "State visit" continues with a copious lunch and a live band playing music from the Balkans.

At the same time the Bulgarian First Secretary Zvikov is here on a state visit to see the beloved Ceausescu. Heightened security creates havoc and confusion. We make it to the National Museum to admire some magnificent treasures, especially the Scythian gold pieces. All is very well displayed against a purple background with proper lighting. When I lose our interpreter Nicoletta, I have finally a few precious moments of freedom of movement. When she reappears she stands before me trembling like a nervous doe. Interpreters and guides are not supposed to lose sight of their foreign guests ever.

At dinner we return to the subject of the Lei account. Mihai impresses upon us that Unicef must do anything to undertake local procurement in Rumania. The idea is that the pioneers should feel that the funds they have so diligently raised should not be stuck in an account. The pioneers would feel frustrated if their efforts remain fruitless in assisting the population of poorer developing countries. In parting Mihai, this elegant Rumanian gives us each a photo book on Bucharest along with a gramophone record of patriotic songs by the Pioneers recorded on the occasion of their 25th anniversary.

The National Committees of the GDR, Poland and Rumania had much in common: they were all controlled and dominated by the State; all three of them were financially weak; their constituency was poor; each mission had been devoted mostly to sightseeing and propaganda, although less so in Poland; and not one major plan was developed with them other than their advocacy for local procurement here by Unicef to use up blocked funds. The Rumanian Committee wanted the help of Unicef to diversify sources of funding to make them less dependent on the pioneers. Bucharest seemed to me the least oppressive of the three cities, perhaps because of relative "independence" from the Soviet empire, its Latin culture and the Latin origins of its population.

The TAROM Tupulev took off almost vertically like a rocket and it was "goodbye to all that" for now. It was the holiday season to enjoy with my little family and to prepare for the Unicef programme orientation journey halfway around the world.

Chapter 5: A glimpse of Unicef in the "field"

The Swiss Air plane rose slowly turning south. passing over Mont Dole (3,800m), where Nadim was having his first ski lesson that very moment. It was early January 1986 and I was thinking how our lives had changed in just four months.

My entry into Unicef seemed to have gotten off to a good start. I was excited when a colleague from somewhere in the world would call to try to "sell" me an innovative project - like Per Engebak from Tegucigalpa with his US $ 400,000 water supply by gravity project - and then how, I in turn, would try to convince a National Committee or PFO New York to fund it. I was thinking how after this orientation trip I would at least be a bit more familiar with Unicef programmes and might then be all fired up to face ministers, parliamentarians and journalists alike to convince them that Unicef deserved three million dollars of funding every day instead of just one. Little did I know that Unicef was to reach Grant's target within a matter of just a few years.

West Africa

The sun was setting over the Sahara with the sands colouring a rusty red. The harmattan[20] made for a fuzzy vision. I realized for the first time that a desert is not just a vast plane of sands, but has some relief of low mountains as well. Perhaps these hills were leftovers of a mountainous past, perhaps to be eroded into sand and dust in another few million years. It was hard to believe that nomads could make some kind of a living in such desolation. Little did I realize then that A. was to come to know well the living conditions and culture of nomads in the Sahara.

---

[20] The dust-swept wind of West Africa prevailing in January–February.

After some six hours the plane touched down in the African night at the international airport of Port Bouet[21]. The Unicef driver took me straight to the Hilton Hotel on the Plateau, the business district of Abidjan. The next day was Sunday, with no sign from anyone of the office except a quick welcoming call from Bertram Collins, the Regional Director. Not knowing anyone in Abidjan, I rested at the pool, reading documents of the Regional Office, but still finding time for Italo Calvino's masterpiece *Le Baron Perché*.

The following morning Collins welcomed me together with Barbara Bentein, who was in charge of my programme of meetings. A most interesting person was Annick Miske-Talbot, regional adviser for Community Development and an expert on nomadic life. No wonder: Annick was married to a Mauritanian anthropologist. The couple had converted their living room into a nomadic tent. Twice a year the roof of the tent had to come off to be dusted, a full day's work. She had written on Mauritania's transition from a nomadic to a sedentary society. I had good conversations with Jack Ling, former Director of the Division of Information, who was on a mission to Abidjan. He had been seconded to the WHO in Geneva in 1982, but maintained his old contacts at Unicef. Ling explained things in a simple and easy to understand way. I told him my trip to the Far East was going to end in Hanoi. Not surprisingly, our conversation moved to Indochina where Ling had spent several years. He gave me a little book he had written on his experiences in Vietnam, a country he loved. He also gave me a copy of *Les Petits Métiers d'Abidjan* by Abdou Touré, about small jobs one finds in the streets of Abidjan.

Waterman Christian Hubert gave me a tour d'horizon of water and sanitation in the Sahel. In those days Unicef had important drilling programmes in these arid regions. Water was often found only at one hundred metres but beyond that depth drilling would no longer be possible.

---

[21] Since 1994 renamed Felix Houphouet-Boigny airport.

CHAPTER 5: A GLIMPSE OF UNICEF IN THE "FIELD"

The next day I visited the old fishing village of Anono with Christof Conrad, the lone Resident Project Officer at the Côte d'Ivoire liaison office. Anono had become an overcrowded shantytown, with immigrants from Burkina Faso, Mali and Togo living side by side with the Ivorians. The Canadian National Committee had funded a milling machine for manioc, a root that has similar attributes as potatoes and is the staple food here. As women used to stamp manioc with long poles, the idea was to free up time and sell some of the manioc at market. If there was an economic gain for anyone, the village as a whole did not develop. Latrines were primitive and were mostly not used. Big red headed lizards had a "moveable" feast with filth. The rather squalid health centre was not something to brag about. Mothers, whose babies were being weighed in hanging baskets looked very young. If this was a Unicef project, it had failed a long time ago.

The next day I flew to Ouagadougou, capital of Burkina Faso, formerly known as Upper Volta. In those days the airport check-in at Port Bouet airport was rather basic. Boarding cards were still written by hand. There was no guidance by ground personnel to the plane. It was only when I was already two steps on the ladder that I was asked to show my boarding pass; and was told that this plane was going to Conakry. One more step and I would have landed in Guinea.

The airport sign welcomed us with *"Burkina Faso, tombeau de l'impérialisme!"* Soldiers were everywhere, looking very young, serious and threatening. The situation was tense. A five-day border clash with Mali had just ended. Mali had bombed two towns on the Northern border, Ouahigouya and Djibo. Burkina retaliated by bombing a town on the Malian side of the border. There were many casualties on both sides. The country was still in a state of emergency with nightly curfews. Streets were surprisingly clean, no slums that I could see. Burkina had a military dictatorship and apparently that worked for them.

Army colonel Thomas Sankara had come to power through a coup d'état in 1984. Now its country's president, he launched a vast immunisation drive which he called "vaccination commando" that triggered vast amounts of development assistance for the country. In my hotel room that evening I saw Sankara, on a black and white TV, dressed in military fatigues and a beret slanted off his head British style, electrifying a large crowd. In a clever nation-building move, he changed the name of the country from Upper Volta to Burkina Faso, "land of upright people". That instilled an enormous national pride in the population.[22] Sankara decreed that each village was to have a health post within 30 days. The response was overwhelming: Most 7,500 villages followed suit with volunteers constructing with local materials. Unicef and NGOs would provide basic medical supplies and train community workers. Bilateral donors could fund essential drugs. The Italian government was already a big donor to Burkina Faso in health and nutrition. A nominal payment system would make it in the end self-sustainable. At the time of my visit, the office was preparing for a visit by the Italian National Committee, hoping to obtain funding.

The Unicef office had been upgraded the year before to country office headed up by a representative. It had project activities in health, water drilling and installation of pumps in rural areas and sanitation, and in pre-school. Nicole Lafrance, the Programme Coordinator accompanied me to several sites.

The primary school was an achievement of the villagers who partially paid for it with the proceeds of milled manioc. Classrooms were in mud huts with thatched roofs so that the children, I was told, would "feel at home". The cycle went through sixth grade but only one in ten children enrolled in first grade would achieve that. The school had a pre-school class of four- to seven-year-olds.

When we arrived, a group of them were sitting under a big mango tree, whose thick foliage protected the children from the burning sun. Temperatures hovered around 45° Celsius. A boy was

---

[22] Webster defines: marked by strong moral rectitude.

CHAPTER 5: A GLIMPSE OF UNICEF IN THE "FIELD"

standing there telling a story to his classmates. He turned out to be a master storyteller, pacing around, using his hands, looking intensely at his audience, and pausing at times, seemingly to create suspense. The children laughed a lot. What a scene. Unicef staffer Patrick Ilboudou translated for me. The story line was as thrilling as the storyteller himself: *"un garçon est chassé par les démons; il court, il a peur, il ne peut presque plus; et du coup frotte contre le dos d'un des démons, qui s'ouvre; il y trouve un oeuf et une grosse pierre; il jète la pierre aux démons et la pierre se transforme en montagne; le garçon est toujours chassé par les démons; il ne peut plus; une fois arrivé au sommet de la montagne, le garçon jète l'oeuf; l'oeuf se transforme dans un immense fleuve; et les démons périssent '* The boy had held the class in suspense for many minutes. The teacher did not interfere; in fact the boy was to do as he pleased. Storytelling is the way African fables are born.

In another spot, a Unicef brigade was drilling a borehole and had reached a depth of 60 metres; and still no water. Villagers stood around in expectation of a major find. The team planned to go to a depth of 80 metres tomorrow hoping to hit water. I was assured that the overall success rate of finding water was around 65%, which is considered high. Someone told me that there would be dancing all around if water is found, an incredible moment to witness. Suddenly I had the inspiration, no idea why, to draw a mask in the sand. As I was working on it, I was surrounded by a large group of children. I thought of Hilde Sigal, A.'s art teacher friend at the Children's Department of the Met in New York. I thought that this might be a nice pre-school project for her in Africa: making sand drawings with children in rural villages.

Nicole Lafrance introduced me to Bernard Ouedraogo over lunch at the home of Representative Stan Adotevi who was out of the country. Ouedraogo, who was from Ouahigouya in the North, had revived the NAAM movement, an age-old agricultural cooperative of young men and women working together, a rather rare occurrence in Africa at that time. When long ago he noticed that at the end of each harvest the young labourers would spend much of their savings on feasting, he thought that some of these savings might be better spent on improving the lives and livelihood of the population.

Bernard Ouedraogo trained the young group in transformation of produce and other income generating projects. NAAM now had a number of community projects with Unicef. I told him about A.'s work in art with children at the Met and he said that Africa had a great need for such creativity to make the children perceive and see. He said that creativity was not always allowed by traditional village elders who feared they might lose some of their power and influence. He said that Sankara, only 35 years old, promoted creativity at the expense of tradition. Neighbouring countries also saw that as a potential threat to old societal norms.

East Africa

A few days later I found myself in a Land Rover going full speed from Dar es Salaam to the highlands of Iringa, Tanzania, a distance of some 700 km. Unicef driver Charles was in a hurry, he drove fast. The road was generally better than the ones I had seen in Burkina Faso. I was going to visit projects executed under the new Joint Nutrition Support Programme (JNSP), a global programme of Unicef and WHO, funded by Italy. Half way we stopped at Mikumi Savannah Camp to debrief representative Urban Jonsson over lunch about my visit with Unicef colleagues in Dar. Urban had come from Iringa and was returning to Dar. He brought my suitcase that had been lost between Abidjan and Nairobi. It felt strange to see it back in the middle of nowhere with half its contents gone, including the camera with pictures from Burkina Faso. But what a relief to find my diary intact and also the first aid kit Nadim had prepared for me!

Urban turned out to be a passionate nutritionist. He said that nutrition needed considerable strengthening in health programmes. It was important that JNSP succeeded. Tanzania was one of the countries that was selected for funding under this programme. Perhaps not so surprising: Unicef had here not one, but

CHAPTER 5: A GLIMPSE OF UNICEF IN THE "FIELD"

two staffers with a strong nutrition background. There was also Project officer Bjorn Ljungqvist, a close friend of Urban's from university days.

Iringa was rich in agriculture, corn and potatoes were the dominant crops. The population needed to be empowered to help combat malnutrition and manage child nutrition. The problem was that women spent too much time working the land and did not have enough time to care for their children. There was not much food variety: the one major meal consisted of corn, potatoes or rice with meat if available. The problem was that the food intake was rather one-sided. Another problem, a Tanzanian explained to me was that when big game hunting was lost for men, a new occupation needed to be found for them. Although some took up farming, most men were just lounging around. GOBI of course was already focusing on the importance of breastfeeding and growth monitoring, but there were many other nutritional approaches required as well, such as diversifying food consumption. For the population of Iringa the poor condition of local roads was a serious obstacle to bring their produce to markets. These factors all contributed to high child mortality rates, a total contradiction in a potentially rich agricultural region. But, at an altitude of 1,500m, there were at least no mosquitoes in Iringa, whereas just down in the valley malaria was rampant.

I stayed at the Baptist Centre run by missionaries from South Carolina. There I ran into some Swiss scientists from the Swiss Tropical Institute, who were running a research institute here. It had been founded by a Mr Geigy, from the prominent Geigy family of the pharmaceuticals firm Ciba-Geigy in Basel. This Mr Geigy did research here on snakes and other reptiles. Then 10 years ago the institute was donated to Tanzania, but was still Swiss-run. Now the emphasis was on medical research for humans. The Swiss joined me on some of the field visits to a school and a training centre. Bjorn Ljungqvist was leading a JNSP session there with a large group of villagers that was in the process of evaluating progress in beating malnutrition, improving nutritional habits and the like. Bjorn was an excellent animator, had a way of listening patiently, taking all his time. It was all very participatory. Everything went on in Swahili that he spoke fluently. It was a couple of hours later that Bjorn explained to me the highlights of the evaluation.

The Unicef base camp was a depot for supplies for water works such as pumps, pipes and drilling equipment. The water engineer was a rough and tumble Irishman. He took me to see an important water reservoir complex, fed by water coming down the mountain. A local engineer explained the ins and outs of water intake and storage, and the management and maintenance of it all. Villages some 70 km away were benefiting from this project. Thinking of the little house on the hill of our farm, where we planned to dig for a well in the summer, I took the opportunity to have the engineer explain to me how to find water, dig a well and channel water through pipes fitted with valves to the little house; and I faxed these guidelines to Nadim and Vanessa for our summer project.

On my last evening at the base camp I had what you could call a beer drinking session with the water engineer. He told me that he himself had set up the camp nine years ago. It seemed that time had come long ago to transfer him but each time he had managed to stay. Here was someone who had "gone native" as the expression goes. He was stuck here. He had married a local woman. Still I could see that he suffered from some form of "island fever" and badly needed company in this desolate place. He said it was time for him to be transferred. But how often had he said that?

At the crack of dawn our driver Charles was already up and about, loading our luggage on the roof of the Land Rover for the long drive back to Dar es Salaam. Not far from the drop-off point he asked if I wanted to visit his family before checking in, as there was still some time to make the flight. I was thrilled to do that; it would be my first visit to someone's home in a village. Charles had a modest house made from mud and some brick. It turned out that

CHAPTER 5: A GLIMPSE OF UNICEF IN THE "FIELD"

this family was quite politically motivated. A *Free Mandela* poster took up most of the wall. At that time Nelson Mandela had already been 23 years on Robben Island. Another poster cried out for the liberation of Palestine. His wife and small children stayed in the background. Time was unfortunately too short to engage with them.

Leaving the African continent that evening with Air India for a stopover in Bombay I jotted down some notes on what I had heard and seen in Tanzania. The country was briefly a German colony until 1918 when it became a British Protectorate. That was Tanzania's luck. I was told that the British allowed a sort of national pride to continue, admitting Swahili as one of the official languages, which they did not allow in the colonies. The British interfered little with Tanzanian daily life and relations between whites and blacks were apparently more or less on a respectful footing. Tanzania had no tribal conflicts – these were often provoked in the colonies – and remained peaceful after independence. In the struggle for independence of Mozambique, Tanzania became a close ally, allowing the *Frente para a Libertação de Moçambique (FRELIMO)* to conduct incursions into Pemba province until it could operate from a base there.

President Julius Nyerere is perhaps best remembered for the successful universal literacy campaign of the 1960s and '70s, for which the entire Tanzanian population was mobilised. Those were the good times. When I was there, USAID had just suspended aid to the country because the government refused to accept conditions of lending imposed by IMF. I saw hardworking families in the Iringa region, children too, who were working the land with the hoe. I came across the Massai, the thinly built nomads dressed in their ankle-long orange robes always walking at a brisk pace with a stick, their oxen hobbling behind them.

Houses were mostly still made of clay, but local brick manufacturing was beginning to take off. Deforestation had become a big problem, but a recently invented simple, round clay stove saved much firewood. In Iringa we visited a sizeable nursery that was part of the reforestation programme. I tasted *ulanzi*, a strong, alcoholic drink made from bamboo and tasting like milk gone sour. I saw in East Africa the greatest sunsets I have ever seen in my life. Hemingway's *The Snows of Kilimanjaro* had more meaning for me now. Notwithstanding the kindness and hospitality I encountered here, I longed to go back to West Africa. I found that people there have a grace of their own. Its women dress in exquisite and abundant colours. Men and women are endowed with an infectious laugh that makes even the most reserved Western listener join in happily.

With these memories safely written up in my diary, I turned to that beautiful ending in Calvino's *Le Baron perché,* that made me wipe off a tear or two.

The Far East

Bangkok was in huge contrast of course to the base camp in Iringa that I had left barely 24 hours ago. Here were cars stuck in traffic during rush hour on the way to the Unicef Regional Office near the world-famous Oriental hotel on the Phraya River. On the Rama thoroughfares *tuk tuks* were weaving in between the heavy traffic. Motorbikes were not yet very common like today.

One of the advisers I met was Jane Hailey, an amusing British woman with a good sense of humour. She gave me an excellent overview of the education programmes in the region. I would later work briefly with her in Abidjan. I ran into Ivo Niehe, the Dutch TV personality who did gala benefits for Unicef. He was in Bangkok to make a documentary, to be shown at the Forum of Parliamentarians in The Hague that I was going to attend a few weeks later. At lunchtime we continued our discussions with him and regional information officer Jack Glattbach on a river barge, munching on pineapple and fried rice.

A most thorough briefing was the session with the regional focal point for Vietnam. I was very interested in gaining a better understanding of the Vietnam War, having been exposed to much American propaganda in the States at the time. For starters, the North Vietnamese called it the "American war". Heleni said Vietnam was still in a miserable state after eleven years of peace. The Europeans were withholding aid as a result of Vietnam for its invasion of Cambodia, and then renamed Kampuchea. There was heavy pressure on the Europeans from Washington not to engage with Hanoi. Only Olaf Palme's Sweden and Australia had the guts to withstand the pressure even during the war years. She said that Unicef paid lip service to giving aid to Vietnam. The Vietnamese population required and deserved massive aid but did not get it. She maintained that Unicef should stress its apolitical side as an argument to increase assistance.

I am forever grateful to Louis Leefers of the Geneva office that Indonesia was included in my orientation programme. Like me, the Deputy Director had family ties there too. And so I finally could set foot in the land of my maternal great-great grandfather Peter William Hofland. Born on the 6th of September 1802 in Jaggernaipora, Madras, India, Hofland immigrated to the Dutch East Indies as a 20-year-old along with other members of his family to Java. The family became naturalised Dutch citizens.

Peter Hofland acquired the estates around 1840 and ran them for 32 years until his death in 1872. This "remarkable Dutchman" focused at first on nutmeg and vanilla. Later he introduced coffee and for years coffee export was the main source of income. When the soil wearied of coffee production, he switched to tea, sugar cane, quinine and teak.[23]

Enter my great-grandfather Albert Mohr. He was the son of my great-great-grandfather Dr Carl Friedrich Gottfried Mohr who was mayor of the city-state of Bremen from 1864 to 1868 and then again briefly in 1871. In 1862 Albert Mohr sailed to the

---

[23] *Journey to Java*, Harold Nicolson, Doubleday & Company, Inc., New York 1958.

Dutch East Indies where he took Dutch nationality. Hofland's daughter Wilhelmine Helene became my great-grandmother when she married Albert Mohr.

At the death of Peter Hofland in 1872, the plantation, by then more than half a million acres (about the size of the province Utrecht in the Netherlands), was run by his two sons. They dissipated the father's fortune with gambling and women in Paris, assuming the names *"Le Comte de Pamanoekan"* and *"Le Comte de Tjasem"*, no doubt to impress their fake friends. When the estates began to have serious problems, a Dutch company was formed to administer them. My great-grandmother along with my great-grandfather Mohr reportedly played a role in saving the company until it was sold to British interests in 1910. That company began to expand tea gardens and plant rubber groves. It was then renamed "The Anglo-Dutch Plantations of Java". I like to think now that that was a bit to honour my maternal great-great grandfather. With that rich family history I vividly hoped that a side trip to Subang could be arranged in the busy Bandoeng schedule.

The Unicef Jakarta office gave an elaborate country programme briefing, ably led by programme coordinator Joe Judd. Unicef opened the office when Indonesia gained independence in 1950. The GOBI[24] strategy was already very developed. Immunization and growth monitoring were most prominent. The approach went beyond GOBI and addressed malaria prevention and control, and nutritional surveillance. What most impressed me was their *"Dokter"* programme in primary schools. Children selected as doctors and nurses would be dressed as such and mobilise their peers on health and hygiene issues. I watched them checking children as soon as they came to school. If not satisfied the "doctors" would send them off to brush their teeth or properly wash their hands with soap. I saw some 30 children brushing their teeth all at once; and then they would check again. This method was health

---

[24] Growth monitoring, oral rehydration therapy, breastfeeding and immunization.

CHAPTER 5: A GLIMPSE OF UNICEF IN THE "FIELD"

education at its best: peer-to-peer. The *dokters* would check for fever and refer to the school's head nurse. I was told that these children often took health and hygiene messages home to mobilise their parents. The Jakarta country team strengthened training for health personnel, to improve quality of service delivery, and thus resolve the present underutilization of services.

One evening I was invited at a buffet dinner given by a colleague from Paraguay, together with some other Unicef colleagues including representative Dan Brooks, an urbane, elegant and well-dressed American, a man of few words and a somewhat dreamy person, living perhaps a bit in a world of his own. Conversations were kept on the light side, mostly about problems with housekeepers, drivers and of course the usual Unicef gossip.

On Saturday morning I took a city tour bus to see some of the old Batavia. Few colonial buildings were still standing. Some whitewashed Dutch houses with red roof tiles were hidden between skyscrapers so far having escaped demolition. The town was very noisy and dirty. The old harbour Tandjong Priok was crumbling and dilapidated. Ancient wooden ships were still being used in the timber trade. The National Museum was the old *stadhuis* during "Dutch Time", the Indonesian expression for the Dutch colonial period. The museum had a small but magnificent collection of old Wayang puppets, a range of splendid Javanese silver inlaid daggers called *kris* and old, worn but splendid batik cloth.

Particularly impressive were the models of Indonesian houses from around the archipelago. The *Dayak*, the original inhabitants of Borneo, now called Kalimantan, built very long houses on stilts (the Dayak house could reach over one hundred metres in length), using ironwood for the structure and tree bark for the walls. The long house was a centre for social life and rituals alike. Each long house has a central stilt that is associated with the ancestor who founded the house. It has sacred significance as the link between the underworld and the upper world. The *Minangkabau* house of West Sumatra has distinctive roofs that look like buffalo horns.

The buffalo is a symbol of status, courage, strength and fighting spirit. The *Tongkonan* house of Sulawesi is constructed in three parts: the upper world (the roof), the world of humans (the middle of the building), and the "under world" (the space under the floor).

On Monday I flew with Information officer Djaradat to Udjung Pradang (formerly Makassar) on the Island of Sulawesi, the former Celebes, to see water pumps and latrines, schools and health centres in rural areas. Unicef groups these activities under an "area-based" programme approach, in which several interventions integrate into one holistic approach to expedite and sustain local development. As we were driving to Central Sulawesi I recognised some of the houses of which I had seen models in the national museum. They were all made of wood and built on stilts to protect them from flooding. I saw a lot of crying babies being vaccinated. Infant mortality rates approached here 170 deaths per 1,000 live births in some areas.

A lot of time is wasted in Indonesia with formal introductions with the local authorities. That cuts into the time to visit project activities. Then they all come along on the field visits, making for an unwieldy group. Therefore it was so refreshing to meet a teenage boy who came up to me spontaneously. He spoke quite good English. We began to have a bit of an exchange, where I came from, what I was doing here; where he had learned this level of English, what did he like best in school. It did not take long before the whole village was standing around us and laughing, which broke the usual monotony of officialdom.

In the evening Djaradat took me in a rickshaw on the way to a restaurant. Squeezed rather uncomfortably under plastic sheeting in driving rain, Djaradat assured me it was OK; he had once fitted his entire family of six into one rickshaw... Now there were hundreds of them swarming all over and we were right there weaving in between them. In almost zero visibility I could not make out the contours of buildings. It was sheer wonder that our rickshaw man found the place. Back at the hotel I heard on my shortwave that

CHAPTER 5: A GLIMPSE OF UNICEF IN THE "FIELD"

the American shuttle *Challenger* had broken up shortly after lift-off, claiming the lives of all seven astronauts. One member of the crew was a schoolteacher from New Hampshire who had been selected to teach American children from the spacecraft. Coming back to the hotel, I took a walk around the swimming pool. The rain had stopped and the stars had returned. But not for these astronauts. I looked up at that bright sky imagining how that crew had perished then and there just hours before.

The day had arrived to visit urban projects in Bandung with National Officer Steve Awin. Traveling some 150 km, I was finally going to get a good view of Java I had heard so much about from my father's two brothers, who had remained in Indonesia after independence. Each year one of the uncles came to Holland on home leave to stay with their younger brother for three months. The uncles talked little about their time on the Burma railroad under the Japanese. They were always deep-frying *krupuk*, a fish-based cracker, until it curled nicely into shape. *Rijsttafel* and *Nasi Goreng* were the usual dishes when the uncles were around. Most talk was about the good days of *"Indië"*, now lost forever.

Far in the distance on my right I noticed a town nestled on a hill. It was Bogor, in "Dutch times" called *Buitenzorg*, which could be translated as "no worries". An exceptionally beautiful suburb, Buitenzorg, at an altitude of 265 m, has nights a bit cooler than Jakarta and had been the weekend playground of the colonial Dutch and other Europeans. Bogor is still famous for its Botanical garden. The *Plantentuin* was founded in 1817 by a German on a plot of land bordering on the grounds of the Governor's Palace, then occupied by Governor Sir Thomas Stamford Raffles. The British had temporarily occupied Java and other Sunda Islands between 1811–15 to prevent their capture by Napoleonic France.[25] Raffles moved the administrative centre from Batavia to Buitenzorg. Wishing to be surrounded by an English garden, he founded the

---

[25] Napoleon had made his brother Louis King of Holland in 1806. Louis was very beloved by the Dutch as a modest person, interested in Dutch culture. He became fluent in Dutch; his son became French emperor Napoleon III.

Botanical Garden and he donated plants from Kew Gardens. In 1826 the Garden received samples of tea trees sent illegally from Japan by a German botanist who worked for the Dutch East Indies Company on the island of Dejima. The Dutch were the only ones allowed to trade with Japan in those days, but this tea export went unreported. Propagation was very successful: by 1833 Java counted more than half a million tea trees. This benefited my family for the rest of the 19th century and even beyond! Regretfully time did not permit a brief stopover in Bogor.

Bandung was a sprawling town with a population of some two million and counting. One of my uncles had worked there just 30 years before representing the Amsterdam based trading company Geo. Wehry & Co. We visited several of the traditional Unicef activities. Shantytowns were spreading beyond the city limits fast. The best I remember was being treated to a full-fledged *Rijsttafel*. To my surprise the hostess spoke impeccable Dutch that was no longer taught in school. Crouched in a circle on the floor, we were some 20 people enjoying this "ricetable", a main dish consisting of numerous side dishes served in small portions, accompanied by rice prepared in several different ways. Popular side dishes include egg rolls, sambals, satay, fish, fruit, vegetables, pickles, and nuts. It is by far the most popular meal in Holland. *Rijsttafel* is a Dutch adaption of *Nasi Padang* from the Padang region of West Sumatra. It is said that the Dutch introduced the multifaceted dish to impress foreign guests with the culinary richness of their colony, at the same time themselves enjoying a wide array of dishes.

Over lunch I told the local officials of my family ties to Subang, expressing the hope to visit, as we were so tantalisingly close. They all were becoming seriously interested in the story. When we sped off, I noticed that our convoy of four-wheel drives was a lot longer than before. I felt sincerely embarrassed and awkward, but it all turned out for the better. As usual we met the local officials first, explaining the reasons of our invasion of Subang. They of course knew the history of the plantation well.

CHAPTER 5: A GLIMPSE OF UNICEF IN THE "FIELD"

After further formalities we headed straight to the ancient cemetery outside Subang. Local vehicles had now also joined the convoy. The cemetery was an overgrown affair. Grass between the graves looked like a hayfield ready to be mowed. Nature had taken back most of the tombstones. I could barely decipher the script on the tombstone of a Hofland brother, deceased in 1869. Children were playing hide and seek among the graves in the overgrown field. One grave stood out, as it was the only one well kept. It was the statue of the patriarch himself, my great-great grandfather Peter William Hofland, founder of the *Pamanoekan en Tjasem Landen*.[26] A huge statue of the former plantation owner flanked by two voluptuous women towered over the graveyard. Here my great-grandmother lay buried next to her father some eighty metres underground. The statue was the work of a Belgian sculptor and was shipped in 1875, three years after the death of PWH. I glanced over my shoulder and saw the group of Indonesians standing respectfully some thirty metres behind, giving me all the time to be by myself in this for me deeply moving moment. Then I descended, alone of course, into the burial site. The light dimmed gradually with each step of the way until I needed the flashlight. Here were the two graves side by side, just simple slabs of stone. It gave me a very eerie feeling to be close to the grandmother of my father, whom he had never known. I spent perhaps ten minutes there, beginning to feel the presence of *Hades*. But at my age I was not at all ready to cross the *Styx*. It was all very weird, but the weirdest was yet to come.

I had asked the Indonesian authorities to see the old house where the Hoflands used to live. We went to see an old priest in town who advised to go and see a Mr K. Sadimoeh, who was a retired personnel director of the P & T Lands. We were in luck, Sadimoeh was home and he invited us all in for soft drinks. He and I sat down on the terrace and the others were all waiting patiently for us inside. He said the house did not exist anymore, it had been destroyed during the riots of 1949, but luckily the superstitious

---

[26] P and T Lands for short.

Javanese had never dared to lay hands on Hofland's grave. Sadimoeh said he had been having dreams in which Hofland had spoken to him, the first time in 1978. My ears perked up: here was real Javanese mysticism at work. Hofland said that he loved the Indonesian people, but was upset that his grave had been grossly neglected. So Sadimoeh took it upon himself to tend his grave that was overgrown like the other graves. Just three weeks before our meeting Hofland told Sadimoeh that he must plant roses around the grave. I said this was entirely possible as Hofland although born in India was ultimately of British descent. In another dream Hofland announced that two P & T directors would be fired on a specific date in December – and indeed they were fired!

Hofland told Sadimoeh that he had died an unnatural death at the hands of those who were after his shares in P & T. I told him this could well have been my great grandmother's brothers, who spent the family money on gambling, drinking and women in Paris and Batavia. In fact after Hofland's death their sister and my great-grandfather Albert Mohr ran the plantation. One day Sadimoeh asked Hofland why he was always wandering about and not taking any deserved rest. "I'll tell you," he said, "but don't tell anybody." Suddenly Sadimoeh reduced his voice to a whisper. Hofland said he had hidden a treasure before he died in a spot some 2.5 km from his old house. As the two brothers could not be entrusted with the family capital, this also sounded very plausible indeed. And then Sadimoeh asked, "How long are you staying? We can then start digging together tomorrow." Sadimoeh knew the exact spot where the house had been. And he insisted: "You see, as family you are a perfect medium that will increase our chances to find it." This reminded me of my father as a young boy participating in séances of calling up ghosts with his cousins. One of them was a girl of 16, a perfect medium who could get the curtains to swing on a sudden breeze and then would talk with the ghosts. I was thrilled to go digging for a family treasure, were it not for an invitation I had accepted from a Dutch diplomat to spend the weekend at his beach house on the Sunda strait. I could not possibly cancel my engagement, if only for bad telephone lines. Sadimoeh begged me to stay on, to no avail.

CHAPTER 5: A GLIMPSE OF UNICEF IN THE "FIELD"

Back at the office in Jakarta it was time for my debriefing. I gave an overview of all I had seen. Djaradat and Steve added details I missed. In the process the debriefing turned into an excellent programme review. This was a very professional country team indeed.

As a last, I briefed them on my own "project", the P & T Lands. I told them about the dreams and conversations Sadimoeh was having with my long deceased maternal great-great grandfather. This mysticism appealed very much to the nationals around the table. As a last, I told them about the family treasure; that I was begged to help find it; and that as family I would probably be a good medium and succeed. I ended by stating that it would be wholly appropriate for the Chief of the Programme Funding Section in Geneva to dig up a treasure. To top it all off, the sound bite came naturally: "and" – pausing a brief second, lifting up both arms to the sky for effect – "what a way to raise funds!" The meeting ended with roaring laughter in which I fully joined – with a few tears in my eyes. The visit to Subang had touched me more than I thought.

The beach house of Dirk Hasselman faced the Sunda Strait that separates Sumatra from Java. On the horizon one could clearly see the tip of the Krakatau volcano sticking out its head just barely above water. Hasselman recalled what we had learned in school, namely the unbelievably powerful eruption of the Krakatau in 1883. The Dutch authorities estimated that 36,417 people perished. A huge Tsunami wiped out entire towns and villages. A good part of the Krakatau islet disappeared in the ocean. The huge and ear-shattering explosion could be heard as far as Alice Springs in Australia, a distance of some 3,500 kilometres. Interestingly, there was also a positive ecological effect. Only after one year grass started to grow again on islets that were spared. Forty years later they were once more covered by dense forest. Nearby regions of Java and Sumatra that were arid before now had suddenly become fertile. This started a process of migration from less fortunate places. Knowing the story, it was strange, even awesome to look at this now quiet monster so near to this beach. When would the Krakatau erupt again? We did not dwell upon it for too long, perhaps preferring to enjoy this typical, relaxing beach weekend, with barbecue and drinks, good company and light conversation. All of them got beach massages, and so did I, the first and last one in my life. The awful smell of coconut oil did me in, it was all too ticklish, and most likely I had no patience for it!

Vietnam

Paul Audat, a bearded French intellectual, who had lived most of his life with his wife Yvonne in North and West Africa, ran the Unicef office in Hanoi. The small office had a very definite family atmosphere, at least among international staff. They were of course very dependent on each other. Yvonne helped out with the typing. It was all a bit with the *Franse slag*[27], with everything delightfully improvised. Often I did not know until the last minute what the programme was, or where I was heading. Perhaps that was due in part to the Vietnamese government partners. But as with artists, it all worked out in the end anyway. Living under a very strict form of communism, nationals had to report once a month to government officials as to what was going on at Unicef. They were all spies so one had to watch out what to say and not to say. Upon going home staff was frisked to see if they had received money or presents that would then be confiscated. When getting a job, even with Unicef, new staff had to hand over the equivalent of ten months' salary to the government. No wonder then that positions in those days rotated often to create more of such revenue. Staff turnover in Unicef was frequent for that reason alone. It all looked like a form of slavery to me.

I stayed at the *Thong Nhat* that was about the only hotel in town. One could not believe that this had once been the luxury Metropole hotel built in 1901 in the old French colonial style. When the communists took over in 1954, the Metropole was nationalised and renamed the *Thong Nhat* or Reunification Hotel. It was now better known for its rat population rather than its beautiful people of the olden days waltzing the nights away.

---

[27] The French would say "à l'improviste", but the Dutch give it a French connotation.

CHAPTER 5: A GLIMPSE OF UNICEF IN THE "FIELD"

On the evening of my arrival I dined by myself in the gloomy and ill-lit restaurant, the only West European surrounded by a handful of Bulgarians and East Germans. The food was poor, to say no more. The man at the reception accompanied me to my room with a flashlight, as a power cut had just come on. On another night, entering after a dinner with the Audats, another power cut had hit the hotel, but this time no one was sitting at the reception and so I had to grope my way upstairs without a flashlight or a key. Somehow I remembered vaguely where my room was. I felt the shape of a hard top suitcase at the entrance, so I concluded that this was my room. I stumbled over a mosquito net but somehow managed to crawl under it happy to land on the mattress. The next day I told Yvonne Audat how I had found my bed with difficulty and that it felt unmade. She said rooms were often rented out to lovers in the afternoon! A junk rating for this once glorious hotel would have been an understatement[28].

One morning at 7 o'clock I was waiting for the Unicef car at a V-junction near *Thong Nat* where two avenues joined. Streets were completely empty at first. Then suddenly, hundreds of bicycles, as if released all at once came around the bend, all going in the direction of where I was standing. It was a very cold and misty February morning. I thought that the bicycle perhaps gave them a sense of freedom, freewheeling all over town without being told where to go. Most of them raced right by me, just staring ahead. But one young boy saw me and screeched to a halt. He spoke a bit of broken English and told me quite openly that he wished to leave Vietnam. And off he went, surely afraid to be noticed. Hanoi was not a city of cars in those days. Only the privileged apparatchiks had access to them, but at this early hour there were none of them yet on the road. The first car that appeared was Unicef.

---

[28] Just one year later the French Pullman Hotels chain entered into a joint venture with the Vietnamese government to restore the hotel to international standards. The hotel was completely rebuilt, regaining the name Metropole. Today it is known as the Legend Sofitel Metropole Hanoi.

That day we were going to see water projects near Nam Dinh, some 90 km south east of Hanoi. The road was in very bad condition. It had been bombed frequently by the Americans but was sort of patched up. Immense craters where bombs had fallen were easily visible from the road. Rusty trucks and buses, their roofs loaded with people's belongings including the inevitable bikes, hobbled along as best they could. The Vietnamese must be very good mechanics I thought. The Unicef driver honked incessantly taking no chances. The weather was overcast and chilly. The Unicef water programme was fairly new in this area. As fresh water was rare in these rural areas – Americans had often poisoned wells from the air – children suffered from waterborne diseases and intestinal parasites. They often showed signs of stunting – their height was below the norm for their age – and other forms of malnutrition.

Rice planting was in full swing. I saw many a pair of women with conical straw hats, who were holding a rope with a pail attached in the middle and scooping up water from brooks and throwing it on to the rice fields. Their swaying movement was like playing jump rope with a child jumping in the middle. Boys with their fathers were tending the oxen ploughing the fields. In the distance I spotted a young boy on an oxen crossing a rice field and coming straight for the road. His clothes were grey and torn but his tiny red scarf provided a touch of colour. Armed with the Unicef camera I jumped out of car and approached him as near as I could in the wet field. The oxen was faster than I was and was suddenly very near. It's really a very impressive animal from up close and I was apprehensive to suddenly find myself on its horns like an incompetent matador. I took the picture fast and ran back to the car. Back in Geneva I had a poster made out of it and had it framed. Since then the poster has hung in every Unicef office that I have occupied.

The field visit included a Vietnamese noodle lunch at a long wooden table with local officials and the water brigade. The locals were a lot less formal than their bosses at the ministry. Broken English was mixed in with Vietnamese, but we all got by somehow, and not least because of the relaxed atmosphere.

CHAPTER 5: A GLIMPSE OF UNICEF IN THE "FIELD"

One evening I happened to sit next to Ambassador Tran Hoan at the official dinner with the government and diplomatic community, on the occasion of *Tet,* the Vietnamese New Year celebration[29]. Formerly ambassador to the UK, he was now the number three at the ministry of Foreign Affairs in charge of relations with the United Nations. An advantage in communist countries is that you do not have to explain yourself from scratch; they have your details even before you come. Mr Tran Hoan seemed well aware of my connection to the United States. It followed that we had a very interesting and in depth discussion about Vietnam and the West. Because of his time spent in London, Mr Tran Hoan struck me as urbane and refined. He was certainly the most relaxed official I met in Hanoi.

Early into the conversation he raised the question of relations with America. I was struck by the fact that there was no hatred in his position; and yet Vietnam had a lot to complain about. Hoan said that he was hoping for a breakthrough with the US and that diplomatic relations would not be long in coming anymore. He said one of the main problems were the Americans missing in action, the MIA's. Vietnam was ready to help in looking for their remains[30]. I said that President Reagan was of course the only one with weight capable to force a breakthrough in establishing diplomatic relations and I thought he might well do this at the end of his presidency that was two years away. I said that perhaps much could advance on the international front if only Vietnam could liberalize its economy and attract foreign direct investment. Later in 1986 Vietnam introduced *"doi moi"*, a policy of economic renovation, gradually shifting the centrally planned economy to a market economy. But diplomatic relations could not begin unless Vietnam withdrew all its troops from Kampuchea.[31] I felt quite at ease to discuss these issues with this charming man who was not afraid to give a frank assessment of the situation.

---

[29] Tet is the most important holiday in Vietnam and can last up to seven days.
[30] In 1988 Vietnam began letting US military search teams into the countryside to look for the remains of missing US service men.
[31] By September 1989 Vietnam had withdrawn all troops from Kampuchea.

In the last hours of my stay Yvonne Audat took me on a tour of the town. The Parisian touch of Hanoi was still very visible in the old colonial buildings on broad tree-lined Hausmann style boulevards. But the war had left scars. With the exception of government buildings, Ho Chi Minh's Mausoleum and some embassies, most structures were quite dilapidated. Ancient churches and pagodas were crumbling. I wrote in my diary that even with just a little bit of paint Hanoi could be one of the quaintest cities its size in the world. We stopped at the market to buy a white hand-embroidered tablecloth plus napkins that Yvonne helped me find. Vietnam is well known for its hand-embroidered cloth. Of course, the conical straw hats were not forgotten. They would come in handy at our farm in upstate New York. I wondered what the farmers there would say, perhaps even, "Ho, ho, the Vietnamese are coming".

There was a thriving black market going on in Dong with the dollar fetching 10 times the official rate of 15. I was sure that the communist government had an interest in the affair. It was now two days before the *Tet* celebrations would get under way. The place was swarming with conical hats. Women were loading small orange trees, the symbol of *Tet*, on to the backseat of their bicycles, spending their last Dong on this important tradition. Japanese cherry branches in full bloom did a brisk business. Surely the Vietnamese had to save up for *Tet* the whole year.

My last image of Hanoi was this tiny wrinkled old woman in a long peasant skirt speeding off on her rusty bicycle, holding a small tree full with oranges with one hand and steadily steering with the other. Such are the images of travel that stay with you forever.

Chapter 6: Sport Aid: The race against time

Just back in Geneva I was already off to Brussels to accompany Jim Grant on a visit to the Belgian National Committee. Grant boiled over with fundraising ideas and shared them on the spot. In this way at dinner he animated the entire table. It was here that I heard of the name Bob Geldof for the first time mentioned in connection with Unicef. My knowledge of rock music did not go much further than the Beatles. Leader of the British rock band the Boomtown Rats, Geldof had made his fame with the Band Aid/Live Aid concerts the year before, raising millions of dollars for famine in Ethiopia and other drought-stricken countries. Grant told us that Geldof had in mind an Olympic event in Birmingham with most of the of the proceeds going to Unicef. A similar event in Los Angeles would also benefit Unicef. Grant's thinking was to link both events as early as this coming summer. This type of fundraising would potentially be enormous. The whole table briefly went silent, no doubt all of us already dreaming of millions of dollars. These potential joint fundraising events turned out to be the blueprint for a much larger undertaking: Sport Aid.

About to board the Sabena plane for New York, Grant put his long crooked thumb up in the air as a sign that things had gone well on our mission in The Hague and Brussels. I must admit that made me feel very good. As only the French can put it so well, Grant was *très cool!* It had been a whirlwind tour that morning with calls on the Ministry of Development and the Belgian National Committee, topped off with an animated press conference. After a hectic two days I needed that most enjoyable and relaxing lunch with John Parr and his ten-year-old daughter and my godchild Alexa at the manège where she rode horses. The entry in my diary reads: *"quite a spirited and spoiled girl: John looks older but finer"*.

Secondment to Bob Geldof's Sport Aid in London

A week or so later I received a phone call from John Williams asking me to come to London and discuss with him and Robert Smith of the UK Committee my secondment to Bob Geldof's Sport Aid team. Did Jim Grant have a hand in this? Sport Aid was going to be a major sports event worldwide, benefiting the Band Aid Trust and Unicef. This sounded fascinating and right up my alley. I remember a fun tête à tête dinner with John, much enjoying his Australian humour mixed in with the fun topic at hand: how to ensure that the partnership of Unicef with Geldof's Band Aid Trust would meet with the expectations of huge income and high, global visibility for Unicef.

Fast forward to London a couple of weeks later: a small group of Unicef staff huddles around our Executive Director in his suite at the Park Lane hotel in London to prepare for the press conference that is to launch *Sport Aid – the Race against Time*. There is Robert Smith, the lean and sparsely bearded Executive Director of the UK Committee; Edith Simmons, his right hand for media relations; and Hélène Gosselin, Regional Information Adviser, Abidjan, seconded to Sport Aid like me. Everybody was in a jolly mood.

At some point the discussion is about which T-shirt Grant should wear under his jacket at the press conference. Two are on Jim's shortlist: one with *"stop children from dying"* and the other with: *"45,000 children dying each day."* The latter version is selected almost unanimously but not quite. I thought that the text should be upbeat and positive and I advise against both. What happened next still makes me smile: Grant tries on the T-shirt, it turns out to be way too big even for this big man; he disappears into his room and locks the door; next thing we hear is the sound of running water; apparently washes the T-shirt; stays away for a long time, steam appearing through the door; We all fear a serious problem and I go knocking on the bathroom door; it's still a few minutes though until he finally comes out with a hair dryer that does not do the job; tries to "iron" it on a stool; I volunteer to take over; Grant getting his camera out and taking my picture – who should

CHAPTER 6: SPORT AID: THE RACE AGAINST TIME

have thought that the ExDir would one day do that. And then it becomes all truly surrealistic with all that steam around the room, a man-made London fog.

It feels like going to a wedding. We are expecting some three hundred "guests" to attend the press conference at the Park Lane Hotel. My diary gives the details: *"Soon after 8 a.m. we brief Grant in his suite on what he should say and not say, certainly not speak in cryptic acronyms like GOBI, UCI or EPI. Then back to the T-shirt again, how should he wear it, over or in his trousers, hiding it as best he can, someone suggesting he could suddenly open his jacket wide as an effect of surprise and so on.* Meanwhile it is waiting for Bob Geldof to show up at the agreed time of ten o'clock. But no, the star is notoriously late – we had been briefed on that one - and finally turns up at 10:40.

My diary: *"In walks Geldof, shoulders pulled up high, simply dressed in jeans and a striped shirt, but OK; he is definitely scruffy but there's something romantic, sensual about the guy"*. He and Jim settle down on an uncomfortably narrow sofa as if they have known each other for years; and we groupies huddle around them, just listening in. Geldof's sentences are full of expletives that Grant ignores totally. He knows the scruffy rock star has a knack for generating publicity.[32] And that was what Unicef needed most. My diary notes: *"Chemistry with JPG very good. Geldof saying that giving through Live Aid was a "rebellious" act: we the people can do better than organisations. Grant agreeing saying there was more people's power in the last year alone than ever before. Geldof says he is sick of Ethiopia and the way it handles its aid; he says that if Ethiopia had had a good PR man they could at least have explained their forced internal migration policy to the world"*. Paul Valleley of *The Times* of London, co-author of *"With Geldof in Africa: confronting the famine crisis"* tells me that he was just thrown out of Ethiopia for exposing the regime's

---

[32] *A Mighty Purpose: How Jim Grant sold the world on saving its children*, Adam Fifield, Other Press, New York.

brutality. The Band Aid people are young, down to earth and refreshing.

The celebrity of the press conference is Geldof, not Grant. I still remember seeing them coming on to the stage – we the "groupies" had taken our seats beforehand. Geldof is wearing a T-shirt with the slogan *"Run the World"* with the new Sport Aid logo on the back – a map of Africa topped off by the torch. He takes the middle seat flanked by Grant and Britain's 1,500-metre Olympic gold medallist, Sebastian Coe. Grant has left his T-shirt in the room, perhaps it was still too large… or he had heeded the advice of the one dissenter.

> The popularity of Geldof's mega events suggested that in the era of celebrity and media power, there were new heights of public attention and action to be commanded on behalf of the developing world, if the right buttons were pushed. This diagnosis of the public mood greatly appealed to Jim Grant who saw an opportunity for "social mobilisation" on a much larger scale.
>
> Maggie Black
> *Children first: the story of Unicef,* 1996

Geldof said the primary goal of Sport Aid was to raise awareness of the continuous need to fight hunger, disease and poverty in Africa. He announced that Sport Aid would run from 17th to 25th May, climaxing with a worldwide 10-kilometre "Race Against Time" on 25th May. That date had been chosen to coincide with the United Nations General Assembly Special Session on Africa and to draw attention to the need to do far more for Africa. Activities for the "Race Against Time" would kick-off on 17th May, when an African runner would leave Ethiopia with a torch lit from charcoal fire in a refugee camp. During the following week, the runner would race through major European capitals until arriving in New York on 25th May to light a Sport Aid flame

CHAPTER 6: SPORT AID: THE RACE AGAINST TIME

at UN Plaza. This would signal the start of 10-kilometre runs all over the world, exactly at 15:00 GMT. Geldof said negotiations were also under way for events to be held in Eastern Bloc countries. *"Music and sport are two things that transcend borders,"* he emphasised. Net proceeds would be split equally between Band Aid and Unicef.

Grant stressed that, *"we want to remind leaders of the world: people do care about Africa."* He said continued aid would help Ethiopia cut its death rate of children in half in the next five years. The 10K run was to symbolise the ten years of famine in Africa and the obligation of the international community to help Africa's transition, *"from famine to rehabilitation to self-reliance".* He illustrated the dire debt situation of Africa by pointing out that the continent received three billion dollars of aid in 1985 but had to pay out double that amount in capital and interest payments. The press conference was widely televised on the British networks of course but also in America, most notably on the CBS morning news. That filled us with hope for massive participation in the race there. But it was not to be. The date of the Sport Aid Race conflicted with the *Hands-Across-America* campaign when millions of people were going to hold hands from California to New York to raise funds in the fight against hunger and poverty in the United States itself.

Sport Aid had now been launched and a huge organisation got under way. Band Aid Trust and Unicef were soon coordinating thousands of Sport Aid focal points around the world. These helped to organise the pre-run, the 10 kilometres "Race against Time" as well as related, which we called "adopted" sport events such as tennis, cricket, soccer and basketball. In the end there were over one thousand of them in the UK alone. First task at hand was the move into office space that the Overseas Development Agency (ODA) had provided to Sport Aid just across Waterloo Bridge, next to the Old Vic Theatre, so tantalisingly close at hand. The office was one large space where at one point tens of young Band Aid volunteers assisted by seconded Unicef staff were squeezed together from early morning to late at night.

Meanwhile I had moved into the Kingsley hotel, a dull place to say the least. The view of my room was on the familiar drab buildings with their brownish red chimneys covered in mist and drizzle. I later upgraded myself and moved to the Clearlake Hotel at 18 Prince of Wales Terrace, Kensington. The closest I got to seeing a lake were road potholes that were never short of stagnant rain water. The place was relatively clean and well run by two Israeli "runaways", who wanted to be far from their Middle East troubles. Equipped with a small kitchen the price of the room was right. On the first Sunday of my stay I turned on the Walkman Nadim had lent me. What a thoughtful thing to do. How delightful it was to be able to listen to a Mendelssohn violin concerto on a Sunday morning in a drab hotel room!

Knowing that I could not handle this work load by myself, I soon brought Bernadette Suffran over from Geneva. She took a room at the Clearlake but later moved to an apartment with Hélène Gosselin near St. James. She was a real trooper, a quiet worker who could be fully relied on. We had a varied group of enthusiasts, most of them young and engaged. The Band Aid/Live Aid concerts and now Sport Aid were the brain child of Chris Long. I found him pleasant, a bit of a dreamy person with a bashful smile, but boiling over with ideas. Then there was Simon Dring, a former BBC TV correspondent, who had been almost shot to pieces when he was covering the Turkish invasion of Cyprus in 1976. I found him rather tense and abrasive, but who knows, it was perhaps a leftover of his traumatic war correspondent days.

Unicef HQ had just hired a consultant for Special Events and Sport Aid was of course a major assignment for him. John Anderson was a meticulous planner, with a quick eye for detail. Although he did not have much of a spark, John was badly needed to balance our media people, who had perhaps too much of it. For them, creative as they were, it was often more ad hoc planning! John Williams, a former journalist started out as overall Sport Aid coordinator for Unicef based at New York Headquarters, but he soon faded in the background. He could now totally rely on

CHAPTER 6: SPORT AID: THE RACE AGAINST TIME

Anderson. Then there was the flamboyant Canadian Hélène Gosselin, another media person, a lively and hard working person who was seconded to London from the Regional Office in Abidjan. There was Elfy, a Special Events officer in New York. Most of the Unicef team in London were media people. Of course they were preparing the press releases and looking for human interest stories around Sport Aid. I always thought that Unicef communication officers had the best and potentially the most creative of all jobs. It was just what you made of it yourself. I always considered Information and Communication the best job I never had!

Sport Aid had enthusiastic and committed young volunteers. Simon Dring's personal assistant was a hardworking and inventive woman, who secured us free stationery by just calling a company from the yellow pages. There were other women who could find us equipment – free of charge – that we could not do without. For example Zoey, a typical London girl with a super commitment and a heart of gold. Zoey was my PA and she took it upon herself to find us a third telex machine on the same day she joined. She even made it work herself. Then she telephoned a contact at Scotland Yard and got a free police escort for Omar Khalifa for after his run, the UK National Committee having booked protection only one-way! Zoey was very quick, her drive was simply enormous and she could improvise marvellously.

Bernadette, Elfy and I were responsible for organising the pre-run of the lone African who was to carry the torch through European capitals all the way to New York. At the same time we were setting up worldwide banking arrangements and sponsorships. Hélène Gosselin linked up with Information officers of Unicef around the world and worked hand in hand with Edith Simmons on press releases, interviews and photo-ops. My group talked daily on the phone with National Committees and field offices monitoring the organisation of the 10K run and their needs for T-shirts or other paraphernalia. The atmosphere at Sport Aid reminded me very much of NBBS, the Dutch travel agency run by students for students in the 1960s and '70s. I worked with NBBS for three summers. Whether it was managing our student hotels or guiding American girls in a VW bus through Europe, we were young people committed to a cause, relying more on improvisation than planning, working many long hours but still having time to party; and sometimes having a crush on someone and falling in love but having no time for it, as time moved on us so very fast.

After a few weeks things were beginning to look bleak for Sport Aid. We still had no sponsor, no runner, nothing; things at the office were still pretty chaotic and disorganised; and time was against us. Meanwhile we were promising the world to the media in press releases and interviews. I warned Geneva of the situation. It dispatched Bob Walwer to strengthen overall coordination. Bob was close to retirement. He was as a painter in his free time which seemed to have kept him young and creative. He thus fitted in very well with the much younger colleagues.

For the 10K run, we were constantly on the phone with the world, plagued by crackling voices and strange sounds. In those days overseas telephone lines were particularly bad with Africa. I often had a phone on each ear listening to two countries all at once. We worked without computers. Fax machines existed but the world was still largely on telex and so were we. My assistant Bernadette remembers "kilometres of telexes rolling out of telex machines" throughout the day. Jo Howe, a communications specialist seconded by IBM, assisted Sport Aid with troubleshooting and maintenance. We usually stayed until 10 pm, to have our last phone calls with New York. And then I would be off and running to the next door pub, usually with Bob Walwer and Bernadette to check out the steak and kidney pie one more time, and hastily swallowing a couple of pints of bitter before the pub closed.

Slowly but surely we were beginning to have some interesting results. We drew up an "adoption agreement" for the related sports in the UK. In the end these adoptions covered hundreds of national and local events including rugby, basketball, gymnastics, tennis and international cricket, even an ice show.

CHAPTER 6: SPORT AID: THE RACE AGAINST TIME

Lots of people came through with side event fundraising ideas. Perhaps the most exotic one was proposed by a parachute jumping instructor. Celebrities would jump from 10,000 feet, with the instructor holding each "passenger" in a bear hug under him while going down. The instructor assured me that the touchdown was perfectly safe. He had already enlisted two celebrities so far who would be sponsored by the public donating money towards the jump with proceeds going to Sport Aid. The hitch was the exorbitant cost of insuring the celebrity for the jump.

We received our *Run the World* Sport Aid T-shirts in time for our jogging through the streets of South London. Jogging was meant to engage the whole office so as to make publicity for Sport Aid, but few joined. Our regular journey took us on a three-mile run several times a week crossing Waterloo Bridge turning right into Aldwych and then Fleet Street, sometimes stopping at a radio or TV station for Chris Long or somebody else to be interviewed. Then on to the Embankment along the Thames, crossing Waterloo Bridge once more and returning to the office at 133 Waterloo Road. Apart from Chris Long, the faithful included Mary Kay, a journalist from Minneapolis, Bernadette, Elfy, and the young and quite lively Tamsin.

Nadim became a RAT regular for the short time he came with A. to London, running in our lunch break in the Sport Aid T-shirt *"Run the World"*. He stood eye to eye with Omar Khalifa, the world famous 1,500m athlete from Sudan, when the latter happened to be in our office to discuss the details of the pre-run. One day we jogged through Westminster and St James as far as Radio London in Marylebone Street. There I was interviewed on the occasion of World Health Day, this year under the banner *"Everybody a Winner"*. I was hoping that perhaps Jack Ling would be listening in and remember our encounter in Abidjan just weeks before. On one of our jogs the *"RAT raiders"* were photographed and the same evening our picture was in the *Evening Standard*. All pre-arranged of course. Motivated by it all, Nadim wrote the Sport Aid story for his school.

One time in between I went back to Geneva on a weekend, taking Mary Kay with me for a press conference to mobilise interest in the 10K run. Arriving late at the house in Trelex the soft clinging sound of the village church bell chimed a peaceful midnight. The kitchen was full of postcards written from Italy but not yet mailed. Among them was a postcard that Vanessa intended to send to a friend in London. It was a beautiful poem by Conrad Aiken on mysticism, of which an extract here:

mysticism but let us have no words
angels but let us have no fantasies
churches but let us have no creeds
no dead gods hung on crosses in a shop
no beads nor prayer nor faith nor sin nor penance:
and yet let us believe
let it be the flower

....

mysticism but let it be the flower
let it be the hand that reaches for the flower
let it be the flower that imagined the first hand
let it be the space that removed itself to give place
for the hand that reaches the flower to be reached
let it be self displacing self
as quietly as a child lifts a pebble
as softly as a flower decides to fall
self replacing self
as seed follows flower to earth

Mary who was from Minneapolis thought that Macalester University in St. Paul would be a good choice for Vanessa to study anthropology. She gave Vanessa some good insights into her life as a journalist. The two girls seemed to be hitting it off well.

Like the London Underground, Sport Aid had its good days and bad days. Simon Kusseff had suggested that we to try to arrange with the investment bank Samuel Montague some kind of banking

CHAPTER 6: SPORT AID: THE RACE AGAINST TIME

syndicate as a novel way to raise donations for Sport Aid. The introductory meeting went well and I decided to inform New York about this potential fundraiser. New York was interested and sent its new Treasurer, a Frenchman and a former banker like me. Together he and I started putting a draft syndicate together in the form of what was called a tombstone in those days. The simple black and white ad does indeed resemble a gravestone and announces the issuance of corporate stock or debt. Such advertisements typically provided the very basic information about the investment to would-be investors.

The first signs of trouble began to appear when I had accepted Montague as the arranging bank after receiving the green light from New York for the tombstone. The treasurer got into a real fit and later blamed it on travel fatigue. Had I stepped on his turf? I do not recall how Banque National de Paris (BNP) was selected later as co-manager. Perhaps the French colleague had had a hand in it. Other major financial institutions would be invited to come on board. Contributions of all these banks were to benefit Sport Aid. The idea was that our Executive Director would announce the Bank Syndicate at the Executive Board session that was going to be held within a matter of weeks and that would be a major coup. Obviously time was of the essence. I felt that much was at stake for Sport Aid for a successful conclusion of the banking deal. It was not to be. The situation became bizarre: on Walwer's computer screen the treasurer singlehandedly changed the venue of signing from London to Dakar, Senegal. He included regional development banks in the tombstone, making this more of a public than private transaction. When he introduced the idea of Central Banks, an exasperated Montague withdrew. The arranging bank had been very patient indeed. But because of all these last minute ad-ons, time had run out. I was not pleased, a key sponsor was now lost. [33]

All sorts of problems could arise in the organisation of the pre-run. It took a long time before a runner was identified to carry the

---

[33] My diary.

torch during the pre-run. In the end the choice fell on Omar Khalifa, a world famous Sudanese athlete. Omar was to light a torch with embers of charcoal from a Sudanese refugee camp and carry it through 12 European capitals to end in New York. There he would light the Sport Aid flame at the United Nations in New York, where it would burn for the duration of the event. A difficult one was to convince Eastern Bloc countries to participate. Poland agreed, but then we got word that they had gotten the date wrong and on-going planning was cancelled… Typical. In the end only Budapest made it. I felt very strongly that Hungary had defied the Soviet empire one more time. That made me think back to the days of the courageous uprising in November 1956 and the subsequent Soviet invasion of Soviet tanks to crush Imre Nagy, so vividly described in James Michener's first novel *The Bridge at Andau* that my father had given to me at that time.

We as pre-run focal points were sometimes dispatched to some of these capitals to solve problems before they could occur. For example there was a heated debate raging in the Italian Committee whether the pre-run should go through Venice or Rome. I sided with the group preferring Venice as the annual Venice marathon could then be linked beneficially with the "Race against Time". Others wanted Rome, arguing that we could then "mobilise the Pope". In Sport Aid we all simply thought that nothing was impossible for us to achieve. Even the wildest proposals such as that one were taken seriously. The Pope's blessing was important to us to get the highest number of 10K runners and Sport Aid adopted side events.

Meanwhile I went with Chiara of the National Committee and Mgr. Umberto and a host of other officials to the Castello Sant' Angelo, where Omar would light the flame. Some 5,000 children were to cheer; letting balloons up in the air, waving Unicef and Sport Aid flags, all for the purpose of a splendid backdrop for the Pope's endorsement. That would also increase our chances for TV hook-ups with other countries. Only Italians can dream up such a show. I myself had not much of a role to play. So I quickly toured

CHAPTER 6: SPORT AID: THE RACE AGAINST TIME

the impressive castle, which is perched on a hill overlooking Trastevere. Alexander VI, the Borghese Pope, used to have an apartment in its donjon. A popular Roman view is that the donjon is the safest place in all of Roma. I thought the Borghese might well have needed all the protection he could get to shield his decadent life from public view.

Many an afternoon Geldof paid a visit to the office with his little dog on the leash, wife and baby girl in the stroller in tow. As soon as Geldof entered Band Aid volunteers would huddle around him. Somebody would turn on the "telly" and play over and over again the Sport Aid theme tune. The tune had been composed by Vangelis (of *Chariots of Fire* fame) especially for Sport Aid and added much to the sense of fervour of the event. It sounded much like the theme song of the film. I can attest that the music also meant a lot to all of us in the office and in fact never bored us. Geldof was upset that we still had not heard about the Pope's participation. As usual, expletives reinforced his point.

Just days before the pre-run was about to begin the atmosphere in the office had become more hectic, frantic and electrifying than ever before. Just days before the runner would land in Madrid I got a call that they had not received the propylene gas from New York. Propylene apparently gives off a nicer flame than propane. We had learned about that too! Suddenly we had to follow up this detail with Germany and New York. The gas had indeed been shipped but was most likely held up at customs. I thought we were crazy to transport highly flammable gas on a plane. And little did we foresee that Khadaffi would be on a state visit in Spain at precisely the same time. In the waning days of the office there were lots of TV cameramen around with interviews going on in every corner. Reuters ran a story with me saying that, "the tendency was now gradually going to be towards long-term development programmes in Africa as opposed to emergency relief." Of course not forgetting that Sport Aid was all about famine and other emergencies.

There was great sentimentality in the air as we knew that in a few days most of us would never see one another again. Telephones were ringing constantly. People were hugging each other for no reason at all or perhaps only to relieve tension. There was still time for last parties *"entre nous"*. Martin, a Sport Aid volunteer, invited us all for a party at his flat with a group of actors and actresses. I was dancing with a girl who got seriously dizzy, I wondered why. Another night the whole office was invited to a famous London disco to promote Sport Aid. The disco was equipped with a lot of psychedelic swirling lights that made your head turn. In the afternoon I already had been asked in the office by Lucie, who was our receptionist, a sweet, dark haired girl, if I could dance with her that evening. And that was after I had told her story of the dizzy girl at Martin's party! Although I was flattered to be booked that far in advance, I was apprehensive – but of course I gracefully accepted – as I am a very clumsy dancer and I was certainly not looking forward to having another girl faint in my arms! The disco was very glamorous and posh. I still see the image of the ceiling above the dance floor starting to descend upon us very slowly with all its lights seemingly swirling even faster. That spectacular ending announced that the disco was about to close. I was looking in vain for Lucie to see if she was OK.

Meanwhile Bernadette and Hélène were far away from these hectic and emotional closing days in London. They had been selected to join Omar Khalifa on the plane to some of the European capitals where he would run with the torch. Khalifa had begun his journey on 16th May, when he lit a torch at the El Moweilih relief camp in the Sudan. My diary notes: *"I must say the picture of Omar Khalifa in the Observer touched me, the lone runner running with the torch casting a long shadow over the sands of the desert"*. Indeed the British have an absolute knack for copyright. Above the photo the headline: *"Flame of hope outpaces the shadow of famine: Omar Khalifa, Sudan's star athlete, sets out across the desert on his Sport Aid run to New York"*. Dramatic stuff but it worked.

Khalifa was then flown to Athens where the torch of Africa and the Olympic torch were symbolically joined. That was the first

CHAPTER 6: SPORT AID: THE RACE AGAINST TIME

time the Olympic torch had been lit outside an Olympic Games. He ran through 12 European capitals in all, greeted by Prime Minister Margaret Thatcher, Prince Charles and Princess Diana, President François Mitterrand, Chancellor Helmut Kohl and Pope John Paul II. On one day, Bernadette recalls, it was a true marathon in itself: Brussels in the morning, Paris at lunchtime (good planning!) and Warsaw in the early evening. Another day it was Dublin, Madrid and Rome, and so on. Budapest was the only East Bloc capital in the pre-run. Meanwhile a sick Geldof had gone off to New York, to attend the arrival of Omar at the United Nations. One more tense moment was lived by the Sport Aid people back in London: would Geldof make it back on time for the run in London? I remember listening to the radio on the morning of the Race. It had been touch and go but Geldof made the night flight alright and then ran the course on Sunday afternoon in London.

On the 25th of May 1986 an estimated twenty million people in some 200 cities and 66 countries ran in the "Race against Time", making it the largest sporting event in history at that time. TV images with proud and happy people running the 10k race flashed live all over the world. Without a doubt the most spectacular TV images came from Ouagadougou, Burkina Faso. To get a decent TV hook-up with a very poor country in Africa was in those days a technical feat of the highest order. Captain Thomas Sankara, the country's young and dynamic President, had ordered his whole cabinet to come out jogging with him; to see thousands of Burkinabe running after their leader through the streets of superhot Ouagadougou, who could ever forget that image?

"I knew you would come," said Vanessa. I had kept my coming back to Geneva a secret to her. I really had preferred to run the race in London, with my children, but I did not want to miss seeing Vanessa perform in a play at school. She had the role of the stepdaughter in Pirandello's *Six characters in search of an author*. The play is a mixture of realism and surrealism until both finally merge into one. The characters become the actors (a destitute family telling its life story) and the actors rehearsing for another play become the spectators. Her role required quite a bit of screaming and she played the part. In fact Vanessa and another classmate carried the play. I thought that she could play any role. She disagreed, saying that she could only play it well if there was something in the part to be found of herself, because then "one acts more convincingly".

Some 8,000 runners showed up in Geneva, a record in those days. There was a lot of excitement all around: the African continent on the Sport Aid flag waving at the participants, with a rock and roll band doing the rest. Vanessa had decided at the last minute to run too. Nadim and his friend Alexis and I started up front. I was carried away and ran really fast. I realised I had let Nadim down. I waited a long time and then he came in last, quite dehydrated. To this very day I have not forgiven my egocentric jogging trip in the *Race against Time*.

For weeks afterwards I kept seeing images of the sentimental goodbye party in the office two days before the race. The atmosphere had been electrifying, full of human radioactivity, sentimentality, and a bit of sensuality and playful jealousy. It had been just like the end of a play. Many talked about their hopes and plans after Sport Aid. Nick Carter, press officer, who was always around and about with a big mouth, was now very quiet as the end was near; Nadia wanted to set up an agency for volunteers to bring business closer to non-profit organisations. I told her about a letter I had written to Per Gyllenhammer, the CEO of Volvo, making the point about the "converging interests of multinationals and voluntary organisations".

Debbie and Lucie, who as reception girls saw and heard a lot, promised to feed me gossip for the play I intended to write about Sport Aid. Lulu, the blond "English schoolgirl" offered to write it with me and wanted to be cast for the main role. Bob Walwer, just back from shaking hands with Charles and Di, was in a happy mood. Overhearing our plan for a play he advised that it should end – like here in the office – just before it happens so it leaves the

CHAPTER 6: SPORT AID: THE RACE AGAINST TIME

audience in suspense. Then there was Chris Long strolling around, immersed with his own thoughts, about to make his brainchild come true; Martin Robinson, of great parties fame; spirited volunteers like Jacqui Shaw, Maggie Mason; Tamsin of the press department, a small girl with a large mouth, member of the infamous RAT raiders, a very charming and funny girl surrounded by a couple of admirers; and Simon Kusseff the intellectual, and brain trust of the moribund tombstone.

The *"Race against Time"* had strongly suggested that time was running out for children. By running across the globe, millions of people had made that point. Most tellingly so, three years later the United Nations General Assembly adopted the Convention on the Rights of the Child. Non-negotiable, period.

Chapter 7: Rise of the Unicef National Committees

The gondola speeds away from the Grand Canal mooring in a show of majestic power. On board is the newly appointed Director of the Geneva office, Victor Soler-Sala; along with Angela, the elegant wife of the Governor of Veneto province; Anna from the regional volunteer committee in Venice; and myself. Turning around one more time we get a glimpse of Aldo Farina and his colleagues standing on the balcony of the local Unicef office, blowing kisses in our direction. Seconds later we pass under Rialto Bridge and are out of sight, leaving Venetian elegance behind us. Soler-Sala declares he wants to move the Geneva office to Venice.

Our mission here had been to determine the venue of the global fundraising workshop of all the National Committees. It was Italy's turn. Aldo Farina proposed Bari, so as to change the venue from always-favoured Northern Italy to the traditionally neglected South. Knowing that all others preferred Venice by far, Aldo's major selling point was that spring comes early to its *Mezzogiorno*! Another reason for our mission was to attend a press conference at the Venice Film Festival where a British filmmaker was awarded the Unicef Committee prize for best film involving children. Under Aldo Farina's leadership the Committee was very strong on advocacy and public relations, but quite weak on fundraising. Support to strengthening fundraising strategies of National Committees was *precisely* my major brief. Perhaps something could be achieved in Italy, but I was not optimistic, because the focus of the Committee was elsewhere.

Origins of the National Committees
Created as a Fund in 1946, Unicef depends entirely on voluntary contributions from member states. As these contributions tend to

CHAPTER 7: RISE OF THE UNICEF NATIONAL COMMITTEES

be highly volatile, raising funds with the public would provide a natural safety net. But would a UN agency ever be permitted to do that? A break-through came in 1947 with the adoption of a Norwegian proposal for a United Nations Appeal for Children (UNAC). The Appeal solicited a one-day's pay for children from salaried people across the globe. By the end of 1948, some $30 million had been raised worldwide with Unicef receiving one third and the rest going to voluntary organisations.

At around the same time the US Children's Bureau, the oldest child-focused government agency in the United States, proposed that a group of influential people come together under a Unicef umbrella to lobby more actively with Congress to secure funding for Unicef. To that end the first Unicef Committee in the world saw the light of day in December 1947. Initially the lobbying idea seemed to work. For example in 1948 the Committee's efforts led to Congress appropriating $35 million to Unicef. But merely remaining a lobbying organisation would turn out to be insufficient for the survival of Unicef. Resistance within the US Committee to private sector fundraising gradually gave way to thinking outside the box: fundraising with the general public became a viable option. UNAC had shown the way.

Interestingly, these transformational developments happened against the backdrop of intense and sometimes emotional deliberations in the UN General Assembly over whether Unicef, which had thus far only temporary status, should be renewed or abolished. The United States position – with Chief of Delegation Eleanor Roosevelt in the lead – was adamantly opposed to renewing the mandate. In the end the US Delegation abstained. Unicef had scraped through with another term of three years. By the time 1953 came around it was almost a foregone conclusion: Unicef was here to stay. On the 6th of October 1953, the UN General Assembly voted unanimously to make Unicef permanent. I would like to think that the growing support to Unicef coming from private citizens in the US since 1947 might well have been an important factor in swaying the US Permanent Mission to finally go along with it. In due time, Unicef was to be recognised as the "lead agency for children". From then on Unicef would carry weight in all matters concerning children worldwide.

And how did the idea of fundraising with the public finally stick? In a way it was triggered by something extraordinary that happened in Prague in 1949, the year the "Iron Curtain" had descended on Czechoslovakia. A seven-year-old Czechoslovakian girl by the name of Ditzka had made a glass painting in school representing a maypole. The girl sent it to the Unicef bureau in Prague with a note from her teacher as a token of thanks to Unicef for the milk she and her classmates drank every day. From there, it ended up in New York. [34] I like to believe that the teacher chose to commemorate the ancient rites of spring[35] rather than Labour Day, so revered by the communist regime. Then a few months later a small number of cards using Ditzka's drawing were produced in New York as a modest way to raise funds. In the end, that led to the creation of the Unicef Greeting Card Operation in 1951. Cards began to be sold in the US by the hundreds of thousands through a network of volunteers. In the early years Raoul Dufy and Henri Matisse donated some of their designs. Over time the Unicef greeting cards have given the agency invaluable visibility and an enormous source of funding around the world.

Another milestone to be remembered was the suggestion by a pastor in Bridesburg, Pennsylvania who, just before Halloween in 1950, proposed to his congregation that instead of only tricking or treating for themselves, children might ask for nickels and dimes for Unicef. This simple suggestion later turned into a major annual national fundraising campaign in the US. From 1953 onwards the US Committee began to actively promote and sustain the Halloween campaign, which has endured till today.

---

[34] *Children and the Nations: The Story of Unicef,* Maggie Black, 1986.
[35] A Maypole is a symbol of spring fertility rites decked with flowers for dancing round on the 1st of May. This celebration came to be overshadowed by International Labour Day.

CHAPTER 7: RISE OF THE UNICEF NATIONAL COMMITTEES

With Europe's post-war economy picking up fast, people in Europe began to take a serious interest in the wellbeing of children in other parts of the world who were suffering in famines and conflicts. Development education was instrumental in raising that curiosity with the post-war generation. A thought then developed to follow the example of the US and create National Committees for Unicef in Europe.

In 1952 Maurice Pate asked Paul Henri Spaak, Belgium's former prime minister, for help. As the first president of the UN General Assembly, Spaak was widely respected. He took up the challenge and began to make the rounds of European capitals promoting the creation of Unicef Committees at the highest levels. The first Committee in Europe – perhaps not surprisingly – was founded in Belgium in 1953. West Germany, Holland and Japan followed in 1955. By 1959 Denmark, Norway, Sweden, Italy, the UK, Luxemburg and Switzerland had all joined.[36] The Committees were created as a franchise, allowed to use the name of Unicef with the proviso that funds raised were transferred to Unicef Headquarters. Its staff are not employees of Unicef. Committees withheld an agreed percentage of fundraising revenues for administrative and operating cost.

The International Year of the Child

Without any doubt a monumental milestone was laid on the 9th of January 1979. On that day, the UN General Assembly launched the International Year of the Child, exactly ten years after the adoption of the Declaration of the Rights of the Child[37]. The event took place *"in a truly celebratory style"* with well-known musicians performing and dedicating to Unicef.[38] The US Committee for Unicef could take full credit for an impeccable launch that was telecast to sixty countries. Unicef was chosen to be in the lead of IYC.

---

[36] *Children and the Nations: The Story of Unicef,* Maggie Black, 1986.
[37] Not to be confused with the Convention on the Rights of the Child which was adopted in 1989 – a legally binding document, whereas a Declaration is not.
[38] *Children and the Nations: The Story of Unicef,* Maggie Black, pages 357–364.

Many countries created national IYC commissions to coordinate a multitude of diverse activities. Some activities were simply a stroke of genius. For example Aldo Farina persuaded the annual Bologna Children's Book Fair to place the 1979 event under the banner of IYC. The result was enormous publicity for Unicef in Italy and beyond. In my time the Committee never became an important contributor to Unicef, but through his Unicef visibility-raising events, Farina was instrumental in that the Italian government became a large donor to Unicef – just when it counted: after all, the Global Revolution for Child Survival and Development needed massive funding.

Unicef field offices began to support governments in undertaking reviews on the situation of their children and the state of social services available to them. Such reviews later evolved into a comprehensive analysis on the situation of children, which in turn became a tool for designing child-focused programmes and state budgeting. Networks of local organisations working for children began to mushroom all over the world. By the end of 1979, there were IYC Commissions in 148 countries. Several Unicef Committees ran joint campaigns with them, which substantially raised the visibility of Unicef. Private contributions to Unicef from all sources reached a record 50 million dollars. When IYC commissions in the industrialised countries closed down when IYC ended, the National Committees took over their sponsors and supporters, winning in strength and depth almost overnight.

My family and I had had some involvement with Unicef during IYC, not realising that six years down the line we would be part of it. This is how that happened. Vanessa was a member of the Meri Mini Players of the First All Children's Theatre. I served on its Board. First ACT had been chosen to represent the children of the United States in a worldwide presentation for the International Year of the Child. One of its performances was taped and aired on the 1979 New Year's Day IYC international telecast, introduced by President Carter. Later in the year, First ACT performed segments of one of their musicals at the IYC press party given by

CHAPTER 7: RISE OF THE UNICEF NATIONAL COMMITTEES

Ambassador and Mrs Andrew Young at the US Permanent Mission to the UN.

Rise of the National Committees
I believe that it slowly began to dawn on Unicef that it needed the National Committees far more than was initially thought – well beyond lobbying with governments to increase funding or selling greeting cards to the public. Grant's Child Survival Revolution and its goal of universal immunisation for children by 1990 made strong allies of the Committees. Direct mail campaigns now had a clear and doable goal they had been waiting for. For once these campaigns were not about war or natural disaster, but focused on long-term health care for children, with immunisation as entry point.

An activity pioneered in Scandinavia, "development education", may well be at the origin of the rise of National Committees. This new approach of educating school children about other cultures was meant to do away with the stereotype notions my generation had of the developing world: poor, underdeveloped and primitive. When I was in high school, teachers took us to the public cinema to watch film footage about life and customs in Africa. To say the least, an imagery of primitiveness was standard pie. Around that time development education began to expose these scandalous sociological fabrications and misconceptions. As late as the early 1980s even diplomats were often still ignorant or misinformed. When I told a senior Dutch diplomat in New York that I was going to work for Unicef, he exclaimed: *"oh, ga je rijst uitdelen aan arme kindertjes!"*[39]

Unicef Committees in Denmark and Finland distributed as early as 1947 materials to thousands of schools, educating pupils and teachers alike to see with different eyes. It stimulated curiosity to the point where schools in the industrialised world built links with schools in Asia and Africa. Development Education informed on issues of inequality, poverty, poor child health and nutrition and

---

[39] "Oh, are you going to distribute rice to poor children!?"

low school enrolment, without forgetting cultural diversity. In the process Unicef's work for children came to be much better understood. Much later Unicef Geneva office created its own DevEd unit.

There was the ground-breaking advocacy work by Unicef's first goodwill ambassador, Danny Kaye. Kaye's association with Unicef nearly ended before it had begun. He was flying from London to New York in 1953 when one of the plane's engines caught fire. Maurice Pate, then Unicef Executive Director, was also on board. Sitting next to Kaye on the journey back to the safety of Ireland and then on to New York, Pate talked to Kaye about Unicef. One of the organization's problems, he explained, was recognition. Perhaps Kaye could help. The result was a documentary, *Assignment: Children*, underwritten by Paramount Pictures, with profits going to Unicef. It was a record of Kaye's tour of projects in Hong Kong, India, Japan, Korea, Myanmar and Thailand, and is estimated to have reached more than 100 million people over time.[40]

In later years other factors emerged that increased the influence of Unicef National Committees on Unicef thinking. Member states began to include National Committees in their Delegations to the Unicef Board. Unicef Committees provided the "institutional memory" to their country's delegation. Over time National Committees acquired more insight into Unicef and its sector programmes in the field. Several Committee delegates like the Swiss Hans Conzett and the Swede Nils Thedin served as chairperson of the Unicef Board.

Later, staff exchange came into fashion. This contributed much to a growing recognition by HQ. My good friend Christopher Cooper of the West German Committee spent six months at HQ. He went on to become its Executive Director ad interim, successfully leading the search for a successor[41]. The Executive Director

---

[40] Source: Unicef, New York.
[41] Dieter Garlach, Executive Director 1989–2006.

CHAPTER 7: RISE OF THE UNICEF NATIONAL COMMITTEES

of the Dutch Committee, Rene Latenstein van Voorst, was seconded as Deputy to Soler-Sala in Public Affairs. The Belgian National Committee seconded their Information officer to Headquarters. Olivier de Greef went on to make a successful career in the field.

Over time the process of information sharing between Unicef and the Committees progressively strengthened. Unicef began to support annual thematic workshops of National Committees on fundraising, information and development education. They began to exchange experiences, creating a strong network under the leadership of its Standing Committee. They began to progressively carry weight with the Unicef secretariat. Unicef needed the Committees who were building up vast networks of thousands of Unicef supporters, making Unicef better known through the sale of greeting cards at strategic outlets.

Unicef field offices increasingly welcomed visits from Committees to show off their projects. Often the national media of the country in question would join on such field trips making documentaries for national television. I remember a film about toys made by children in Kenya from local materials, and how attached they were to them. The film contrasted that with children in Holland casting aside toys when they were getting bored. Here were two messages: Ownership, and Kenyan children had it, because they had made the toys themselves, but the Dutch did not. Consumerism was the other. Dutch children suffered from it, the Kenyans did not. This was development education at its best.

Workshops of the National Committees with the Unicef secretariat did much to cement working relations. This way Committees gained enormous insights in the policy and strategies of the organisation. In my day there were two types of workshops: Information (which included Development Education) and Fundraising. My Section was the focal point for the Global Fundraising Workshop. On my watch we organised three: Oslo (1986), Bari (1987) and Warsaw (1988). In that period National Committees contributions globally increased to over 55 million dollars. The meeting in Bari launched the debate on raising funds with corporations. In Warsaw the Committees endorsed a proposal for a global fundraising strategy to be developed by the Director of Programme Funding Office in consultation with National Committees. I was going to be the focal point for that in New York. The Warsaw meeting recommended that Committees should establish a special rapid response fund for emergencies – an idea of my Programme Funding Section, developed after attending donor conferences on Angola and Mozambique.

The Committees began to be seen as indispensable partners in elevating Unicef to a major agency for children within the UN family and the NGO world. Global goodwill ambassadors Danny Kaye, Harry Belafonte, Liv Ullmann, Tetsuko Kuroyanagi[42] and Peter Ustinov talked with authority and emotion to governments, National Committees and the media about what they had witnessed during often very hazardous field trips in Africa, Asia and Latin America.

One day Jim Grant let me in on a secret few people knew. Being Dutch I was often send to Holland on various assignments. On one such occasion I participated in a Unicef/WHO/UNFPA conference on immunization in the Hague, the topic that had then all our attention. Jim Grant was there, along with Marco Vianello-Chiodo and Allegra Morelli of Public Affairs. After the meeting Marco asked me on the spur of the moment to accompany Grant to Brussels by train for a crucial meeting with European Commissioner Lorenzo Natali in an effort to get funding for immunization in Ethiopia, Somalia and Sudan. As we were driving on the way to the railway station Holland Spoor in The Hague, we passed the Bankastraat where the Unicef Committee had its offices at the time. "Could we see the office, have we got time," he asked. We jump out, tell the driver to wait and run like two robbers after a hold-up at a bank to the Unicef office with Grant

---

[42] Renowned actress, writer and TV personality in Japan.

CHAPTER 7: RISE OF THE UNICEF NATIONAL COMMITTEES

greeting everyone as best he can, and some twenty minutes later we are back in the car.

I thought, no wonder our Executive Director is in such excellent athletic shape. Ah, but we had not figured with Dutch traffic lights that can be stubborn as the Dutch themselves. Running on to the platform I could just see the curved back of the train moving teasingly slowly out of the station. We jump back in the car and are driven to Brussels by the Unicef Committee driver. Side by side in the back of the car, Grant tells me he will travel on to the home of Audrey Hepburn in Geneva to ask her to become Unicef Goodwill Ambassador. Grant seems happy as a child about meeting her shortly. And then out of the blue he asks me what I think about it all. Me? I was astounded, why ask me? It was typical for Grant to spring such surprise questions, it had happened to me before. Then it dawned on me that it was perhaps because of Hepburn's Dutch connection, which he knew certainly something about.

I said we in Holland were proud of her Dutch past. I remembered very well how she often recalled the famine of winter 1944-1945 in Holland and how she had benefited from food and medical relief through Unicef as a child after the war. I had myself benefited from the very same program as a five-year-old. Although much younger than Audrey Hepburn, I also had a vivid memory of the famine which we, as a family, had to endure for many months. Dutch people had exactly that in common with her. I was therefore genuinely thrilled – and it showed on my face – to see her join Unicef.

I was one of a very few who was in on the secret, but not for long. Jim appointed Audrey Hepburn Goodwill Ambassador for UNICEF soon thereafter.

Before going in to meet with the Commissioner, I telephoned my close friend John Parr at the European Commission, in order to be able to brief Grant beforehand. After many years in Brussels Natali still only spoke in Italian. It turned out to be a rather disappointing and superficial meeting. This rather spark-less man, a role model for bureaucrats, was not at all in the mood to commit funds to Unicef. No matter how convincingly Jim Grant pictured the health risks for children caught up in the emergency, the Commissioner remained unmoved. He greatly regretted that his friend Claude Cheysson, former French minister of Foreign Affairs and now Commissioner for North-South relations, was away on mission in the Far East, as he would surely have preferred to call on him instead – most likely with more tangible results.

Unicef in Geneva created a Special Events section to coordinate the programme of goodwill ambassadors who supported galas and other events organised by our Unicef Committees. I once met Liv Ullmann at a lunch hosted by the Geneva office. She struck me as a most refined woman with a soft voice. I met Peter Ustinov on a few occasions, as we will see later; but regretfully never Audrey Hepburn.

By now the Unicef communication machine was in full swing with the Committees playing their part very well. In 1984 the West German Committee became the first to appoint a national goodwill ambassador. That was the popular actor Joachim "Blacky" Fuchsberger, a flamboyant personality endowed with lots of flowing hair. He was the centre of many a gala for 25 years. Dutch entertainer Paul van Vliet became national goodwill ambassador in the Netherlands in 1992. He has hosted many benefit performances for Unicef up until this very day. I knew him well from my student days in Leiden back in the 1960s, when he was already a most gifted entertainer. How surprised and happy I was to hear his voice in a radio programme for schools introducing an interview with me on the situation in Mozambique. Indeed the national ambassadors gave a considerable boost to Unicef visibility and fundraising.

National Committees began to step up media relations, linking the Unicef response to relief and rehabilitation with the need for funds. Direct mail income focusing on emergency relief soared. A

CHAPTER 7: RISE OF THE UNICEF NATIONAL COMMITTEES

declining global economy, civil conflicts and wars, drought and floods affected children in Africa far more than other regions in the world. Africans often lacked even the simplest means to cope. Any progress small or big could simply be wiped out overnight. A school damaged in a flood might take months to repair; or a school still intact could be requisitioned to house displaced people. In both cases children would not be able to attend class for many months. Children enlisted as child soldiers would be children no more, ever. Stark images of hunger and malnutrition filmed with Bob Geldof in Africa raised millions with the Live Aid concerts and Sport Aid.

At the time when I took up my post in Geneva, the drafting process of the United Nations Convention on the Rights of the Child was in full swing. For Unicef, the drafting focal points were Kimberly Gamble in New York and Marjorie Newman-Black in Geneva. That was a full time job. Adopted exactly ten years after the 1979 UN Declaration on the Rights of the Child, the Unicef Committees began to make use of the Convention in advocacy and fundraising. In this respect, the committees collaborated most effectively with their own national media. Global and national goodwill ambassadors supported these efforts. The impact the CRC had on progress for children can be illustrated in that free and compulsory education became the norm; considerable progress in school enrolment was achieved, in particular for girls; and free healthcare for children under five and pregnant women became the norm, to name a few examples. The CRC principle of "the best interest of the child" became a tool to promote pro-poor budgets and greater protection for families in the form of cash grants to the poorest.

The power of money was a deciding factor for the growing influence of the committees with the Unicef Secretariat, and their contributions were rising fast. When I joined, Unicef was still a small organisation with annual revenues of around $300 million. Although in those days the National Committees accounted for only 15% of Unicef's income, change was in the air. By 1990 their share had risen to 25%.[43] In 1989 the Japanese Committee became the first to contribute 100 million dollars.

Amazing fundraising ideas

During my time in Geneva and New York, there were fundraising ideas galore, but many never materialised. Some were outright crazy. Perhaps the most illustrious of all these ideas had its roots on Moscow's Red Square.

On the 28th May 1987 an 18-year-old German, Mathias Rust, flew a Cessna all the way from Helsinki via Iceland into Soviet airspace out of sight of the Soviet radar system. He landed next to St. Basil cathedral, after first swooping low over the Kremlin and 'Krásnaya Plóshchad'[44], the very seat of Soviet Russian power. Climbing out of the cockpit to greet the crowds that had gathered around him, Rust simply said, "I am here on a peace mission from Germany." To me that phrase had almost as much significance in its simplicity as the one by Neil Armstrong when he stepped on to the moon and said: "it's small step for a man, but a giant leap for mankind". Mathias Rust's feat had enormous consequences for the Soviet military. Some even say that Gorbachev jumped on the occasion to clean up the bloated military. Within a few days the Soviet minister of defence was forced to retire. The head of air defences was fired. Over the next few months some 150 people lost their jobs in government.

Rust was released in 1988 after serving only 14 months in jail. The signing of the non-proliferation treaty by Reagan and Gorbachev provided a pretext for this gesture of goodwill. Even before the plane came back to West Germany, I heard on one of my regular visits to the Committee that a businessman had proposed to buy the plane and auction it off with the proceeds going to Unicef, estimated as high as one million dollars. With this brilliant idea I walked into Victor Soler-Sala's office. Not surprisingly

---

[43] Not long thereafter Unicef shattered the glass ceiling, reaching annual revenues of one billion dollars.
[44] Red Square.

CHAPTER 7: RISE OF THE UNICEF NATIONAL COMMITTEES

he thought I was mad, and he rejected this idea outright, fearing a diplomatic scandal. At around the same time the CEO of the MCM fashion label of München wanted to buy the plane and use it for publicity and advertising[45]. I do not know if this was the same businessman. Chancellor Helmut Kohl, who was good friends with Mikhail Gorbachev, stopped him in his tracks, fearing a serious diplomatic incident. The plane was later tracked to Japan and can now be seen in Berlin's Museum für Transport und Technik.

A sailing race from Marseille to Algiers seemed a crazy idea but doable. Special Events was working on this, along with the French Committee and Unicef Representative Ekrem Birerdinc in Algiers. Only wealthy yacht owners would be invited to participate, of course at a hefty fee. Hundreds of yachts were expected to sign up. Potential amounts of 50 million dollars in revenues were floating around. In the end the cost of the investment turned out to be huge, the logistics would simply be a nightmare, the level of participation uncertain and the idea was quietly dropped.

I heard Jim Grant himself once talk about a "1990 Club" for immunization at a dinner with one of the National Committees. The idea was for a membership limited to 1990 members with three groups of very large contributions, consisting of 1,000, 900 and 90 persons respectively. The magic number was of course the year in which universal child immunisation (UCI) had to be reached. The group of 90 would be benefactors paying the largest sum and have special privileges. All these people would be private citizens. Grant wanted Reagan and Gorbachev to be chairing. Everyone around the table cheered this idea, seeing millions. I was the last to be asked. I said that since governments are cutting back and funding was the raison d'être we should not include representatives from governments, it would simply be the wrong strategy. He stared at me with these piercing blue eyes for ten seconds. I honestly thought he would disown me there and then. But no, just silence. But in the end the 1990 Club never happened.

---

[45] Telephone interview with Dieter Pool, former West German National Committee member, 23rd October 2017.

A DESTINY IN THE MAKING: FROM WALL STREET TO UNICEF IN AFRICA

A donation in kind to be remembered

When Jim Grant travelled through Geneva, he would almost always call an all-staff meeting to brief us on developments, just like David Rockefeller did at Chase after trips abroad. I was fascinated to listen to our Executive Director, who always remained his enthusiastic and positive self. I believe that Grant was a deeply emotional man who simply rejected the notion that some children are destined to grow up in misery.

Grant had come to Geneva straight from Angola. Often an informal drink was organised for him to meet staff in a more casual and informal setting. It seemed to me that was what he liked best, mingling with his own people. He pulled me over and said that he had just been on a field trip to internally displaced people in the mountains of Uombo, the fief of rebel leader Jonas Savimbi. Grant was visibly upset and very worried. He had seen shivering children without any clothes. He had stared hunger and disease in the face – once again. With the onset of winter in the Angolan highlands, time was of the essence. The Dutch Committee had already sent 200,000 blankets but he said that this was not nearly going to be enough. I still see this big man towering over me with glass in hand, saying with great emphasis, "We *must* have clothes". It took me a flash second and I replied without thinking, " I will find you the clothes."

The following morning it literally dawned on me how difficult this promise would be to keep. Collecting clothes from the public would have been a nightmare; and time was of the essence. So I contacted some of my former business contacts. I called the European HQ of Levi Strauss in Brussels, and of another jeans maker, Blue Bell International. Blue Bell happened to have a liquidation shipment of 154,000 pairs of brand-new jeans, sweaters and T-shirts destined for Venezuela that had just been cancelled. We could have them at two dollars apiece; and, oh what luck, a fully loaded container was sitting in the port of Antwerp ready to be shipped. Unicef Angola coordinated the shipment at the receiving end. The vessel sailed to Luanda barely ten days after Grant's

CHAPTER 7: RISE OF THE UNICEF NATIONAL COMMITTEES

request. Record time. And this is how Grant could inspire people to do the job well and fast.

Then I too once had a crazy, but perhaps not that crazy a fundraising idea. When a representative of the Red Cross and Red Crescent Society in Moscow came to Geneva, I looked forward to challenging him on the ultimate symbol of that divide: the Berlin Wall. The Society was acting as our National Committee, but its structure was obviously state-inspired. Sergei and I first warmed up a bit, talking roubles, the usual story, trying to find ways to unblock them for Unicef. Then I changed the subject. I said that in my view the Wall was worth a lot of money as it is and should be taken down to capitalise on that. It would be a great way to raise funds for Unicef! I went a step further and observed that, once gone (I expressly avoided the if), it could be sold brick by brick, with even some graffiti art on the Wall's West German side to boot. Sergei drew an extended "ahh", a convenient and suspensive expression that merely acknowledged the arrival of the observation – and no more.[46] As I was hoping for more, I kept silent and then Sergei said rather sternly: "ahhh, that's the Western way of doing business. "

When Berlin youth on both sides took the Wall down with their own hands in 1989, I wondered if Sergei would think back to our discussion that very moment. Of course pieces of the Wall quickly spread throughout the world, a memorable souvenir for those visiting the area or as a collectible to mark the end of the Cold War. Chancellor Helmut Kohl presented one piece of wall to President George Walker Bush as an official state gift. A Wall bricks trade began to flourish.[47] What a pity that no funding scheme was ever built on these bricks for Unicef!

---

[46] Taking a leaf from John Morley's *The Life of Gladstone* (MacMillan & Co Ltd, New York 1905): "the Duke of Wellington appears to speak little; and never for speaking's sake, but only to convey an idea, commonly worth conveying. He receives remarks made to him very frequently with '*Ha*', a convenient, suspensive expression that merely acknowledges the arrival of the observation – and no more".

[47] Today, the larger pieces measuring over 30 cm on each side are still fetching several thousand dollars.

The hurdles of Unicef doing "business with business"

Fundraising with the corporate world was a tricky one. "Business" was simply a dirty word when I joined. Business was looked upon as something wicked. Unicef was far more at ease with like-minded organisations that were not out for profit. But Jim Grant saw further ahead. He started hiring people from the private sector for senior positions- and I was one of them. Slowly the anti-business culture started to change. Bypassing his colleague from the banking world, Soler-Sala hired a professor from Durham University in Yorkshire to submit a report on the matter. He was Professor Robin Medforth-Mills, son-in-law of exiled King Michael of Rumania. Mills had been a professor at Durham University in Yorkshire, and now lived in Geneva with his new wife, Princess Elena, near the old King, doing consultancies for the UN.

As a former professor of geography, Mills was not at all equipped in matters of corporate fundraising. I had almost daily sessions with Mills to brainstorm on ideas. I developed a list of companies that might be open to working with Unicef. We looked at the IKEA model that raised funds for Unicef through merchandising techniques; to the UK Committee that was developing *Change for Good*, a coin collection programme on airplanes that was later implemented with British Airways; we looked at modalities of sponsorship; we put together a blacklist of companies with whom Unicef would never work, for example companies employing child labour; after the Bhopal disaster, Union Carbide was of course on everyone's blacklist[48].

Partnerships in development with corporations with investments in developing nations seemed a doable proposition. Where corporations had operations in the field, we began to look at potential for joint project activities in health and education. But things were not that smooth in Africa. At a conference with business leaders in Geneva I ran into just-retired Frits Philips, the son of the founder

---

[48] "Even if Union Carbide offered me one million dollars, I would never accept it", Grant once told me.

CHAPTER 7: RISE OF THE UNICEF NATIONAL COMMITTEES

of Philips Gloeilampen NV. He was a philanthropic idealist. He told me that Philips had just closed a transistor radio assembly plant in Arusha, Tanzania. The plant was created to take advantage of the free trade association between Kenya, Uganda and Tanzania; but obstacles of red tape, for example to obtain approval to pay in dollars for parts shipped from Eindhoven, eventually took the subsidiary down. Frits Philips was very disappointed. He had wanted his company to be among the first of multinationals to start manufacturing in Africa. But the times were not ripe for it. From 1988 I stepped up my involvement with companies in Europe. I had meetings with IKEA in Älmhult, Sweden, Philips Gloeilampen in Eindhoven and the NMB Bank – later ING Bank – in Amsterdam for collaborating with Unicef in one way or another. It felt as if I was back as a banker calling on his customers. In between I always made a stop for a few days to cheer up Mam with stories from far away.

As much as Grant wished to court business, he was not afraid to confront companies when that would be in the best interest of the child. Unicef battled the pharmaceuticals for years to lower the price of vaccines. Unicef and the WHO did not shy away from confronting infant-formula companies – in particular Nestlé - that were aggressively promoting their formula in areas with poor hygiene without warning against the risks of dirty water in poor and impoverished areas. The International Code for the Marketing of Breast-milk Substitutes sponsored by the WHO and Unicef prescribed a total ban on free distribution to women in hospitals and health centres with the exception for medically approved purposes controlled by health personnel. Governments were responsible to inform about infant and young child feeding, in particular the advantages of breastfeeding in strengthening the immune system of the infant.

Although the infant-formula companies lobbied fiercely against its adoption, in the end they grudgingly accepted it. But very few countries passed legislation to enforce the articles of the code. Here then was a case where the WHO and Unicef were up against the corporate world along with voluntary organizations with very valid arguments. A climate of mutual distrust between "them" and "us" lingered on and it never disappeared altogether. Meanwhile the agencies adopted another strategy: they actively promoted breastfeeding to pregnant women – this was already part and parcel of the GOBI approach – out of fear that the Code by itself would not be effective in turning the tide towards mother's milk. Most notably, hospitals and clinics were awarded the designation "baby-friendly" when they had shown proof of promoting breastfeeding, improving hygiene, training of health personnel, and providing for a more caring environment.

Much later I developed at HQ a global corporate fundraising strategy for the Programme Funding Office with Sasha Bacic. Over time I befriended this proud Croat, who had been special adviser to Jim Grant on Africa. Sasha was a former Director of PFO and was now embedded as a consultant. He was not in good health and could be somewhat bitter at times. But I will never forget our geopolitical discussions, in particular his prediction that the departure of Tito would lead to the break-up of Yugoslavia. Most of our discussions were about the cold war that was soon to end. Sasha had been Area Representative in Dakar at one time, covering countries where there was no office. He was instrumental behind the scenes in getting me to Africa.

Much later a realization began to take hold that there was much mutual benefit to be had in public/private partnership arrangements: *"Roll Back Malaria"*, initiated by Unicef, the WHO and the World Bank; and the Vaccine Alliance GAVI, inspired by the Bill and Melinda Gates Foundation, were pioneers in that respect. Initially the thinking in Unicef was that all fundraising should benefit our own organization. In later years Unicef's thinking began to shift: it was all about the importance of leveraging funds for children. Such funds, even if raised by Unicef, did not necessarily have to transit through Unicef as long as non-governmental organisations considered the "best interest of the child".

CHAPTER 7: RISE OF THE UNICEF NATIONAL COMMITTEES

From the family's vantage point

A. and the children had made much of the transition to a new life in Switzerland. Vanessa and Nadim were both happy at the Chataigneriaz campus of the bilingual *Ecole Internationale de Genève*. There was a lot of sports and theatre. Vanessa brought our puppy Labrador Balik, "Nadim's sister", in a bag on the train from Paris. A few times Nadim brought her to school and the pup was allowed to sleep under his desk. She loved snow and went on cross-country ski trips with us, trying to sit on our skis.

For the first time, Nadim went alone to visit Vanessa who had become an au pair in Paris, enjoying a ride on the then brand-new TGV. She had found a nice apartment next to Musée Picasso, but the building was rather squalid. The table was laid out for a nice dinner, with candlelight of course. She was working nearby, doing art with children, just like her mother had done in New York. Once I looked up Vanessa in Paris alone. She showed me the *péniche* where she had performed an ABC of characters with a theatre group just a few days before. Inside there was an exhibit on dance; when we came back up again, there was improvised dancing on deck, sensual movements of girls making use of the props of the barge and the passive participation of the audience: girls dancing and falling over seated men. Vanessa loved it. I gave her Baudelaire's "*Les Fleurs du mal*" and Vercors' "*Le Silence de la Mer*". I left her at the *péniche* with a sad pinch. She was still so young to be away from home.

Nadim was always on to something new. One day he bought a 10-year-old Solex and fixed it up with the help of Enrique, our neighbour in Chataigneriaz. Nadim was not much of reader in those days, bringing our avid bookworm Vanessa to desperation: one day she piled up a stack of books in Nadim's room and exclaimed, "READ THESE!" A. volunteered for a while with Monika Knofler in the Art department of the Greeting Card Operation. On my travels through Europe I made it a point to spend a few days with my mother. She always put on a brave face, trying to make the best of it alone in her new one-bedroom flat in

Naarden. But her eyes belied a deep sadness, she missed my father immensely.

Selling the sales book
The orientation trip in West and East Africa had been time and money well spent. When meeting with donors in Europe I could now speak with some feeling and understanding about Unicef's work in the field. I for one could very well understand that the French Committee wanted to adopt autonomously some projects in Senegal and Mali, without going through the New York channel. But the problem was that Unicef had other resources at hand called "supplementary funds" that were applied to specific projects developed by our country offices. Hundreds of these projects, labelled "noted" for the fact that they were noted in an annual "Sales Book", were then shared with National Committees, and other donors for funding. Unicef policy prohibited Committees to apply part of their income on "noted" projects of their own, so as not to lose a part of that valuable type of income for Unicef HQ. There was a lot of haggling between Soler-Sala and the French Committee on this. The French had already undertaken funding of several projects in Francophone West Africa without informing Unicef beforehand. That raised the level of tensions with the Committee. I for one could feel for the French position on this issue as it gave them valuable visibility with their constituency; and besides, their contributions to Unicef increased significantly each year. So why bother to bother them? I thought the Unicef policy was short-sighted. In later years the rule was somewhat relaxed. When a heavy earthquake hit Italy, the Italian Committee was allowed to raise funds for it.

Galas were an effective way to raise funds and publicity for Unicef. I attended one such event, hosted by Dutch TV personality Ivo Niehe along with Peter Ustinov. Queen Beatrix who had been *beschermvrouwe*[49] of the Committee when still a Princess, continued to support Unicef with her sheer presence. A small group from

---

[49] Transl: patroness.

CHAPTER 7: RISE OF THE UNICEF NATIONAL COMMITTEES

Unicef had come to attend, Soler-Sala, Jean-Marie Benjamin, Information Officer Tony Carvalho and myself. A couple of hours before the curtain was raised, the agent of Charles Aznavour had thrown a time bomb into the affair: he wanted to have thousands of dollars more – and if not, his client would not go on stage. Ivo Niehe and Soler-Sala were visibly upset. Once on stage we were really "moved" to hear Aznavour speak so eloquently about children in need. Ustinov and Niehe were strutting all over the stage introducing artists and cracking jokes. I best remember the *Bangles*, a rock band who performed their catchy hit *Walk like an Egyptian*, the singers walking in one row with both hands stretched out at the level of their chin, just as the figurines on the painted vases of the pharaoh dynasties. I will never forget the two suppers we had with Peter Ustinov. He made us laugh all the way through the meal, cracking Russian jokes one after the other. To think that Ustinov still had had to go on stage after this "private" performance is now hard to imagine.

The study on the Geneva office

I had come to the conclusion that my post was an unnecessary duplication of efforts between Programme Funding Office in New York and my Section. For every funding issue I had to refer back to the senior programme funding officers in New York. It so happened that Karl Erik-Knutsson, former Deputy Executive Director for Operations and now Regional Director in Nairobi, was conducting a study on the Geneva office with a view to streamlining operations. In September 1987 he came to Geneva to study workflows, reporting lines, budgets and fundraising results. In a closed meeting I explained to him the reasons why my post should be abolished. Knuttson fully agreed. I gathered I must have been the first UN official to abolish his own post without the prospect of another! The Director was transferred to New York after only two years in the job, along with the overall National Committees coordinator and myself. It was a watershed of top management leaving Geneva for New York HQ, lock, stock and barrel; and somehow I believe that I had a hand in it in no small way. But this obviously did not endear me with Soler-Sala during my last year in Geneva.

Nearing the end in Geneva

Back in Geneva, I returned to writing on sovereign debt. Inspired by my orientation trip to Africa I gave the article the title *"Africa's debt: resolve now or pay later"*. The article was published by the *NRC-Handelsblad* to coincide with the opening of the IMF-World Bank annual meeting in Washington. Former Le Monde journalist Claire Brisset, who was Information officer in Geneva reworked all my articles into one and got it published in *Le Monde Diplomatique* with the shock heading: *"Quand le tiers monde subventionne le développement des pays riches"*. Even our local upstate New York newspaper *The Oneonta Star* ran a story about me with the headline: *"Former banker says forgiveness can help Africa: recommends banks forgive 101 billion dollars in debt"*. Peter Hall, a former financial writer on Wall Street turned independent film maker and a frequent guest at the farm, advised me to take the subject of debt a step further and write about the potentially positive impact of trade with Africa on jobs in the OECD countries. Writing became my salvation, once again. I felt a lot better already, liberated in a way.

Meanwhile, Victor Soler-Sala had completed the analysis of my performance and character: "Mohr is weak, not a leader, but a gentleman with impressive baggage". At least that. Strangely enough, it all rang true. I was left out and walked upon by the Spaniard and let him do it too; in comparison to my first year in Geneva, I was vastly underutilised in relation to my capacities but I did not protest enough; impressive baggage, yes that I had, even to the point that I could look aloof and overstudious, which was only partially true; Perhaps I gave the impression of being a gentleman, but I simply laid back too much, even to the point that I was thinking of leaving the organisation. I was looking forward though to being at HQ for a year, which would not only round out my second two-year contract, but perhaps might bring me closer to Jim Grant and his entourage. That in itself could perhaps set the record straight.

At the Fundraising workshop in Warsaw, Marco Vianello-Chiodo introduced me to former Dutch MP Suzanne Bischoff van

CHAPTER 7: RISE OF THE UNICEF NATIONAL COMMITTEES

Heemskerck[50], who had succeeded Marco as Director of PFO. Marco himself had been promoted to Deputy Executive Director, External Relations. Suzanne practically endorsed me there and then, saying that she looked forward to having me in her team. That was a welcome recognition to which I was no longer used. She turned out to be a great support that entire year. Although I advised her a lot on the pitfalls of her new surroundings – Sasha Bacic was supportive of her too – she was transferred to the Greeting Cards Operation after one year. Several people had turned against her and this made her unsure of herself. I thought she was never given the chance. Susan left Unicef after her two-year contract had come to an end.

I drove down from our farm to New York and had taken Nadim with me. It was a chance to show Nadim the nerve centre of Unicef. As we were both waiting at the reception area on the thirteenth floor for my meeting with Marco to finalise my transfer, guess who comes by: Mr James P. Grant himself! He takes time to have a chat with us and soon Nadim changes the subject to our upstate farm, telling Grant the specifics of our family life there. He is genuinely interested. I thought he looked thinner, but well-tanned. I inform him that I was going to see Marco to hear about my future. Nadim whispers to me that, on walking away, Grant almost inaudibly said to himself that he "will do something now". And at that moment Grant turns around going in the direction of Marco's office. Marco is apparently not in, because he comes straight back out, going into the men's room. I then figured out that the decision had been made there.

Marco announced that I would be at PFO for one year. If I did well, I would get a permanent contract. End of interview. The Venetian ended on a remarkable note, saying that he could be soft and sentimental, but that he was basically hard and ambitious. That sounded quite Machiavellian. But the biggest revelation was

---

[50] Susan Bischoff was a former member of Parliament for the Dutch centrist party D66, cofounded by Geb Rignalda.

that I reminded him of his father; who had excellent qualities but no "push" and "could not sell himself"[51]. After his father died people realised his qualities, but then it was rather too late. Indeed I always felt that my relationship with Vianello-Chiodo was uncomfortable. He later said that I "had no spark", perhaps true during that one-year at HQ when I was treading carefully through a morass of unknowns. But I admired his creativity and interests. He was definitely "original". For example, when we were in Dakar for a regional meeting several years later, Marco asked at lunchtime if I was interested in going with him to the *Centre Culturel Français (CCF)* across the street to buy some *sous-verre* paintings from the Senegalese artist who was famous for this, Gora M'Bengue. I must admit that I had never seen or heard of *sous-verres*. But I was curious and followed the fast-paced, long-legged man as best I could. The colours of these paintings are vivid as they come in Senegal. They reminded me of the little shapes Marco painted with magic markers on small pieces of paper during plenary sessions, at times when he was utterly bored. Then he handed them out to a few participants. I was a recipient once.

When I returned from the meeting, I spotted Jim Grant and Nadim near the elevator, just the two of them, once again engaged in animated conversation about life at the farm. Then someone approached him, presumably to have lunch, and the short meeting was over. As always, Grant took all his time to listen to a child, just posing a question here and there. I thanked him for his decision to assign me to New York, vowing, "I will prove Victor wrong". Grant answered mysteriously, "Together we will prove him wrong".

Meanwhile A. had agreed to exchange her green card for a US passport. I was already working on a plan B, creating ahead of

---

[51] My good friend Richard Barber of my INSEAD promotion (1969) advised me before going into an interview with Ciba-Geigy at the INSEAD campus to "sell yourself". Perhaps because in the end I did not do that, I was not hired for a Finance post in Basel!

CHAPTER 7: RISE OF THE UNICEF NATIONAL COMMITTEES

time this parachute back to America, and the idea was that through her I would get my green card back in no time if I left Unicef. We prepared a great naturalisation party at the farm. Nadim had bought an old American flag at Kip's barn for one dollar. That flag had still only 46 stars. The Gourlaouens happened to be in New York and joined in the fun. Neighbour Karen had made a cake with the flag as its design; we organised a soccer match which became an annual event from then on; A. was goalie; Bernard in good Breton tradition scored four goals; our Labrador Balik never let go off the ball so that she was disqualified in later years for too much ball possession, locked up in Nadim's room and crying all through the match. The party had Ron singing Bob Dylan songs; the Blues playing an old Celtic string instrument and harmonica; the children giggling, Heidi, Brandy, Solvay, tiny Esa; Ty Coburn sulking in a corner; and Carole Gourlaouen laughing as only she can.

We lived on 668 Greenwich Street in the former Post Office that was now remodelled to receive the yuppies[52]. Daily routines settled in fast. A. was often at the farm with Balik. She was overseeing the transformation of the garage into living space that doubled the size of our living room. The new space got three large windows side by side, almost to the floor offering a magnificent vista on the field. Nadim and I were alone in Manhattan surviving on take-outs at the Chinese. Tofu and bean sprouts were standard fare. In the beginning we biked through the Village at night as two boy scouts on a mission. We rented movies, such as *The Africa Queen* with Spencer Tracy and Katherine Hepburn, getting in the mood for our own Africa adventure. We listened to Sting, Dire Straits and John Lennon. I tutored Nadim in French, so he would keep it fresh if we were going to Abidjan or perhaps Niamey. On Friday nights we would pick up the Jeep Cherokee from the rooftop parking on the Hudson, pack it with beer and sandwiches and drive 170 miles straight to Otego to join A. in the quiet beauty

---

[52] young urban professionals.

of the farm. Vanessa called from Friends World College, sounding so happy. FWC was a college on Long Island that had an interesting programme for anthropology and sociology students. From day one, students made their own programme guided by their professors. Students studied at the Long Island campus the first year, then continuing research at the various FWC campus locations abroad. Vanessa thus continued her multicultural experience that she had picked up in the melting pot of New York.

We organised an art exhibit in our apartment for painter Rebecca Alston, Hans van den Houten's wife, who sold several paintings and gave one painting, "The Birth", as a thank-you present to A. Rebecca became rather successful later and could more or less live off her art.

Nadim advised me that I should bike to the office to keep in shape. My route was via Hudson Street on to Eighth Avenue crossing over into the garment district. From there up Third Avenue to 44th Street and First Avenue. Biking in Manhattan gives one an exhilarating feeling. Swinging over from one side to the other on a big Avenue when cars have to stop for a light, there's simply nothing like it. When all else is blocked, there's always the sidewalk. Few Unicef colleagues biked to the office in those days, programme training guru Alan Silverman was one of them. My diary: "It's some revolutionary feeling, beating everyone at his own game". Sometimes I was caught in the rain going home, but my thin suit would dry overnight and I would wear it the next day as if nothing had happened; just like Jim Grant who was known to wash his suit at his hotel under the shower and wear it the next day! It was his way to travel light with just carry-on luggage. Once at lunch break I biked over to the Met, craving for some cultural outing in between the uncreative bureaucracy of Unicef HQ. A. had started working there again in the children's art classes of Hilda Siegel. She took me to see *The Georgia O'Keefe's retrospective*. On the way back I grabbed a sandwich and devoured it on the curb to gain time. A smiling gentleman stopped by and asked: "Do you need a dime?" Not known for dressing well, I probably looked as if I did.

External Relations

At its session in April 1989, the Executive Board requested that Unicef conduct an evaluation of its external relations. In this context Headquarters organised the first joint Global Information/ DevEd and Fundraising workshop with the National Committees to listen to their needs and concerns as input to the evaluation.

Jim Grant opened this important meeting. He predicted that universal immunization would be beyond just immunization: it would motivate government leaders for other global goals. He thought that the upcoming Jomtien Conference on Education for All would be to basic education what Alma Ata was to primary health care; in other words, the beacon to follow. There were several important decisions that would further contribute to the growing importance of National Committees in the Unicef family in the years to come. National Committees were each to establish a Universal Childhood Immunisation (UCI) task force liaising closely with the UCI task force of Headquarters in annual progress reviews and training. The Committees committed to fundraising with corporations, for example through voluntary payroll deductions. Harold Fleming, PFO focal point for emergencies, urged Committees to be better prepared with information and fundraising when on-set natural or man-made disasters happened. As had been already agreed upon in Warsaw, he urged Committees to establish an emergency fund. Development Education experts proposed an annual technical meeting on development education, possibly leading to a permanent third thematic workshop. Unicef and the Committees were asked to jointly establish an overall strategy for development education activities.

For the first time, the Secretariat invited the Committees to identify candidates among their midst for the new senior post of Development Education Officer. Many Committees strong in DevEd had developed excellent links to national education. The Standing Committee of, in effect its management group, was mandated to evaluate the whole issue of media visits and study tours in the field to achieve better planning, coupled with targeted information-sharing among Committees, including PFO and Programme Division.

The External Relations Evaluation came out two months after I had left New York for Africa.[53] One major finding stands out for me: "The quality of the consultation process between NYHQ with National Committees and governments in industrial countries is the key to its advocacy and fundraising effectiveness". Furthermore, the evaluation called for "a special partnership arrangement between Unicef and National Committees to define rights and responsibilities of each partner, designed to allow for diversity of the Committees rather than to impose uniformity." These words were proof to me that the influence of National Committees was growing.

A new beginning looms on the horizon
The day of the 21st March 1989 was a new beginning for me when Stan Adotevi, the Regional Director for West and Central Africa called and offered me a senior post in economic analysis, *adjustment with a human face* and focal point for relations with the African Development Bank. Unicef and ADB had just signed a Memorandum of Understanding for a close partnership in development, essentially health and education. My diary of that day: *"I am very moved to go to Africa. I cannot believe the change in life we have made: from banking to development. The old Africa hands in Unicef, Paul Audat, Sasha Bacic believed in me and saw me there. They supported me through thick and thin. And now it is going to happen"*.

In hindsight I was perhaps a bit of an idealist about Africa. For instance I wrote in my diary that I believed in Africa as the next market; that to kick-start the African economies, total debt write-off and new debt with stronger conditions and oversight would be the solution. And then, smart investments would ultimately weed

---

[53] *The Evaluation and Analysis of UNICEF's External Relations Policies and Functions,* Samir Basta, Director, Evaluation Office, Unicef New York.

CHAPTER 7: RISE OF THE UNICEF NATIONAL COMMITTEES

out development assistance. In the context of today's investment interest in Africa, this was not entirely unrealistic after all.

People said that I had "no field experience." I saw that as an advantage as I was not rooted in the old development assistance mode. And people who did have field experience, did they have it when they were sent there for the first time? Then I wrote in my diary, "What is assistance anyway? How to place a pump, construct, teach, vaccinate, and weigh babies?" I decided I would be a freethinker and stress self-reliance by way of the twin engines of social and economic development. Create capabilities in people and they become masters of their own rights. As the mantra goes, instead of giving a man a fish, give him a fishing rod. Meanwhile I picked up a copy of René Dumont's *"L'Afrique étranglée"* that was lying around the house. It promotes changing the way we live by decreasing *"inégalité"*. In the midst of these reflections about development, a well-known New York head-hunter called proposing me for a job in banking. That was going to be the last time any of them would call. My mother called to say she was coming in June, her third visit to America, and this time she wanted to spend most of the time at the farm.

By the end of the 1980s the world was witnessing historic events that were going to be crucial for children. The Berlin Wall had fallen, turning the world upside down with the end of the Cold War and the subsequent disintegration of the Soviet empire. Only nine months before, Gorbachev had delivered his historic address before UN the General Assembly. I remember some of us dashing off to the communication room at Unicef HQ at 14:30 to watch. Gorbachev sprang a total surprise on the world, announcing that troop levels of the Soviet Union would be reduced unilaterally by half a million soldiers, and the volume of conventional arms would be cut considerably. By agreement with the Warsaw Pact six tanks divisions would be withdrawn from the GDR, Czechoslovakia and Hungary, and would be disbanded by 1991. Soviet forces situated in those countries would be cut by 50,000 persons together with 5,000 tanks. The remaining division would become "unambiguously" defensive. It was a "benign bombshell" and the whole world applauded. "One would like to believe, as he put it so well, "that our joint efforts to put an end to the era of wars, confrontation and regional conflicts, aggression against nature, the terror of hunger and poverty, as well as political terrorism, will be comparable with our hopes."

There were more positive signs on the world scene. Leaders had agreed to a 1990 Summit for Children committing Heads of State and Government to setting a series of development goals to be achieved by the year 2000. The Convention on the Rights of the Child had come into force as a legally binding instrument; Unicef joined the World Bank, UNESCO and UNDP in organising a major Conference in Jomtien, Thailand that would soon adopt a framework to reach for "Education for all". Universal Childhood Immunization was on track to be achieved, saving millions of children every year. About this time Unicef was beginning to build a "grand alliance of people's power for children" with new strategic partners such as trade unions, national parliaments, artists and intellectuals, national NGOs and youth associations. The media became the glue that held it all together.

Because of its massive needs, Africa soon became the corporate priority of Unicef. By 1990 more than a third of Unicef assistance was allocated to the continent. Full-fletched country offices headed up by a Unicef representative sprung up all over West and Central Africa. There was a huge need for qualified staff to boost Unicef's presence on the ground. Grant called them "gold medallists". French was not widely spoken in Unicef, making it complicated to find qualified Francophone candidates for West Africa. And that had been my chance.

Chase Manhattan Plaza with the "Four Trees" by Jean Dubuffet
Photo: Richard Levine/Alamy stock photo

Entrance of Société Générale branch at Rockefeller Plaza

UNICEF Executive Director James Grant chairing launch of Operation Life Line Sudan in the presence of United Nations Secretary General Javier Pérez de Cuellar and the Sudan delegation
Source: UNICEF photographer

United Nations Executive Director James Grant negotiating with leaders of the Sudan People's Liberation Army (SPLA) in Southern Sudan, 1992
Photo: UNICEF/Jeremy Hartley

UNICEF Deputy Executive Director for Programmes Richard Jolly talks with Rwandan refugee children near a UNICEF-installed waterpump at the UNICEF-assisted Benaco Camp for Rwandan refugees in the remote Nagara region. 1994.
Photo: UNICEF/Margherita Amodeo

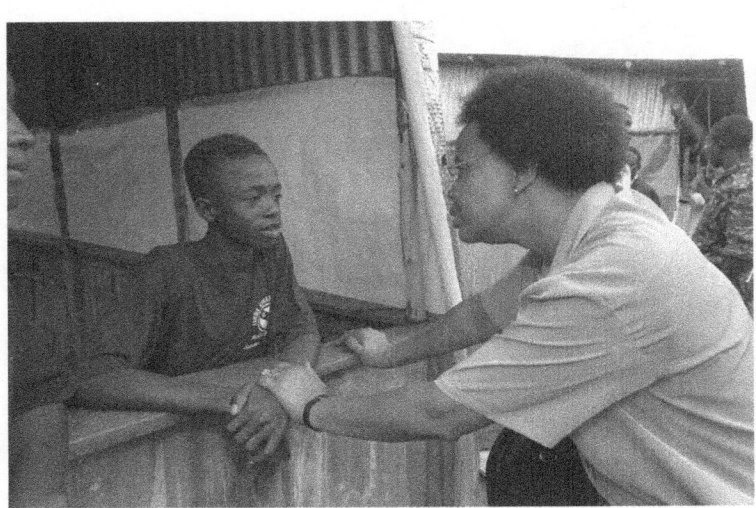

Graça Machel speaking with a former child soldier during a visit to a UNICEF-assisted camp for demobilized child soldiers near the capital Freetown, 1995, as part of her global work to carry out a two-year UN Study on the Impact of Armed Conflict on Children.
Photo: UNICEF/Robert Grossman

Audrey Hepburn and Paul van Vliet at Danny Kay Award, 1992, the moment Audrey asked Paul to become goodwill ambassador of UNICEF Nederland.
Courtesy: UNICEF Nederland

President of UNICEF Italy Aldo Farina showing his new UNICEF publication *MondoDomani* to James Grant, 1984
Courtesy: UNICEF Italy

President of the U.S. Committee for UNICEF Dr Gwendolyn Baker speaking at a luncheon at the National Press Club in Washington DC, sponsored by UNICEF and the Overseas Development Council, 1993.
Photo: UNICEF/John Isaac

Sudanese world renowned athlete Omar Khalifa running for Sport Aid past St. Peter's Square with the Olympic torch on the way to the United Nations in New York, May 1886
Courtesy: UNICEF Italy

Women's horticulture project near Senegal River, Mauritania, 1990

Women's horticulture project near Senegal River, Mauritania, 1990

With Goliath and his gang of street children in Nouakschott, 1992

Tuareg children on a boulevard taking a break from begging, Abidjan 1992
Photo: UNICEF/Giacomo Pirzozzi

Annette with her Tuareg children and women in Gobelet, Abidjan, 1992

The multigrade classroom in Gobelet, Abidjan

A's painting project with Tuareg children at our home in Rue Lepic, Abidjan

Painting by 11 year old Chaidi, 1993

Nadim in a village near Man, North East Côte d'Ivoire, December 1989

Checking the purchase of a Malian blanket with Hamidou, Djenné, Mali, December 1990

Drafting peace education project with Saad Houry and Irene Galamba at a mini-retreat in Inhambane, June 1994

Saad Houry and Hamidou Bidiga, sharing a light moment at our home in Rua Dom Afonso Enriques, Maputo 1994

Taking a break with Shob Jhie at the UNDP/UNICEF sponsored
Seminar on Sustainable Human Development, 1995

My office at UNICEF Maputo, July 1997
Photo: Hamidou Bidiga

João keeping up the production of model bicyles for his lucrative business, front porch of the house at Rua Dom Afonso Enriques, Maputo, 1995

Cover of the Profile of Donors to UNICEF in Mozambique, 1996
Photo: UNICEF/Ruth Ayisi

Teacher addressing class during recess, Porto Alegre,
São Tomé Island, 1999
Photo: Bernard Gourlaouen

Classroom in Porto Alegre, São Tomé Island, 1999
Photo: Bernard Gourlaouen

A *roça-dependencia* on São Tomé Island at the foot of the Pico São Tomé

Challenging field visit, São Tomé Island, 1999
Photo: Bernard Gourlaouen

Our farmhouse, a haven of peace, that was built as a watercress farm in 1810 and remained with our family for 23 years

The "vista" at the farm in Upstate New York

Vanessa on the front porch studying for school, 1984

Nadim on the wooden bridge leading to the cabin on the hill, 1985

Acting in "Adam and Eve" a one-act play written by Claire White for the two-day theatre and musical event at the farm, August 1983

A quiet moment with my mother in Upstate New York, June 1989

My father painting the bay of Roquebrune-Cap Martin, Côte d'Azur, August 1956

It took my father seven winters to build this model of the Mayflower

Chapter 8: Ghostbusters of West and Central Africa

From the early 1980s world attention began to shift to Africa as a continent with huge investment potential. At the same time social indicators such as poverty, illiteracy, child mortality and malnutrition were still at unacceptably high levels. Meanwhile the continent had gone through multiple periods of drought during the '70s and this situation worsened in the '80s, most notably in the Sahel, Ethiopia, Somalia and Southern Africa. At that time the Board asked Unicef to submit a report on what Unicef should do better to respond to these emergencies and implement programmes for long-term development.

Fouad Kronfol, the newly appointed chief of the Africa desk was put in charge to study the situation. It was a turning point in Unicef assistance to Africa. Programme activities in African countries were until then served from thinly staffed regional hubs in Dakar and Nairobi. For the Africa desk to be able to support a beefed-up Unicef presence in Africa in long-term development as well as emergencies and all other issues related to Africa, the section was grossly understaffed. Kronfol's most risky proposal was to upgrade some 25 small country offices to full-fledged representative offices. Somehow he was able to convince Grant to "take advantage of the political climate". Kronfol had read that very well: the Board enthusiastically approved that proposal, which included the establishment of a large number of posts.[54] The Board even complimented Jim Grant for his vision. Grant's relations with the Board had come a long way since more difficult

---

[54] "How Jim Grant put Africa on the Map", contribution by Fouad Kronfol in *Remembering Jim Grant: Champion for Children,* European Center for Peace and Development (ECPD), Belgrade and Roberto Savio, Other News.

CHAPTER 8: GHOSTBUSTERS OF WEST AND CENTRAL AFRICA

times early on. The Africa desk became the largest of all geographical sections. Now the challenge was to find qualified representatives for all those upgraded offices. That did not happen without hiccups of course.

All this had been going on shortly before I joined Unicef. Four years later I myself was assigned to West Africa to help strengthen managerial and programme capacities. But some at HQ were sceptical about that, seeing me more in a Headquarters role, because "Mohr lacks field experience". Again I was bent on proving this notion wrong, I could perhaps learn fast. I began by agreeing with HR to take a step back: I accepted to be downgraded to from P5 to P4[55]. That was highly unusual in the organization, it was – as the French put it so well – *reculer pour mieux sauter.*

In my last days at Headquarters I said goodbye to Dr Nyi Nyi, the Director of Programmes, who, as a most trusted "trooper" of Jim Grant, had been put in charge of leading the drive to achieve universal immunization for all children by 1990. Nyi Nyi's desk was notoriously cluttered with piles of files stacked up high, behind which the diminutive man was working almost invisibly. But he knew exactly where to find what he needed. As I was going to be focal point for building up relations with the African Development Bank, he miraculously pulled out the Memorandum of Understanding that had just been signed and he reeled off my tasks based upon this agreement. Seeing me out of the door, Nyi Nyi said he had enormous appreciation for Deputy Regional Director Shob Jhie, both as a leader and a human being. That sounded good, because Shob would be my new boss.

Then I went to say goodbye to Fouad Kronfol who had just been appointed Director of Human Resources. I submitted to Kronfol that I had a serious problem with my job description. The title was Regional Analyst, Economic Analysis and the content was about

---

[55] P5 is the most "junior" of the senior management posts. Above that come D1 and D2.

programme monitoring and evaluation, formulation of "innovative" action plans and coordination with external agencies to "elevate/expand Unicef's cooperative horizons". There was some reference to inform about changes in political, demographic, economic and social trends "having direct and indirect bearings on Unicef assisted programmes". At the same time I was to be the focal point in macroeconomics, structural adjustment and monetary policies. Kronfol said not to worry, stressing that JD's often had flaws. Passing quickly over this what he saw as a non-problem he said, "Just latch on to three people: Shob Jhie, Saad Houry and Christian Voumard. They are the people in that office who count". I heeded his advice and have not regretted it ever since. I have learned enormously from them – and fast.

I asked Kronfol for his views on Africa and whether he had any hope for the continent. I remember that he answered with a flat "No". Corruption, low levels of education compared to the success of the Asian "Tigers" and brain drain were some of the factors. With my high hopes for Africa I was taken aback and wondered if I were perhaps wrong. By the time I reached Abidjan I pushed the thought out of my mind and went enthusiastically at work.

At the Regional Office in Abidjan there were three offices next to one another on the fifth floor. I was in the middle office, sandwiched in between Saad Houry, the Regional Planning Officer and Lewanika, our Education colleague from Zambia. I was usually in before the other two. Lewanika was usually next; one could hear her from far away singing Christian hymns down the last stretch. Very soon I plugged my ears the minute I heard her from far away. That high-pitched celestial singing was too much for me to start the day with. When she sat down, the voice would linger on a bit and then suddenly stop.

For three months I was getting fed on stacks of country office annual reports, situation analyses, mid-term reviews and documents of the Executive Board relating to our region. There were always endless training workshops going on in Unicef. There was one at the *Hotel du Golf* only days after I arrived. I shall be forgiven that I do not remember the topic. Participants were all young and eager people, Africans, Europeans and some Americans. I remember meeting there for the first time Denis Valot from Niamey, Pascal Villeneuve from Brazzaville, Hervé Peries, the young pharmacist based in Nouakchott and Muriel Glasgow, a water and sanitation project officer who had just been promoted to head up the Lome office. Alan Silverman from New York was the trainer. Coffee, baby croissants and orange juice were served on the terrace near the swimming pool under a burning sun. I was dripping water like a hippo climbing out of the Limpopo River. I noticed that the others did not quite suffer the same fate. No doubt they were used to the humidity by now. That's what luckily happened to me soon afterwards too.

For days I was reading totally undisturbed, hardly anyone came to my office, if only for Saad Houry who kept feeding me new reading assignments. Many years later Saad told me that Shob at first had no clue what to do with me, and what role I should play in the team. No wonder with such a confusing job description! My first tangible assignment was to put into practice what I had read: I was to write the 1989 annual report of our Region for the 1990 Executive Board. I wrote the political and socio-economic overview and edited the contributions of the Regional Advisers into a comprehensive document. Hans Narula telexed Shob from HQ to thank him for a concise and well-written report. This encouraged me much, but at the same time I realised that there was a long way to go before I would be able to "latch on" to the three "gold medallists". With this I had become a victim of my success, becoming the scribe for our Region almost overnight!

One day Saad invited me to lunch at his house. It was a very welcome invitation after this non-stop reading that had made a bit of a zombie out of me. I told him I first had to fetch Nadim from school though. He stared at me in disbelief, because he thought I meant his son, who also happened to be called Nadim. And how could I know his name? I explained why we had named him after a Lebanese friend from our INSEAD days. We laughed together at Saad's totally normal confusion. It was the beginning of a long lasting friendship.

When Lewanika left the Regional Office for good I inherited her office, cleaned it out of dust and old documents; and had a wooden bench made by a Togolese furniture maker, to fill up an awkward corner. Unicef photographer Giacomo Pirozzi designed it. I often took a short nap on it at lunchtime with the door locked, feeling completely refreshed afterwards. The natural wood coloured bench blended in well with the wooden panels that lined the walls. When Shob came by on one of his rare visits to someone's office, he made an obscure remark that seemed to hide strong disapproval, something like: *"what do you need that for, a bed in your office?"*

My very first travel in the region was to Bamako, the capital of Mali, where I was going to run the regional programme and evaluation workshop with Saad Houry and Ibrahim Jabber. It was January 1990. Mali was officially still a Marxist country with Moussa Traore its president since 1968. Relations were still strong with the Soviet Union. Endless waiting at airports in our region had one advantage: one could pick up on the local news. For two hours we waited for our luggage – Air Ivoire was in a dispute with the baggage handlers – so I had ample time to look around. A group of Saudis were descending from a military plane that had come in from Tombouctou. The Saudis were financiers of the new bridge over the Niger and were here to lay the first stone. Chinese workers were going to build it. Meanwhile the harmattan had covered the sky grey with Sahara dust.

The Grand Hotel in Bamako– not so "grand" in those days – was the venue for our workshop. The aircon in my room was heating rather than cooling, it was noisy and leaking. This was already my second choice of a room and I was moving on to the third.

CHAPTER 8: GHOSTBUSTERS OF WEST AND CENTRAL AFRICA

I maintained this "selecting-a-room-by-trial-and-error" method throughout my years in Africa.[56]

I was in Bamako of course mostly to learn. Saad was delayed because of a problem with his plane and I had to take his slot on the Situation Analysis, one of the very first modules. I had just a few hours to prepare my presentation. I think it passed all right, but it was certainly not an inspiring talk. Little did I realize that years later I would write the first draft of the situation analysis for two West African countries! The workshop lasted two weeks, an inordinate length of time. Working groups continued to work ambitiously in a climate of overkill. Always the same people talking, always the same people silent. There was just too much on the plate, and that began to seriously tax our attention span.

A major problem for us turned out to be the visit of Pope John Paul II to Bamako. He was due to arrive on a Sunday, just when we had concluded the first week of the workshop. There were only very few Christians in predominant Islamic Mali, but excitement was equally great among Muslims. Unicef was unexpectedly asked to leave the Grand Hotel and move the workshop to a conference centre with accommodation facilities up on the hill. We reacted in disbelief in the face of this serious lack of planning for a Papal visit. Saad tried to negotiate with the authorities for us to at least come back to the hotel after two days, but to no avail. We lost more than half a day relocating venue and accommodation. For the Marxist president this visit represented a much-needed boost. The country had grown weary of hollow Marxist promises and the on-going Soviet robbery of their gold reserves. Mali was turning increasingly to the West until the *coup de grâce* came for Traore the following year when he was overthrown and locked up in the desert jail of Kidal.

---

[56] The record was at the Sheraton in Abuja. I changed six times in one month until A., who came to visit at Christmas time, got it right. With mounting insecurity in the region I took on the habit to scrutinise a hotel room assigned to me, based on tips from UN field security officers (FSO's). More than once I even looked under the bed.

The family adapts – quickly again

It did not take A. and Nadim long to adapt to the new environment. In fact she soon ran into some Burkinabe children in a shantytown near our hotel. Imagine the setting: a simple table under a palm tree with A. teaching them how to mix colours and paint.

In fact, when I arrived three weeks after them at my new duty station, they already knew their way around. A. had found us a three-bedroom house in the Riviera III section of Abidjan. For weeks we waited for our furniture to arrive. Meanwhile we slept at night in the living room on mattresses. One night a heavy tropical rainstorm woke us up, as massive rain had flooded the house. Our mattresses were floating like small boats through the living room!

The house had a small, rather nondescript garden. It was there when we learned of the watershed news coming from South Africa. It was lunchtime on that sunny, historic day of 11th February 1990. I had placed the shortwave radio against a tree in the garden of our Riviera III house for better reception. It was a live broadcast of Nelson Mandela walking to freedom out of the prison in Cape Town with wife Winnie Mandela. After 27 years in jail, mostly on Robben Island, he could finally raise a fist in triumph while thousands of people were cheering him on. Again we listened to a memorable event of great geopolitical significance, this time from South Africa, which possibly signalled the end of Apartheid. I thought back to the Free Mandela poster I had seen at the home of Charles, the Unicef driver in Dar Es Salaam back in 1986 – the first time I had heard of this great man.

Unicef had recommended a guard to me, but Nadim had a young man in mind from Burkina Faso. His name was Hamidou and he was already guarding the house before we came, sleeping at night on a piece of carton in the garage. He was rather enterprising, running a *"dépôt de pain"* at the street corner. His friend Salif ran a *kiosque* next to it with first necessities such as soap, salt, sugar, coffee, tea, mineral water and soft drinks. Nadim started making ice cubes for Salif in our freezer! I followed our son's advice.

CHAPTER 8: GHOSTBUSTERS OF WEST AND CENTRAL AFRICA

Hamidou was a good "hire" as this story will tell. Our Labrador Balik was in her element. From five o'clock she would lie in the front garden of the house with the soccer ball at her front paws, waiting for some street soccer with Nadim, Hamidou and me. Meanwhile social life with Unicef colleagues began to flourish: dinners, beach trips on weekends, tennis, all made for quick integration. My diary observed: "A. is totally absorbed by West African literature."

Nadim went to school at the American School ICSA[57], and was put in charge of the Year Book 1989–90. In the first weeks his class experienced a terrible drama: Yoyo, a very lively classmate died suddenly of heart failure, possibly related to drugs. Nadim liked her drive and her sudden death made a lasting impression on him. In the school newspaper *The Ivory Eye* a friend of hers wrote a beautiful poem about her: *"your smile which puts the sun to shame"*. It was strange to hear the sounds of the funeral service coming through the open window of my office on the *Plateau*[58] from the church next door and realizing that Nadim and his classmates were all there.

First impressions of Côte d'Ivoire

On weekends we often explored local markets with Hamidou. The biggest one is Adjamé, a popular neighbourhood of Abidjan on a hill overlooking Cocody. It is a bustling market of thousands of merchants selling from small *kiosks*, mothers with babies on their back, colourful boubous, with the one-track railroad to Ouagadougou overgrown with weeds running right down the middle. The stench of urine and rotting produce is strong in places and one has to hop over puddles of stagnant water after the rains. Literally anything can be had in Adjamé, from fruits and vegetables to construction materials and baby foot games. Chickens are beheaded as you are buying them, still warm when your cook prepares them. A bit more "chic" was the covered market at Cocody,

---

[57] International Community School of Abidjan.
[58] The business district of Abidjan.

where middle class Ivorians and Europeans go bargain hunting. Hundreds of tailors are doing a brisk business, manning a battery of black Singer sewing machines there. A. was a frequent customer of Diallo, who made her long, cool skirts with handmade embroidery at the hem.

In a letter to Sasha Bacic, my old mentor at PFO, I wrote: *"My family and I have now a much better understanding of the issues and the problems. For instance, we discovered that the so called 'African solidarity', so much made mention of in international fora, is often a drawback on development: each time an entrepreneur is successful, he has his entire family on his back. In fact a great deal of intra-family begging is going on here. Nigeria must be the dirtiest country, Mali has all the culture, Burkina Faso and the Gambia the friendliness, Senegal the attitude of superiority, Mauritania is at the crossroads of Moor and Peul civilisations"*.

In a letter to my good friend Richard Barber from INSEAD, I wrote some other impressions of my new duty station: *"There are many images that you may never see on television: babies carried on the back of their mothers in a colourful sling; bright colours of women's pagnes[59]; poor or not poor, people's smiles and hearty laughs; shoeshine boys shining shoes as if there is no tomorrow; burying relatives is almost an everyday affair with fewer tears shed it seems than in our society; small children everywhere often run around totally by themselves; babies sucking mother's breast in the middle of a traffic congestion; beggars pooling lucrative business ventures; street kids running along empty taxis ready to open the door for a white customer, hoping for "une pièce"; and then the contrast: the Concorde flying low over Abidjan, returning its 90-year-old leader from France...."*

My new Sony shortwave radio kept us up to date with the astounding news coming from Europe. The Berlin wall had fallen,

---

[59] Pagne is the typical cloth of Côte d'Ivoire, which women buy to have dresses and boubous made by their personal tailors..

CHAPTER 8: GHOSTBUSTERS OF WEST AND CENTRAL AFRICA

Erich Honecker and his wife had fled to Moscow and from there to dictator-friendly Chile. The aftermath of *"die Wende"* was enormous"[60]: hundreds of thousands *Ossis* moved West. Financial pressure on West Germany's citizens increased with a tax surcharge to fund the reunification. Rumanian Dictator Ceausescu was executed outside Bucharest along with his wife.

At Christmas 1989 we drove in our new Peugeot 309 to Man, 600 km North West of Abidjan, getting a good feel for this lush country. We saw typical Yacouba villages with their round huts and thatched roofs, and forests perched on hillsides, often perceived by the Yacouba as sacred. We felt rather awkward intruding on people's lives, in a way taking a "snapshot-peek" with Western curiosity. Nadim even said: "never again".

That very evening we heard on the evening news that a small band of Libyan-trained rebels had just invaded Liberia from Odienne, no more than 100 km away from where we were enjoying our holiday in utter ignorance. The rebel leader was an Americo-Liberian by the name of Charles Taylor, who had once been President Samuel Doe's procurement chief. It was the beginning of a 16-year long civil war. Some 60,000 Anglophone Liberians fled to Côte d'Ivoire in a matter of weeks; and none of them spoke French. It did not take long before the conflict became sub-regional: As Taylor tried to consolidate power in the North of Liberia, neighbouring Sierra Leone fell to a Taylor-backed armed rebellion in 1991, the Revolutionary United Front (RUF). Taylor smuggled small arms and militia into the country to destabilize the situation. As RUF consolidated control of the diamond-rich areas of Sierra Leone, an armed insurgency also backed up by Taylor flared up in neighbouring Guinea. Clearly, everybody was going into "blood diamonds".

---

[60] Christopher Cooper in a letter dated January 1990.

A DESTINY IN THE MAKING: FROM WALL STREET TO UNICEF IN AFRICA

Tempted by a new development bank for Eastern Europe
The liberation of Eastern Europe that was now in progress fascinated me. James Michener's first historical novel *The Bridge at Andau*, a present from my father when I was 16 years old, had made a deep impression on me. At Leiden University I had taken as one of my electives "The Rise of Communism in Eastern Europe". And now the tide was turning. The Iron Curtain was coming down. Could I be involved more directly in one way or another? At the initiative of President Mitterand, a project was under way to establish a European Bank for Reconstruction and Development (EBRD). I was apparently still not totally sure about staying with Unicef, so I decided to ask the Dutch Ministry of Foreign Affairs for advice. Peter van Vliet, then spokesman for BZ, whom I knew from my student days, advised me to submit a background file that the ministry would forward to the EBRD. And indeed I received an interim letter from the Bank: "We will certainly keep you in mind when we start the recruitment process". I was dreaming on doing five years in London. This was after all where my international banking career had begun. My idea was to then afterwards teach at the many private and public universities of Upstate New York, to write and make candles and live at the farm. I soon forgot that I was ever interested in yet another bank, again run by a Frenchman, Mitterand's close adviser Jacques Attali. My diary: "It seems that ERBD has turned me down. A. must be delighted, no more banking in this family, never!"

I had really no time to think much of it, already so absorbed was I in my Unicef job around West and Central Africa. I also had more job satisfaction, I began to be knowledgeable and I received ever more requests from country offices to come and assist with programme and operational management advice. No looking back, full steam ahead! In a letter to my mother in 1991 I wrote: *"Looking back on six years in Unicef, I feel to be in the right place. I made many friends; my work pleases me, although Saturdays and Sundays have lost their traditional meaning. These are often travel days or there is stuff to do in the office. And now I see that you also are doing work for Unicef! Great!"* My mother had become a volunteer for the local Unicef Chapter in Hilversum selling greeting cards from home. So now there were three of us for the price of one! Two years later in another letter to my mother I judged that my transformation was now complete: *"I am now totally Unicef; when I reveal my previous career, everyone is dumbfounded; nobody understands how a former banker has been able to transform himself so totally"*.

Worsening political climate in West and Central Africa
With worsening political indicators in Côte d'Ivoire, the new decade did not look promising for the country and its sub-region. 1990 was the year the country was expected to achieve immunization for all its children, but political and economic signs were not encouraging. The old president Houphouet-Boigny was aging fast; coffee and cocoa prices dropped on world markets at a steady pace; just at the time when Côte d'Ivoire had become the third largest cotton producer of Africa after Egypt and Sudan, prices started to tumble. Living standards in Côte d'Ivoire had dropped significantly from the early 1980s. By 1990 the number of French advisers to the government had dropped by half, to 20,000. Moreover hundreds of French business people started to leave. The struggle for *waré*[61] became more intense, and banditry was on the rise.

Meanwhile thousands of students in Abidjan began to demonstrate against new austerity measures the government had imposed against the backdrop of its legendary corruption at the highest levels, with millions of dollars stashed away in European banks. It came at the time when President Mitterand had declared at the 1990 Francophone summit in La Baule that Africa should engage on a path of democracy, but as he counselled, *chacun à son rythme*. The university was closed for more than a month, risking *une année blanche*. People clamoured for multiparty democracy and a multiparty system. Pamphlets or *"tracts"* began to appear, with facts about Côte d'Ivoire nobody dared to talk openly about.

---
[61] Money in Bambara.

Our friend Yacine Diallo supplied us with the newest issues. Circulation of Laurent Gbagbo's opposition paper reached a circulation of 12,000 copies a week at 500 CFA a copy.

By 1992 the unrest had taken on a new dimension. Cars were set on fire. Laurent Gbagbo was in jail. His Toyota Landcruiser was burnt. A couple of days later friends of Nadim took his picture sitting behind the wheel of the burnt-out vehicle. The opposition accused *loubards*[62] paid by the government to have been the instigators to discredit the opposition. Peaceful marches were quelled with teargas. The President called interest groups one by one for consultation: traditional and religious leaders, women, farmers, business leaders, and community groups. In the midst of these troubles, Pope John Paul came to inaugurate the Basilica in Yamousoukrou. Although there was the usual public enthusiasm surrounding the holy visit, questions were raised how this exact copy of St. Peter's had been financed. In the end Houphouet-Boigny put these rumours to bed declaring that he had funded the cathedral entirely from his own funds. Other rumours had it that the Basilica was sinking into the ground by one or two centimetres per year.

With a total debt of 15 billion dollars and a population of some 11 million people[63], Côte d'Ivoire was at that time the most heavily indebted country per capita in Africa. Put in a different way, the government had to borrow in order to fund the gap created by the capital flight of its leaders and the wealthy middle class. Throughout the year things got progressively worse. At one point young soldiers occupied the airport for several days, buses went on strike and recruits brandishing guns held up private cars. The President was frequently in Paris, presumably for medical treatment. Student leader Guillaume Soro went on hunger strike

---

[62] Hooligans.
[63] Four million were immigrant workers, mainly from Burkina Faso, Mali and Ghana.

CHAPTER 8: GHOSTBUSTERS OF WEST AND CENTRAL AFRICA

in prison. The University was heading for *une année blanche*[64]. A. continued driving through town, but was constantly scared to lose our Peugeot 309 to mutineers. When we finally got a working telephone after many months of requesting one, landlines were constantly cut during riots. In those days making a successful phone call was a real treat in any case. Shortly after I had left Abidjan for good, President Houphouet-Boigny died. A month later, the CFA franc was devalued by 100%.

The unrest was not limited to Côte d'Ivoire. Civil strife in Togo, Liberia and Zaire forced regional programme reviews to be cancelled altogether. Niger and Nigeria were all stirring and becoming unsafe. One of my missions to Mauritania was cancelled due to sudden political unrest. Even oil-rich Cameroon was tense. I had landed in Douala and was driven after sundown to the capital Yaounde on a bandit-infested road, a two-hour drive. Luckily there was an armed guard in the passenger seat, but at the same time it gave me a most unpleasant feeling.

On that same mission, I spent a Sunday with one of the Anglophone drivers in Labe, formerly called Victoria. I took him to lunch at the old British Atlantic Hotel to know more about the history and present situation of the two Anglophone provinces in a predominantly Francophone country. From him I began to understand the simmering tensions between the Anglophone minority and the Francophones. Labe, formerly Victoria, is a natural deep-sea harbour. It would have made economic sense to develop the harbour there. But instead, the predominantly Francophone government had developed the sandy harbour of Douala. But this port has to be permanently dredged at a huge cost in order to guarantee access to large container vessels. Discrimination against the Anglophones was flagrant. Very competent Anglophones would often be bypassed for higher office. A border conflict involving the potentially oil rich Bakassi Peninsula between Nigeria and Cameroon, was resolved by the International Court of Justice in favour of Cameroon.

---

[64] A "lost" year.

Programme missions to country offices

I remember vividly the joint mission to Kinshasa, to assist Zaire – as the Democratic Republic of Congo (DRC) was called then – in mapping out strategies for the next country programme. Under normal circumstances country offices submit a five-year strategy plan for review and discussion with the regional team. In a highly volatile and uncertain planning environment such as exists in emergency countries, Unicef would propose much shorter periods.

Considering the complexity of the country programme, Deputy Regional Director Shob Jhie decided to come with an almost complete regional team. To our great surprise there was no strategy paper awaiting us to prepare us, just an anthology of speeches by the representative, from which we were to distil the strategy of the future country programme. Shob Jhie was not pleased; and ordered a group of us to remain in Kinshasa to effectively put a strategy paper together with the country team. Marta Mauras, Chief of Africa Section, Saad Houry, immunization adviser Claude Letarte and Michel Sidibe from the Unicef sub-office in the diamond-mining town Mbuji-Mayi and I worked for ten days with the team in working groups by sector, drafting late into the night.

A funny thought once occurred to me at Dakar airport. I was walking on the tarmac behind Shob, Saad and Christian Voumard on the way to board a plane, behind the very same colleagues of whom Kronfol had said I should "latch on to". Suddenly I saw before me three Ghostbusters – Saad had a backpack on his back and that made me think of the movie – with me following in fourth position. Of course we were not here busting ghosts, but we did a fair amount of other types of problem solving, attaché case in hand. Like the movie, we tried to fix everything, made enemies here and there, but people loved us anyway. For example, in some offices we noticed that there was a fair amount of discrimination against national officers. In that case Chief Ghostbuster Shob Jhie then had the task of calling the representative in question to order. In programme implementation, we the regional advisers could sometimes detect that behind the wording

CHAPTER 8: GHOSTBUSTERS OF WEST AND CENTRAL AFRICA

"activity implemented"; the actual implementation was more "financial" than "operational". If money had been advanced to the government for an activity, it was often noted as "accomplished" even though its beneficiaries had not seen anything yet. Here we seriously questioned the country team to set the record straight. That was often painful.

This teamwork created a bond amongst us. Shob was by all means our great leader. He could gauge our moods. Waiting in the lounge at Dakar airport I was visibly upset after some harassment by a Senegalese customs officer. Shob noticed, pulled out his whisky bottle, poured the last drop in the bottle's cap and said, "drink this, this will calm you down" – and it did. Saad was a most caring person, always taking care of passports and Laissez-passer's like a tour operator. He himself was often held back briefly at customs and questioned because of his Lebanese passport – in spite of his Laissez-passer. Shob had a good appetite and loved to eat the big gambas and crabs of Dakar. During a mission with the team in Ouagadougou I suggested we dine at the *Eau Vive*[65], a restaurant run by nuns that simply had the best food in Ouaga. Shob was eager to try it, but when I said: "there is only one thing, Shob, midway there is an *Ave Maria* performance followed by prayer". Shob refused and decided we all settle for the hotel menu.

Nobody knew Shob could sing softly, sentimentally and most melodiously. One evening at a colleague's dinner table he began to sing out of the blue some Korean songs. They were based on ancient poems and he delivered them in a soft, melodious, sentimental, almost sensual way that surprised us all. On top of that he had an astonishing range. I never heard him sing again. There were many gifted colleagues in Unicef who could surprise on social evenings like this one.

First steps in desert sands
One day Saad asked me to go on mission to Mauritania in his stead because of other commitments that had suddenly come up.

---
[65] Water of Life.

It was my first mission on my own. The first thing one notices when touching down in Nouakchott is sand, with some cluttering of green spots of trees struggling for survival.

Fetching me from the airport, the husband of colleague Debbie Dishman drove his car straight into a sand bank until it could go no further. A group of Mauritanians rushed to the rescue and in no time pushed us out of the trouble spot like a car stuck in a snowstorm on 79th Street and Park Avenue. My hotel was El Amane, a simple but agreeable place, breathing a North African ambiance. Simple wooden furniture, a very hard wooden bed base and a lovely courtyard decked with rather unkempt *Bougainvillea*. It had sparse furniture and an alcohol-less bar. El Amane was the very first hotel of Nouakchott. Its setting could have come straight out of a Somerset Maugham story.

Nouakchott is a city that did not have the benefit of city planning to say the least. At independence in 1960 it had 5,000 inhabitants; thirty years later it counted half a million. The first houses were built too near to the ocean and were all crumbling.

The town is a melting pot of white and dark Moors, Poulah, Wolof and Hassani. The street scene of Nouakchott is something to behold: Mauritanians dressed in boubous strut around like the old Romans; small tents serve sweet mint tea, poured consecutively in three small glasses; goats walk unguarded and eat carton boxes and plastic bags, excellent for milk production I am told; there are few cars, most very old; stores are the typical Mauritanian kiosk, a tiny opening through the wired fence, with the products rather invisible behind the merchant; heavy-set women lounge on the floor of a friend's store, resting their head against a pillow; there is a first – and so far only – traffic light installed two years ago, but sandstorms have knocked out its lights a long time ago. Dust is like dry drizzle, it does not go away. Walls of houses disappear and then collapse, if sand is not shovelled off in time. I am reminded by Jorge Borges' novel *The Book of Sand*: a man taken prisoner by a woman who wants him as her lover. The man

CHAPTER 8: GHOSTBUSTERS OF WEST AND CENTRAL AFRICA

shovels sand for her every day. For years he is planning his escape. When he finally sees a ladder leaning against a wall in the courtyard, he is motionless and does not use it.

Another day the office car takes me to a "raw" settlement 10 km out of Nouakchott, an absolute desert no-man's land, where there is no water, health, or food, no nothing at all. There is a makeshift health post consisting of a group of tents. People look destitute here. It's a flagrant violation of the most basic rights of mankind. I am told that eventually some 250,000 people are going to be resettled from a shantytown near Nouakchott for the sake of construction of proper suburban houses. When I pass the deserted area where the shantytown had been just weeks before, all I see are light blue plastic bags littering the ground with some lifted up high in the air by strong gusts of the desert winds.

At El Amane I check out the local newspaper for the weather forecast of the day. We are going to the Senegal River, on the border with Senegal. The forecast is truly unique: *"réduction locale de visibilité par vent de sable"*. Just one year before 50,000 Poulahs (Peuls) were thrown out of Mauritania via the river into Senegal just because the Moors wanted their cattle. At night Poulah often come back over the river, trying to take their cattle back with them to Senegal. Relations with Senegal are tense. The Senegal River is not wide at all; one could almost jump over it. Women cultivate the fields and irrigate them with water pumped up from the river. They seem motivated and sing all the time. In every village we go to we share a meal, usually goat meat.

Here I plant my footsteps for the first time in the red and yellow sands of the desert. All day long I am wearing a Tuareg style cloth wrapped around my head to protect me from the hot sun. It feels surprisingly cool inside it. With project officer Boucoum I climb a sand hill. Sand is amazingly well packed and one does not sink into it at all. Then and there I develop an idea to boost Mauritania's exports: export desert sand to the US, package it under the label *"Sahara Sandbox"* complete with wooden lining and sand to make sandboxes for children. My father, an advertising man and a creative graphic artist in his free time, would have loved to design the packaging. I scoop up some red and sandy coloured sand to show the family and, why not to potential buyers in the US? Up on a sand hill Boucoum turns on his shortwave radio: at that very moment Cameroon scores against Argentina in the opening match of the World Cup. We do a bear hug, it is a magic moment. On the way back to Nouakchott, the sandstorm that was in the forecast hits us on cue. We drive by the beach and spot the colourful *pirogues*[66]. The Mauritanian coastline has one of the richest fisheries reserves in the world, but Spanish and Japanese overfishing has greatly reduced the catch for local fishermen. Young men, even boys push them over the surf, then jump in and are pulled into the boat by strong arms. A dangerous occupation and many drown.

Another day I go back into the desert with Hervé Peries. He is simply the best person to be on a field trip with. Hervé has developed a deep love for Mauritania. In fact Hervé's wife Yasmina is Mauritanian. Today we visit a small oasis. There are very few tents. Seen once, these images stay with you forever. Sticks are upholding colourful cloth that is patched together like an American quilt. Inside the tent there are pillows and rugs to sit or lie down on. There are two women and a young girl, serving us tea continuously. Hervé points to some greenery in the far distance and explains: "Unicef and UNDP have a tree planting project here to contain the desert sand from encroaching on this oasis". Hervé discussing some issues the women are bringing up. We sit here listening to their concerns and take all our time. I absorb the calmness around us. What a different life! Nearby, mules tied to a long rope continue their heavy work of pulling water out of a well with a rubber bucket cut out from a tire.

The Mid-Term Review of Mali in 1991 may be more remembered for what followed rather than the event itself. Shob himself led the team that included Saad Houry, Jacques Adande and myself.

---

[66] Fishing boat of modest size used in Africa and Oceania.

CHAPTER 8: GHOSTBUSTERS OF WEST AND CENTRAL AFRICA

Jacques, a most elegant and amiable man, always told me stories about African cultures, gave useful historical and political insights. A big moment for him came when, as a young 22 year-old trainee at the Benin Ministry of Foreign Affairs on an orientation tour of several embassies, President Kennedy had shaken hands with him and his classmates at the White House. Jacques simply knew everyone and everybody everywhere. When running through airports with him he still found time to greet all the people he knew. Like a candidate campaigning for the highest office.

The conference room at Hotel de l'Amitié was filled to capacity. We were on the home turf of the Bamako Initiative. BI was an initiative by African Health ministers to accelerate primary health care health care through communities", as a follow-up to the ground-breaking 1978 Alma Ata Conference on "Health for All". The Mid Term Review took stock of progress made in Mali. It was not doing too well. At a UNICEF suboffice there had just occurred a big theft of the BI cash representing revenues from sale of drugs. One idea namely was to revitalise primary healthcare by generating funds in communities through the sales of drugs. But people began to stay away as they no longer could afford the high cost. Another impediment was the high cost of training community health personnel. Local health authorities were supposed to stand behind the communities, but had only a virtual autonomous budget. National "catching-up" immunisation campaigns drew these people to lucrative short-term jobs, which was disruptive in building a routine, decentralised health system. One day no one spoke about BI anymore and other strategies came about to accelerate child survival and development. Many countries began to adopt free health care for children under five and pregnant women.

It all seemed a normal, routine review, but strong rumours of an imminent coup circulated in the hallways. As we were meeting, A. and Marinette, who had joined us on this mission, spent time at the market. They learned a lot from the market women; something was bursting in Malian society. I thought back to a remark a

Unicef driver from the Bamako office once had made to me a year earlier. Pointing to a group of luxurious houses in the distance, he said: *"Nous les appellons les maisons de la sécheresse"*. These had been built for the elite with donor funds during the 1973–74 drought emergency.

Moving on to Dakar we missed the coup by just a few days. The market was destroyed and many children and women were killed. A harrowing thought crossed my mind that A. and Marinette could have been there at the wrong moment; and surely they must have met some of women who were killed. Moussa Traore was overthrown and locked up in the prison of Kidal.

The Dakar office proposed to support the Imams in improving the structures of their dilapidated environment. The issue for me was that many of the Imams of the Koranic schools forced the Talibé (student) children to beg in the street during the day. They had to bring home a certain daily sum, and if that failed they could expect corporal punishment and deprivation of food. The Talibés often had a harsh life both in the street and in the coranic school, which was supposed to be a "protective, learning" environment for them. I thought the office approached the problem from the wrong angle. How could it focus on the aggressor and not on the victims? Was it not better to provide formal education or vocational training to keep them from the streets? The issue was very sensitive in predominantly Islamic Senegal.[67]

Our multi-country mission ended with the Gambia. Surangkana was in charge of the office. The programme was small and did not take up much time. In the evening she hosted a big dinner in a restaurant, attended by one of the ministers. A. had the best part of this trip: the office had arranged a field trip for her to visit school gardens along the Gambia River. She spent all day in a *pirogue* on the Gambia River, accompanied by a Dutch UN Volunteer who was in charge of the project. It was then that I got the idea to push for vegetable gardens in schools elsewhere in Africa.

---

[67] Giving alms to the poor is one of the "Pillars of Islam".

CHAPTER 8: GHOSTBUSTERS OF WEST AND CENTRAL AFRICA

When on mission I would sometimes go on a field trip of my own on weekends. One Saturday I travelled with Unicef Gambia driver Lamine Camara to his village. On weekends he is a farmer, tending his fields of millet, maize and cassava. I had bought a *pagne* for his wife for the occasion. One problem though: Lamine has three wives. Two wives would surely get jealous. So he asks me to give it to his mother instead. This way village peace would be maintained. Not at all! Now the three wives are angry… Lamine knows I love the Kora. As a surprise he gives me a couple of tapes of Gambian Kora music that he has recorded especially for me. Long after that, I got a letter from him: "My mother cannot forget you, she cannot pronounce your name and she asks, "Where is Mr Moro haha!"

Another day it was off to Nigeria. Lagos airport is a most chaotic scene. One is immediately accosted; you feel an arm around your shoulder, as if you have been the oldest of friends. "Welcome to Lagos"; "no thank you, I have a Unicef driver"; "look, my car is just over there"; "I don't see it" – and so on for a bit. *Un vrai dialogue de sourds,* as only the French can say it. Until I see the driver with the familiar Unicef sign with a degree of relief. Meanwhile I watch the "Mama Benz" women checking in huge cartons, sacks and bags, shouting and being shouted at, it's all very messy, not to say unruly. They are called Mama Benzes because they drive around in a Mercedes Benz and are usually very well off. The term originated in Togo with batik clothes traders[68]. These women are very wealthy, but you would not say so when you see them. They often perspire heavily and are generally voluminous, but that is because they carry extra pagne under their clothes to carry even more than their bags can hold. I know because I once saw a Mama Benz undress herself in the middle of an airport and literally tens of pagnes appeared and were repacked in bags there and then. Benz women take planes and sell all over West Africa. The worst

---

[68] Batik was introduced to West Africa by the Dutch colonists of the Dutch East Indies. A son of the Fentener van Vlissingen family founded Vlisco in 1846 and appropriated the wax printing technique of the colony. In the late 1880s Vlisco's vessels began to sell batik in ports of call in West Africa on the return trip to Holland.

is to sit next to one – as happened to me many times – because they need in effect two seats, so yours too. The story goes that these women once lent their fleet of Mercedes Benzes to the President of Togo to accommodate state visitors during a summit of the Organisation of African Unity.

I had come into Lagos airport on a local flight from Ibadan where I had been making preparations for an evaluation workshop at IITA (International Institute for Tropical Agriculture). The Rockefeller and Ford Foundations founded IITA to research how to improve yields and make drought-resistant crops. It has excellent lodging and conference room facilities. It also had a good number of tennis courts, a major attraction, and a pool of course. I visited a food security project run by women, who were busy peeling, drying and storing cassava. On Sunday morning I toured the 1,000 ha IITA grounds with Russ, an Americanized Sri Lankan, a "burgher" of Dutch descent. The Dutch had briefly colonised Ceylon hundreds of years ago and several Dutch families had remained behind. We watched kingfishers, herons and other water birds with the field glasses; and then went for a Sri Lankan meal at the home of Gamini Abeysekera, our Unicef man on the spot, with more Sri Lankans. Never saw so many in my life, all tucked away in Ibadan. They strike me as a proud and gallant people. The women seem to remain in the background, leaving the men conversing among themselves.

Driving from Banjul to Senegal's Casamance province the scenery changes completely from arid to lush and green. For years the province tried to secede from Dakar making the place quite unsafe. Indeed the darker skinned Jola have nothing in common with the dominating Wolof of the North. In fact Portugal lost possession of Casamance when a border was negotiated between the French colony of Senegal and Portuguese Guinea (now Guinea-Bissau) in 1888. Claiming economic discrimination and neglect a movement for independence came into being. Insecurity and sporadic violence persists. Casamance is the fruit and vegetable basket of Senegal.

CHAPTER 8: GHOSTBUSTERS OF WEST AND CENTRAL AFRICA

Casamance River looks more like a lake of the *Loosdrechtse Plassen* of my youth. Before boarding the *pirogue* I watched the poor, overloaded thing, packed with people, and suitcases and bags balancing close to the water's edge. With occupancy rates of well over 100 per cent capacity, ferry business is flourishing in Africa, but far from safe. I was not looking forward to having to swim ashore among the crocodiles. The Unicef driver from Bissau was waiting for me at San Vicente. I can't recall if there were any border formalities. Seemed there was more water around us than land, at least for a while.

The capital Bissau is a quaint Portuguese town with red tiled roofs and white washed walls. Some modest renovation was going on here and there, but otherwise, dilapidation reigned. The programme meetings with the Unicef team were gruelling and lasted for four days. Gone were the days when Shob was leading the group. I was now all by myself, trying to stimulate a rather dull team. I was happy to be back on the ferry just as the sun was rising. It was strange to wear a dark blue linen jacket and a tie, as if I were going to an important meeting with government. Unicef driver Lamine Camara drove me straight with Surangkana, the head of the office, to Zinguichor, where we finalized her Board document. Surangkana was a serious and thorough colleague in her work but there was always time for dinners and parties. In fact she was most hospitable and had a great sense of humour. We became good friends. The last evening in The Gambia I spent with her on "fish and chips" on the beach with her friends Mario and Belinda from Rome who worked for an Italian NGO. Sadly enough, the Gambian coastline was seriously eroding caused by trucks "stealing" tons of white sand for construction.

We regional advisers were used to crisscrossing the region from one end to the other. Now it was off to the Central African Republic of infamous Emperor Bokassa.[69] This is a diamond-rich place, hot and very humid, with dark forests and Pygmies, just

---

[69] Deposed in 1979.

north of the Democratic Republic of the Congo. I joined Saad and immunisation adviser Claude Letarte to participate in a programme review meeting with the government. All three of us had a fever and were dizzy and miserable during the proceedings. Still we did what we had to do. My diary: "This trip was killing; I got some virus there, perhaps malaria – not the place to get stuck; only one plane a week; Unicef meeting, awful bickering and lousy work presented".

Then all the way west again, to Cape Verde, 500 nautical miles off the coast of Dakar. After a hard day's work with the head of Unicef Praia on her pet programme, street and working children. There was a huge problem of migrant children going from one island to another, sometimes trafficked against their will, exposed to abuse and neglect, not to mention the dark dangers of the ocean itself.

After work, I settled down on a steep cliff above the bay at a restaurant called *"Poeta"*, enjoying the sunset over the ocean. I loved the old Portuguese lighthouse and rocky cliffs sticking out their paws into the bay. Some small boats were lying sideways and half under water in the marine cemetery. In the morning I had visited a pre-school, laughing with the kids, then offering no plan to make their lives better; more worried about one's speech or report rather than doing something good. I was thinking that now as I was finishing Catcher in the Rye: *"even if you did save a life (as a lawyer) you did it only to be a terrific lawyer, with everyone slapping you on the shoulder, full of admiration when the trial was over"*. Elsewhere in the book Vanessa had marked a passage which was in the same vein: *"Game, my ass, some game; if you get on the side where all the hotshots are, then it's a game alright – I'll admit that. But if you get on the <u>other</u> side where there are no hotshots, then what's the game about? Nothing, no game"*.[70]

---

[70] *Catcher in the Rye*, J.D. Salinger

CHAPTER 8: GHOSTBUSTERS OF WEST AND CENTRAL AFRICA

Family matters

Just before home leave I moved into an apartment in Rue Le Pic in Cocody, below the McGuinty's, a JPO couple from Ontario. The one-bedroom apartment had two balconies in the living room, one of which looked out on a valley covered with palm trees and underbrush. The building had a tennis court and a long swimming pool. We bought lounge chairs that could be wheeled around and later added a ping-pong table. Our new friend Yacine often came by with her nine-year-old Bintou. I gave her one of the bracelets from Djenné, which look very good on her dark skin. I think West Africans have something distinctly elegant about them: Hamidou, the "prince" from Burkina Faso has a style about him. Helped by Nadim, the family thinks that he dresses now better than me. That's not too difficult as I am no Pierre Cardin. Then Salif and many other Africans have a grace that we have long since lost. Bijou, in saying goodbye for the summer, gives me a white rose. I leave it in the apartment in the hope of finding it when I return from home leave.

Summers at the farm were simply refreshing. Once Nadim had a surprise in store for me: he had made a vegetable garden along the old stone wall of what was once a barn with a stone path and grass alongside; we canoed with Peter Hall on the Susquehanna river from Otego to Bainbridge with blue herons and ducks racing us, a hedgehog was busying himself with household chores; of course we tipped over when we ducked all three to one side to avoid an overhanging branch. On this peaceful day in August, Mikhail Gorbachev had been taken prisoner in a military coup in Moscow that soon fizzled out.

We made hundreds of tapers and votive candles to bring back to Africa; and the soccer party was as good as ever, with two-year-old Nile Mitchell already on the field! Naturally, my family was "forced to listen" once again to me reciting the Chinese poem written hundreds of years ago, *Watching the reapers,* about a student who comes home from the big city for the summer holidays and watches the serfs with a degree of shame till the soil.

When summer at the farm was ending, I returned with Nadim to Abidjan in time for his final year to start. For the first time he liked his class and teachers from day one. That could also be a bad sign. Indeed the International School of Abidjan (ICSA) was a lightweight school but a lot of fun for him. He bought himself a Peugeot moped, riding the 12km to school; was bartender at a Unicef party thrown by IT officer Steve Fazio; and organized a camping trip to Jacqueville for his school. He was clearly in his element, growing up fast as a young man. At this point of his very last year in school, we had lost count of the number of schools he had been to. A. became an expert in stringing old beads into a chain. She could spend hours on the markets of Abidjan, Bamako and Ouagadougou, searching and selecting, and talking with the old men selling them. Gradually she could tell a fake from a real old one. She started giving names to each necklace like *le sophistiqué, le triste, le blasé, le sérieux, le frivole* and many other names. Meanwhile Vanessa was in Hangzhou, China for her senior year at Friends World College. FWC was a Quaker college that stressed the humanities and had campuses in India, Costa Rica, China and Kenya as well as London and Paris. It later merged with Long Island University but the ideals it stood for continued.

One Christmas, we took a holiday on the Niger River in Segou, Mali. We all agreed that Segou would be lovely to have a small house and "feel Africa". The mosque in Djenné was simply stunning. Wooden poles sticking out of the walls are holding the structure in place. They serve as permanent scaffolding for easy access: maintenance is on going. Nets are fixed high up inside to catch bats that would otherwise ruin the walls with their excreta. Their screaming is rather unsettling. Mopti, 460 km northeast of Bamako was the next stop. This is the town where the Niger and Bani Rivers meet. A bustling town, I called it the Rotterdam of the savannah. *Pirogues* going about in all directions, Bobo's selling fish and other goods. Nadim's knack for business showed once again. He bought a fair number of Fulani, Bambara and Dogon blankets to sell in the US. He was lucky to find a magnificent ancient wooden puppet for only 200 dollars. Malians are great

CHAPTER 8: GHOSTBUSTERS OF WEST AND CENTRAL AFRICA

puppet players. In a way it was sad that Nadim was getting away with buying a piece of the old tradition. A Bozo fisherman took us on a sunset trip on the Niger that ended a long trading day for the family in style. The river's edge is lined with well-tended vegetable gardens. At that hour women and men water the gardens through a handmade irrigation system.

I think this trip made Nadim even more determined to leave Cooperstown, New York and finish high school in Abidjan. I was happy in one way, but apprehensive in another: the International Community School of Abidjan (ICSA) was an absolutely low-level learning environment. I was worried how Nadim afterwards could ever be accepted at a decent college. Our autodidact A. reminded me then that school was not the only thing that counts in life; and so it was decided. Nadim was enrolled in his old class, now in 12th grade in Abidjan.

Meanwhile my mother's health was deteriorating fast. She was admitted to the hospital, with a fast beating heart, fighting her awful emphysema. I felt terrible, being so far away, but relieved that my sister and brother were around her along with her grandchildren.

The trade in Mopti gave Nadim the idea to establish a little business: Africa Imports, established at Briar Creek Road, Box 279, Otego, NY 13825. The blankets from Mali and Korrhogo sold like *petits pains*. In Kumasi, Ghana he bought a whole supply of baskets. His main customer was a fruit and vegetable barn near Otego, which resold them to its customers. Nadim's products had a special corner there. When he got his US driver's license at 16 years, Hamidou and he went on buying trips to Mali and Burkina Faso. One day on the way back the customs officer held them up asking for money to allow the goods to be imported in Côte d'Ivoire. Nadim refused and they spent the night there. The following morning a Tuareg customs officer showed up for morning duty. And Nadim asked him point blank: *"Est ce que tu connais Annette?"* By that time A. was rather well known in the

Tuareg community of Abidjan as we shall see shortly. *"Oui bien sûr"*, answered the customs officer. *"C'est ma mère"*, Nadim said rather sternly. At that point the customs officer quickly waved them through. It pays to know the right people in far away places! In his last school year Nadim taught English to a Lebanese businessman three times a week. This was a very lucrative affair. The man learned fast and Nadim earned fast. The Lebanese came three times a week, always bringing a shiny platter with delicious Lebanese food. He consistently left the platter behind. The man briefly ended up in jail for some felony or other. And so the tutoring came to an abrupt halt.

Another time, Nadim and Hamidou, this time with A., drove all the way from Abidjan to Agadez in Niger. Little Mohamed was of the party, going back to his village that he was going to restore. In many ways Hamidou was our *garde de corps*. In Agadez they rented a four-wheel drive to go further north. Nadim did some six hours on a camel without a saddle sitting behind the Tuareg to bring water back to the camp. But all he found was a crate of coca cola. With A. in the car, blankets and baskets bought in Niamey made it back safely through customs to Abidjan.

Life with the Tuaregs

Meanwhile A. had found her calling in Abidjan. One day a young photographer, Giacomo Pirozzi, the new junior professional officer (JPO), invited A. to join him on a photo shoot with Tuareg refugees from Mali and Niger who lived in rather miserable circumstances in a *bidonville* called Washington in the *Deux Plateaux* neighbourhood. While Giacomo was shooting his photo reportage, A. had time to speak with the women and children about their problems. They had considerable health issues, such as diarrhoea, malaria and acute respiratory infections and malnutrition. Skin wounds caused by infections and malnutrition were rampant.

The children longed to have a classroom. I remember her coming home that evening determined to try to do something, especially in art so as to make them forget their misery. She added a second shantytown to her work terrain by the name of Gobelet. That's where she established a primary school. Children from Burkinabe migrants who lived in Gobelet were also admitted. She found a very motivated Ivorian teacher who doubled his income by teaching afternoons. The Tuareg children were very good learners. Jacques Bignancourt of ENDA-Tiers Monde, Dakar[71] and Madame Chantal Bouquier of the French Consulate provided funding.

A. even arranged a donation in kind that generated income through art; and she lost no time in achieving that too. She contacted her friend Muriel Silberstein at the Children's Department of the Metropolitan Museum of New York who introduced her to the public relations person at Creola in Pennsylvania. He was a man with deep feelings for charity. When the first package arrived in the pouch from the company, it read: *"For Annette's Africa children"*. For the next three years these packages provided paint and brushes, crayons and drawing paper. Through ENDA and the social services at the French embassy she found a Tunisian doctor with whom she went on Sundays to vaccinate, treat skin diseases and de-worm "her" children. She handed out soap to the women. Sunday afternoons the children would often come to our apartment in Rue Le Pic to paint and to do handicraft. We would let them swim in the large swimming pool, which greatly angered our French neighbours.

Another of her projects was to restore a village in Niger, 150 km North of Tahoua. She raised a considerable amount of money. Many of our friends were very generous, even those far away, like our good friend John Parr in Brussels and Peter Hall in New York. A young Tuareg was sent from Abidjan with these funds to organize this. Instead he vanished with the money in the desert mountains to join the rebels. Now A. and I were both working for children, albeit in two very different situations. Even in Africa it was "two for the price of one."

---

[71] Environnement et Developpement Tiers Monde

A major event was the multi-media exhibit about life and culture of Tuaregs at the Centre Culturel Français that A. organised with Pirozzi and two Tuareg community leaders. The exhibit was called *Itinéraire* and was an enormous success. Giacomo had made the brochure. His photos lined the walls of the CCF. Next to the photos were poems about the desert. A video film was shown on life in Gobelet and Washington, and children begging in the street. Drinks were on hand of course. Tuareg music filled the rooms. The children had painted a large collection of well-wishing cards with images of Tuareg life in the desert. Monika Knofler of the Greeting Card Division came to look at possibilities to include some in the annual greeting card collection. Children had decorated Bic pens, armbands and key rings with coloured plastic wires. Tuareg artisans sold silver jewellery and leather baskets. The children made considerable money. What they made A. took to Paris and New York and was sold there as well. There was a write-up in the daily paper *Fraternité Matin*. Life of the Tuaregs became her life's passion.

Death of a colleague

In May 1991 I was invited to a farewell dinner at the home of Rebecca Belanger for Surangkana, who was leaving the Gambia for an assignment in Human Resources at HQ. There were some other guests from the Quebec community in Abidjan. Rebecca was a totally bilingual consultant. She wrote the Situation Analysis of the Gambia, the best one I had read until then. Her husband represented Canada and a group of other countries at the African Development Bank. I happened to sit next to Françoise Levesque of the Canadian embassy, who was an education specialist at the Canadian International Development Agency (CIDA) in Abidjan at that time. In talking with her at length about the challenge of education in our region I began to feel that she might well have the qualifications for the vacant post of Regional Adviser, Education; and I strongly encouraged her to apply. She was rather speedily confirmed in the post.

Although I had not had the chance yet to go on mission with her, her reputation spread quickly through the region where I passed through. For instance, I was most impressed by comments from the Mauritanian Education Ministry, which heaped praise on her creative approaches. I recall that they particularly welcomed her point of view on the importance of instruction in the maternal language, at least in the first grades. One morning we got the terrible news that Françoise had died overnight of a fatal attack of meningitis in her hotel room in Bamako. She had called reception in the middle of the night asking for medication for her pains, which turned out to be fatal. Françoise had been with the team barely one year. In no time at all she impressed with her professionalism and warm personality. Her passing away was a huge intellectual loss for the region. Saad was still in Abidjan at the time, waiting to leave for Canada to complete requirements for immigration to Canada. We sustained each other. Together we visited Françoise's sister, who had come to Abidjan to arrange her affairs. It was simply heart-breaking.

The promise of a new millennium

The year 1991 kicked off the new decade that stood in the light of the development goals to be reached by the year 2000. The UN World Summit for Children had been held the year before. Until then, summits referred only to face-to-face meetings between the Presidents of the United States and the Soviet Union. That "glass ceiling" had now been broken for the sake of children. UN development summits became the new "fashion"[72]. 71 heads of state and government and 88 ministers adopted a Declaration on the Survival, Protection and Development of Children and a Plan of Action committing member states to a series of survival and development goals[73]. Some of us in Unicef were against this rigid goal

---

[72] The Earth Summit (Rio de Janeiro, 1992) and the Social Summit (Copenhagen, 1995) are important examples.
[73] Reduction of infant and under-five child mortality by a third; reduction of maternal mortality rate by half; reduction of severe and moderate malnutrition; universal access to safe drinking water and sanitation; universal access to basic education and completion of primary education by at least 80 per cent of primary school-age children; reduction of the adult illiteracy rate to at least half its 1990 baseline; and improved protection of children in especially difficult circumstances.

setting; Shob Jhie and myself were among them. My thinking was that development should accelerate, yes, but global goal setting made little sense in Africa, a continent of rich diversity. Africa as a whole suffered from weak human capacities, massive brain drain of talent and low levels of education compared to Asia and Latin America. Moreover, in the rush to reach the coverage targets, these were often an impediment to building up routine and durable health systems. The extra money that could be had in the forever short-lived polio campaigns understandably distracted health personnel.

The "All Africa Consultation with James Grant" was a strategy meeting of Unicef Representatives and regional teams. This meeting came just months after the World Summit for Children. The stage was set to push the Representatives to greater heights in reaching other global goals now that universal childhood immunisation had been a great success. In fact one can now say that the year 1990 had been a turning point in development. Thanks to UCI, development goals got a far sharper focus. The Education Conference in Jomtien, sponsored by the World Bank, Unesco, Unicef and UNDP, had just set a framework to advance education for all. In September 1990 the Convention of the Rights of the Child had come into force when a sufficient number of member states had ratified it. Child rights were now the linchpin of our advocacy, "in the best interest of the child". Unicef had its work cut out, but the time frame to achieve was very short to achieve some of these very ambitious and sometimes unrealistic goals.

The meeting was held at the UN compound Giri Giri, a beautifully landscaped 300-acre plot of land where most UN agencies have offices. There are flowering trees like the splendid Jacaranda, an abundance of roses and tall bougainvillea and lots of places to have a warm lunch or sandwich.

Grant opened with a big pep talk, urging everyone to start working on the goals. I was included in the team of rapporteurs led by Michael O'Reilly, the Regional Monitoring and Evaluation

CHAPTER 8: GHOSTBUSTERS OF WEST AND CENTRAL AFRICA

officer in Nairobi. As a rapporteur one is of course concentrated on what is being said. It is easy to miss something important. The audio can of course be replayed but one should not have to depend on it, as transcribing is very time consuming, at least for me. One does that only when in doubt. Sometimes a speech of intervention fascinated me so that I replayed it several times, until I got it right. I still remember the electrifying speech by Stephen Lewis, former Canadian ambassador to the UN, and now adviser to Pérez de Quellar on Africa, who hammered out these words in the keynote speech: "We can't let Africa go, we can't let the world get away with it; and the world, if given the chance, would get away with it". It was populism of the best kind. With the Unicef audience almost cheering him on, this went down very well. Lewis blamed everything on the West, singling out the failure of the United Nations Programme of Action for Africa Economic Recovery and Development (UNPAERD) – as if the Africans themselves had nothing to do with it. At the same time it was pretty patronizing too.

Representatives pledged to advocate with their respective host governments to put in place a National Plan Action for Children, in effect a strategic road map to achieve the goals. Unicef HQ was to develop a tracking mechanism to follow progress of nations towards reaching the goals.

I remember the ambiance and people swirling around our leaders, Grant, Jolly, Marco. Grant always managed to greet you, and would often put his arm around you. In fact, coming from him, this warm gesture from this driven man was an encouragement for me and I am sure many others. Such gatherings were great for looking for your next assignment. I myself did a bit of that too at times. Shortly before coming to Nairobi, Shob had offered me the post of Community Development, returning me to my previous level of P5. I had not yet accepted his offer at that point. Regional Director Mary Racelis, who was close to Grant, thought that I might be a good candidate for the Rwanda Representative post. Kigali had refused the *agrément* for a Belgian colleague just weeks before.

Marco Vianello-Chiodo, now Deputy to Grant, revealed to me that Unicef was having some problems with the Dutch government: three senior Dutch staff members had just left: my former boss in PFO Suzanne Bischoff; Economist Rolph van der Hoeven who returned to ILO after a two year secondment with Richard Jolly; and René Latenstein, who had given up his leadership position of the Dutch Committee two years before and now wished to rejoin his family in Holland. Marco said that Unicef could thus ill afford losing another Dutch national. At least that... I told Hans Narula that Shob had offered me the regional post of Community Development. Narula was in the Programme Division and a champion of area-based programming. He thought that Community Development should not be at regional level but in country offices as a support to area-based programmes. That gave me food for thought.

For the first time since my interview with Richard Jolly in 1985, I had some good interaction with him. At a special evening session on *Adjustment with a Human Face*, I had made an intervention about the sovereign debt issue. The following day I found myself in a working group on Programme Funding and he and Marco were also in that group, and that did not hurt. Jolly later complimented me on my ideas: one of these was promoting a sovereign debt reduction scheme at the African Development Bank. This was not an entirely new idea but an idea whose time had come and it needed considerable pushing. Jolly said that we were both close on the issues.

Since 1985 he had taken his *Adjustment with a Human Face* quite a bit further down the road. The 1989 Unicef State of the World's Children Report gives a clue. The report devoted a major part to what was appropriately labelled "Children in Debt". Building on a quotation by former Tanzanian President Julius Nyerere, "Must we starve our children to pay our debts", Unicef maintained that that question had in practice been answered with 'yes'. One only had to look at malnourished children to realise that they were already paying the price. The report went on to say that a large

CHAPTER 8: GHOSTBUSTERS OF WEST AND CENTRAL AFRICA

part of economic adjustment policies were failing in two major ways: they placed a disproportionate burden on the poorest and most vulnerable, with children bearing most of the brunt. The second failing was that adjustment policies of that time failed to restore economic growth. In effect, Unicef was in no way denying the importance of growth, arguing instead that *Adjustment with a Human Face* did not at all mean to introduce more welfare fare in a stagnant economy. There was simply a wider argument for a different, two-pronged approach to the whole adjustment process, not only to seek to protect the poorest and most vulnerable, but very much also to "contribute to a quickening of economic growth of a kind to which smaller and poorer producers could contribute to and benefit from".[74]

A few months later Unicef launched the "Debt Relief for Child Development" Initiative, the brainchild of Richard Jolly and Stephany Griffith-Jones. I was in New York at the time and attended a couple of meetings as an observer for the Programme Funding Office. As a former banker, I was keenly interested of course. The initiative combined sovereign debt reduction with assuring that the resources freed up from debt service would be committed by recipient governments to improving health, nutrition and education of the poorest and most vulnerable children. The very first transaction was with Midland Bank in December 1988. The Midland Bank forgave all its loan exposure to Sudan, amounting to some US $ 800,000 for use by Unicef as counterpart funds in health, water, sanitation and reforestation programmes in Sudan's Kordofan Region. At about the same time the Inter-American Development Bank and Unicef launched an initiative for human capital development in the 1990s funded through a social investment trust fund, to enable IDB member countries to borrow at IDB and buy back well below par their external debt in the secondary market.[75]

---

[74] State of the World's Children Report 1989, Unicef
[75] Griffith-Jones, Stephany: Debt Reduction with a Human Face: The IDB and Unicef Initiative, 1989

Richard gave me some useful advice: as a Rapporteur of meetings, to write reports with a touch of humour to lighten the text. I could not agree with him more. In fact in a letter to my mother written around that time, I told her about a style of writing I already had adopted: *"In all my report writing for Unicef I attempt to apply a bit of a journalistic style, so as to minimize United Nations jargon that usually makes for rather dull and dry reading"*.

Back in Abidjan I briefed Shob on my prospects for Kigali – and in the same breath confessed that I knew absolutely nothing about community development... And, I ventured to say, "should it not be dealt with only at field level?" His only answer was that it was easy and I would pick it up quickly. He said excessive specialization as an attribute was not a *sine qua non* for Urban Affairs, children in difficult circumstances or rural development, all areas of my new responsibility. Few in Unicef had that expertise in any case, he added. So the pull from my region to keep me there turned out to be very great indeed. In the end I accepted the regional post, not knowing then that that decision saved me from witnessing first-hand the genocide in Rwanda of 1994. That thought still haunts me today.

Community Development was not a programme but a strategy cutting across all sectors to involve people in making their own decisions. Community development underpinned area-based programmes that were mostly in rural areas, but could easily be applied in urban areas as well. The pillars of my job were urban programming and children in especially difficult circumstances (street and working children, children with disabilities, child soldiers, HIV/AIDS orphans). Padmini at HQ became my mentor. I learned much from her. Area-based programming targeted specific zones for a series of mutually reinforcing interventions in health, water and sanitation, education, economic activities and specific protection for vulnerable children. A drawback was that neighbouring non-intervention districts were not advancing as fast, which could lead to gross geographical inequality and local rivalry.

CHAPTER 8: GHOSTBUSTERS OF WEST AND CENTRAL AFRICA

As a first step, I joined Shob at a Unicef consultation on area-based programming in Harare. In Unicef there was a network of colleagues promoting the area-based approach, whereas others favoured a national approach at ministerial level with services available to the whole population, for example immunisation or formal education. Shob's strategy was that I might be able to impress this closely knit group if I produced a good report. Apparently this was the case, because I did cross a crucial bridge in my Unicef career. In the process I became a champion for community participation and empowerment. About to begin this new assignment, I thought of Unicef colleague Grace in Abidjan, our women's adviser, who could read someone's future in the palm of a hand. Six months before she had predicted that the stars looked particularly good for me in April 1991. How right she was! Her stars were not too bad either: right around that time Grace moved over to the African Development Bank, gaining a big promotion as their new Women's Affairs adviser.[76]

Called Salisbury by the British, Harare struck me as a small provincial town somewhere in the South East of England. Low white washed buildings, shops in arcades, lots of green, and a major park. On the day before the meeting, I checked out Harare Park, to see what locals do on a Sunday. Armed with area-based programming documents to prepare myself, I took in some impressions. A group of British women were singing hymns under a tree. I watched some others neatly dressed in all white outfits, rolling a ball over grass cut short like a green, scoring points. It looked a bit like a game played at a garden party during high tea. Let's say, a bit of a mix between bowling and croquet[77]. I asked some Zimbabweans the name of this game, but they could not tell. Although Zimbabwe had been independent some eleven years, the scene still looked decidedly colonial. In the distance the voice of

---

[76] IT Colleague Steve Fazio had joked that Grace was "going from BAD (Banque Africaine de Developpement) to worse".
[77] The origin of croquet is a 16th century French game called "paille-maille"; whence the name of the London Street Pall Mall, where it was played; Oxford Encyclopedic Dictionary.

Vera Lynn was crooning *"Land of hope and glory, mother of the free, How shall we extol thee, who are born of thee? Wider still and wider shall thy bounds be set. God who made thee mighty, make thee mightier yet..."*

I now began to realize that Shob must have been in a hurry to fill this post. We knew something was in the air as Shob had begun to count the number of countries in our region he had been to, often a sign of impending re-assignment. Two months later he announced that he was going to be transferred to HQ. His assignment was to work on a programme management tracking system that in somewhat revised form is still in use today. I was very sad to see him go, I was going to miss his leadership, the camaraderie with the other Ghostbusters in his hotel room, sipping a late night scotch. On one such evening Shob made the point that a "merger" of oriental and western values would make for a better world. I believe he was absolutely right.

As part of the orientation for my new post, I visited area-based programmes in Kitui, Kenya that lies on the road to Somalia. Water is a scarce commodity there. And the very day that I am there, Danida[78], having uncovered a massive corruption scandal announces that it suspends all assistance to water and sanitation projects in Kenya. Strangely enough the authorities do not seem at all disturbed about it. Women are weaving baskets and selling them, grinding corn in a Unicef provided mill as if there is no tomorrow, and making steady money at that. Have I encountered the poorest of the poor? No, on the contrary. I was thinking of Robert Chambers' book *Rural Development: Putting the Last First* that Dick Heyward, the Unicef guru on community development, had recommended to me along with stacks of other books. Was I engaging myself in what Robert Chambers has called "development tourism" and "project bias"? In Chambers' words: "Project bias is most marked by the showpiece: the pet project or model village specially staffed and supported, with well briefed

---

[78] Danish International Development Agency.

CHAPTER 8: GHOSTBUSTERS OF WEST AND CENTRAL AFRICA

members who know what to say, sited at a reasonable but not excessive distance from the urban headquarters; such projects provide a simple reflex to solve the problem of what to do with visitors and senior staff on inspection. Once again, they direct attention away from poorer people".[79]

I was out of touch with the real poor and I felt a cloud of shame descending on me. While I was talking to the villagers, my mind wandered off to a life of mine that was so far removed from theirs. In Nairobi, I spoke with very poor children in a community school who might otherwise have been in the street. My diary explains, "I spoke with them and enjoyed it." That, I am afraid, sounds very much like development tourism indeed. But my diary called me to order a few days later, and this is the gist of it: that I should teach and motivate – and *give something back for what I have learned from them.* Even this sounds hollow.

Only a few miles from the centre of Nairobi, there is the neighbourhood of Kibera, the largest urban slum in Africa. The landing corridor of Jomo Kenyatta International airport is right above it. Planes land right above your head at an altitude of just a few hundred metres. I went there on a fact-finding mission with the Undugu Society of Nairobi. Undugu ran community schools in slums and have integrated projects there in urban farming, income generating activities, water and sanitation and so on. Most of Kibera's residents lived in extreme poverty, earning less than $1.00 per day. Unemployment rates were high. Many lived with HIV/AIDS. Domestic violence and rape were common. There were few schools and many children were not in school. Scarcity of clean water and poor hygiene brought diarrhoea and cholera.

Indeed hygiene was appalling. Open sewer systems were common throughout the slum. Although the community had constructed latrines with the support of the NGO, the doors were locked.

---

[79] Robert Chambers, *Rural Development: Putting the Last First*, Longman Group UK Ltd, 1983.

At my request they opened one and I saw that they had never been used. On the positive side, urban farming was flourishing and small fields well-tended. There was some animal husbandry, with goats and chickens roaming around. Organic waste was used to make compost.

Investors in urban farming are usually middle class businessmen seeking a good return. Women play an important role, since they can combine more easily agriculture, food processing and selling at markets with household tasks. Studies done in the early 1990s found that urban farming did not drive down malnutrition rates among children, as it should have. More than half were stunted in some areas, well above the 1991 national average of one in five[80]. Several women engaged in trades such as renting out stores, selling kerosene, grinding kassava and marketing fruits and vegetables. They looked well off. But are the poorest of the poor involved and getting out of poverty as a result of urban farming? No, not really. A "trickle-down" effect perhaps? Maybe to some extent, but don't hold your breath. Does truly participatory development exist where the poorest of the poor are listened to? A tormenting question: Has my life's career simply gone from business development to development business? Were most project activities I have seen so far in fact a case of project bias?[81]

The Maradi Consultation on Participatory Development
The trip to Nairobi and Kitui was well timed, coming as it did on the heels of a "Consultation on Participatory Development" in Arusha, Tanzania. That workshop took under the loop how community participation as a strategy could accelerate development. This helped me to develop our own consultation one year later. Cynthia Court, Dutch wife of our Representative in Chad, Alan Court, had come over to Niamey to assist me with ideas for

---

[80] Mboganie-Mwangi, Alice and Foeken, Dick, University of Nairobi and African Studies Centre, Leiden University: *Urban agriculture, Food Security and Nutrition in low income areas of Nairobi, 1996.*
[81] The then French minister of Cooperation Bernard Kouchner, co-founder of Médecins sans frontières (MSF) called that *"Business Charité"*.

CHAPTER 8: GHOSTBUSTERS OF WEST AND CENTRAL AFRICA

content and logistics. I deliberately wanted the workshop in the field and preferably as far away as possible from Niamey – so that we could see community development in action and put an interesting field trip on the agenda. My eyes fell on Zinder, some 1,000 km East of Niamey towards the border with Chad.

Zinder struck me as a forlorn and forgotten place. It was unbearably hot. There was no hotel that could conveniently receive our group; air conditioners were fickle at best. The only conference room was too hot and too small, even for our small group. On the way back we stop in Maradi, on the Niger River and "only" some 600 km from Niamey. We check out the airport, it's an all-grass strip so our plane can land and take off softly, so the authorities assure me. Other facilities are much better all around compared to Zinder. Several weeks after my visit, I heard on the BBC that the Imam of Zinder blamed the absence of rain on girls wearing miniskirts, lambasting Western mores in the process. He then encouraged the religious police and others to admonish these girls. When the situation got out of hand and became violent, the Imam issued a second statement, cautioning: *"ça suffit"*[82]. The next day it rained for many hours…

In Maradi we had a selected, motivated group that studied the relationship of several different themes with community participation and development under the overall guidance of Padmini. She had in-depth knowledge on community approaches to development, including in urban areas. Urban was her specialty. External resource persons were Bernard Ouedraogo founder of the NAAM movement in Burkina Faso; and a representative of the Bangladesh Rural Advance Committee. BRAC did much for the advancement of community development. It had innovative approaches in extending loans to the rural poor to develop small businesses.

Unicef staffers Bintou Keita, Ndolamb Ngokwey, Hervé Peries, Michel Sidibe, and Denis Valot were all enthusiastic area-based

---

[82] Enough is enough.

and community participation converts. One of the workshop themes was related to emergencies. Could community development exist in an emergency situation? We concluded that even in the case of enduring conflict, a huge opportunity existed to engage civil society. We had a case like that in West Africa. When the Liberian government lost control, several private organizations filled the void and became the principal partner of Unicef. Although the government retrieved that role after the conflict ended, it now had stronger private organizations to deal with.

One afternoon was devoted to a field trip. It was excruciatingly hot. We sat under the one and only tree of a village for many hours listening to the concerns of villagers and how the community was organized. Denis Valot led the session and translated in French. We drank litres of mineral water. When the consultation ended, I briefed the local authorities on our conclusions. I ended with something Thomas Sankara had once said: *"Il faut être un peu fou pour vouloir changer le monde; moi, je veux être un de ces fous"*. Because that was what our group really wished to do too.

Workshops and consultations in Unicef sometimes "brought people closer together". Maradi was no exception. There were three men rather enamoured by the same young participant. There was Michel Sidibe; and Alfonso, information officer from Lagos. I kept my own feelings rather to myself. Alfonso was the clear favourite of hers and I must admit, they made for a stunning couple. When I told them so, Alfonso simply commented that she resembled his wife. One evening Alfonso said that this evening was a good one to watch falling stars. The Maradi sky was crystal clear, suddenly we noticed a very sharp ray of light shining onto Earth that went around in circles and disappeared altogether after half an hour. We both agreed that it was not a falling star but an unidentified flying object, a UFO therefore, just like I had seen seven years before, when Vanessa and I were driving one late evening on the rural road from Franklin, NY to our farmhouse, a one-hour drive. Then the UFO followed our car all the way to the farm and disappeared over a neighbour's hill.

CHAPTER 8: GHOSTBUSTERS OF WEST AND CENTRAL AFRICA

Mauritania, one more time

Of all the countries in West Africa, Mauritania fascinated me the most. Where else can one see two soldiers holding hands or someone pushing someone else's car out of a sand hill? Where else in an office can you get served three consecutive glasses of very sugary mint tea and another round for the asking? Where else can you witness a presidential campaign with veiled women promoting their candidate from tents and offering passers-by tea through the night?

Early in 1992, I was asked to come and help with the Situation Analysis, in particular the section dealing with children in especially difficult circumstances. That was a target group that the Executive Board had singled out at its 1986 session as extremely vulnerable[83]. Padmini had joined me on this mission. The presidential campaign was in full swing, and the streets were crowded with white and black Moors. I was told there was considerable tension among the ethnic groups, especially in that the blacks claimed to be far more numerous that the official census would have it. That was a no-no.

One evening after dinner the driver showed us how the presidential campaign was being conducted. It was a most unusual campaign to witness, at least for our eyes: very colourful, with tents of political parties all over town promoting their candidate. It was all very animated in half-lit Nouakchott and it lasted till well after midnight. The moment was historic: these were after all the very first democratic elections for the country. One could feel that there was great excitement all around. We passed one large tent and the driver slowed down. There were only women and Padmini asked the driver to stop. We went in the tent and got a royal reception. Tea was offered and the women enthusiastically explained their part in the campaign. Padmini was in no hurry at all to go to the hotel. We stayed for some time to take it all in. On the 24th of

---

[83] These were children, the main focus was at first on children living and working in the street or street children; children affected or infected by HIV/AIDS and other vulnerable children.

January 1992, incumbent President Maaouya Ould Sid'Ahmed Taya was elected easily in the first round. Accusations of rigging would never leave him and eventually he was overthrown.

In between programme meetings Padmini and I paid a visit to the Minister of Justice to discuss the state of juvenile justice in Mauritania. Padmini told me that this was the first time that Unicef called on a Minister of Justice on such a sensitive issue. First we went to the old Fort that housed the prison to get an idea of the situation. It was here where Antoine St Exupéry had written parts of *Terre des Hommes*. The overcrowded situation, the squalor in which these children had to live was not to be believed. The cement floor served as their bed. The children had almost no exercise and lived side by side with adults. At night the guards bullied them into stealing on their behalf outside the prison walls. The minister listened patiently to Padmini who pleaded with him to at least separate these children from the adults and build juvenile centres with a focus of reintegrating them in society. The Minister seemed receptive to this idea but stated that the government lacked money to do so. Talking about *"un monde digne de l'enfant"*.[84] But one year or so later, the Minister had found a way and the children were indeed separated. So at least we had achieved that.

Representative Sergio Soro asked me if I could write a story for the Situation Analysis about street children in Nouakchott. I thought there was plenty of "material" to develop a story and so I agreed. The office supported a *Centre d'écoute* funded in part by the French National Committee. Caritas was also working with street children. I spent several evenings at the *Centre d'écoute* to get a feeling for how they live. Most children would come here by themselves through word of mouth or along with other street children. They learned Arabic and French and could stay overnight if they wished. Some attended the new *écoles de rattrapage* that made them reach sixth grade in half the time.

---

[84] The slogan for the Global Movement of Children as promoted by the United Nations General Assembly's Special Session on Children, May 2002.

CHAPTER 8: GHOSTBUSTERS OF WEST AND CENTRAL AFRICA

There was Biri, a black kid, very upbeat, who taught me a little boxing; Ousmane, also black, about 10 years old, who had just arrived from the East, hidden in the undercarriage of a truck and who seemed to possess all the street wisdom ever invented; there was Goliath, his *nom de guerre* of the street, because he was the fastest thief among the children. Goliath showed me how to pickpocket but all I remember was that it was fast and very clever. One evening they treated me to some very entertaining theatre and it was of course all about themselves and how they live in the street. He did not look like a street child the way I had come to know them; in fact he had a rather soft and dreamy look. And he admits: *"j'ai fait tout, tout"*, and that, I was told, includes prostitution, although he did not say that. Goliath admitted to excessive cheating when playing poker, boasting of a friend who lost badly to him: *"je l'ai vidé"*[85]. He had become a fisherman of sorts, fishing at night in the port, sleeping there and selling the catch of the night to his customers in the morning. The day before we went to the place where the huge trucks are parked. He showed me the secret hiding place for kids, above the tyres, with just enough space for body and feet; but the head had to rest on a separate steel bar. Like this these children hitch rides over hundreds of kilometres, unseen by the drivers, from the Malian border to Nouakchott, no doubt filling their lungs with sand and dust all the way.

These were the children of François Lefort, priest and medical doctor. A very amiable, sociable and intellectual *Breton*, he seemed to me a little out of place in that environment. I was already aware of his work because the French Committee's Paul Audat had sent me his book *La vie réconciliée*. The book had won the annual award of the French Unicef Committee at the 1989 Nancy Book Fair. One evening I went with the children and Badu the moniteur of the *Centre d'écoute* to look for Lefort. His van was parked outside the Catholic Mission. Lefort never locked it so they could sleep in it at night. Biri and Goliath climbed in and found their friend *Quinze-Ans*, totally drugged. He had just returned to life in

---

[85] Freely translated as: "I cleaned him out".

the street, contrary to his own advice to his friends. I asked Goliath what he might have been up to and he said: *"les ambassades, ce sont ses amis"*. That's all he said, leaving the rest to my imagination. I left them there with Badu to wait for their priest and protector who no doubt was enjoying a gourmet meal with his friends, the missionaries.

Resource person in regional and global consultations and seminars

I was a resource person in several regional and global workshops and consultations in Europe or the US. One was the biannual Congress on Child Abuse and Neglect held in Chicago. The first part was a "pre-Congress" at the university of Chicago on the theme "Children in war" in which some one hundred people from all over the world participated. We heard presentations by Shrifra from South Africa (children under Apartheid); Sultan from Mozambique (children affected by war); Carlos, a former street child from Bogota; Adriana, education specialist from an ONG in Bogota; Kathy from rough South Chicago; Marina from war torn Croatia and others. Clarence Shubert, CEDC expert in Padmini's Urban Section at HQ spoke on behalf of Unicef. The Pre-Congress was a relatively small gathering of the think tank type and was the most productive. The Congress itself was a much bigger event, with more than 2,000 people attending. At the opening ceremony, a children's choir from Chicago sang gospels. TV talk-show host Oprah Winfrey made the keynote address and disclosed emotionally for the first time how a distant cousin had abused her at the age of nine. In that same week she hosted a compelling TV documentary titled *Scared silent: exposing and ending child abuse*. For two days we listened in plenary to one presentation after another, with little debate or discussion other than in the hallways for networking and exchange of business cards.

The 1992 ILO Conference on Child Labour in Dakar effectively launched the close cooperation between ILO and Unicef on this issue. Countries presented case studies of children working under harsh conditions. Excesses were noted in Côte d'Ivoire where

CHAPTER 8: GHOSTBUSTERS OF WEST AND CENTRAL AFRICA

children worked on cocoa plantations and in gold mines; in Zaire over 100,000 children worked in the gold and diamond mines. I had prepared a speech for my Regional Director, but instead he asked me to go to Dakar to deliver it on his behalf!

In 1993 I participated in the Global Seminar *on Street and Working Children* at *Spedale Innocenti* in Florence, the Unicef Research Centre on Children. Innocenti had been a gift of the Italian government. Six years earlier I had attended a very lively debate of the Executive Board on Innocenti, a home in Florence built in 1494 for babies born out of wedlock. These children came from all social classes, but especially the poor. By the 16th century Innocenti was home to some 1,000 children. By 1984, the number had dwindled to nine. The Italian government wished to donate part of this splendid building to Unicef with the proviso that it should become a research centre on children named "The International Child Development Centre". Several delegations were wary that the running cost would turn out to be high. The German Committee made the statement that it was a "proud" donation, but would entail huge running cost for Unicef. In spite of a very mediocre presentation of a badly prepared project, the resolution was passed. The French delegation pointed out that there already existed a renowned research centre on children, namely the *Centre de Recherche pour l'Enfant* in Paris, so there was no need for a second one.

Training guru Alain Silverman and Victoria Rialp of Urban Section at HQ had prepared the content and modules of the seminar with great professionalism. Participants came from all over the world. The seminar was a key milestone in the new collaboration with ILO on child labour and lasted for ten days. The final report was written by Maggie Black, author of *Children and the Nations*. After reviewing the situation of these children in several case studies, the focus was on practical approaches to adopt with a view to improving their protection and development. Participants from Latin America – far ahead on these issues – shared their rich experiences. The debate also took other children in especially children under the loop, such as orphaned and abandoned children and children with disabilities.

Roger Hart spoke on maximising children's participation, a subject he had researched for his book *From tokenism to citizenship*. A lively discussion followed between sceptics and proponents. Very few dissident voices on the subject, but some words to the wise were expressed: Miguel Ugalde, our man on the spot in Ibadan, said that there was a great risk that adults could manipulate participating children. I myself was rather sceptical too. Children's participation thus far was based on one-time events such as Children's Parliaments that met on child development resolutions once a year on the occasion of the International Day of the Child of the first of June. I made the point that "children's participation must lead to a better chance for children in life; it should not be an end in itself. If they do play a participatory role, they must be able to see the light at the end of the tunnel."

As in any seminar, we were split up in working groups. I forget what the assignment was about, but on one of them Maggie Black and I worked out a sketch about street and working children. In hindsight I am sure now that I was inspired by the funny theatre sketch of Goliath and his friends about daily life of street kids in Nouakchott. We made it quite humorous, rebellious and showed the bright character of these kids. Rather than continue on the street child doomsday scenario, we filled the sketch with happy and humorous moments that do indeed exist among them. We played it out in plenary much to the delight of the whole group.

Regional programme networks were not entirely new in Unicef in those days. Early on I decided to create a regional network of CEDC experts in which I included external resource persons to enrich the debate. The idea of such networks was to exchange ideas, experiences, best practices and ideas for collaboration. With my PFO background, I thought that fundraising was also a regional issue; and made it part of the agenda.

CHAPTER 8: GHOSTBUSTERS OF WEST AND CENTRAL AFRICA

I had seen in other regions that they sometimes developed sub-regional programmes on a particular theme. These addressed cross-border issues, such as health issues like outbreaks of polio and measles or emergencies in war affected areas. Sub-regional programmes were also a way to fundraise successfully for "unpopular" countries. I thought the time was ripe for such a programme for working and street children. I hired an international consultant from Venezuela, a former Unicef regional CEDC adviser, who assisted me in formulating a draft regional CEDC programme for several West and Central African countries. We included activities such as technical training, literacy, access to health mobile teams, and access to accelerated education. In West Africa there were border issues such as migrant and trafficked children that a regional or sub regional programme could also usefully focus on. Everybody's a winner; no? No, not this time. In those days country offices mostly wanted to make their own programmes and fund them only the way they saw fit. I could see their point in some ways but generally it was short-sighted. With a slight knock of the hammer on the green-clothed table, Chairman Kul Gautam ended my hopes for an innovative and accelerated approach to child protection[86].

Two years after the first All Africa Representatives' meeting, a second consultation with Jim Grant was held, again at the UN Giri Giri complex in Nairobi. Grant looked thin and haggard. The lines of his face were quite a bit deeper, and it looked as if his suit had outgrown him by a several inches. I got to speak with him only briefly, surrounded as he was by his HQ entourage and dragged into the next side meeting. Our Goodwill Ambassador Audrey Hepburn, on whom Grant had increasingly relied, had died of cancer just days before. Just months before, her last field trip had been to Somalia. In spite of her illness, sheer courage and determination pulled her through. A few months later Grant was operated on for cancer of the liver; and his time began to run out. But I did not realise then how bad his condition really was until much later.

---

[86] Regional or sub-regional programmes became a feature in later years.

Emergencies on the African Continent were the major theme of this consultation. Africa was now facing far more emergencies than ever before. That was a threat to long-term development. I participated in the working group on emergencies. We brainstormed on prevention of and response to emergencies. Hans Narula proposed that I should be the one to present our findings to plenary. It was 9 pm and I had 15 minutes to juggle my notes before I faced a plenary of some 150 people, among whom Grant, Jolly, Marco and the rest of the top of Unicef. I began by listing the emergencies that the continent of Africa had experienced since the late 1980s and early 1990s. Somalia had been without a government since 1991. Warlords in different parts of the country literally and figuratively called the shots. Somaliland split off and declared itself independent. Mohammed Farrah Aidid was killing U.N. workers, including Unicef staff. Aidid's goal was to control the country by controlling all the food. The Americans were determined to kidnap or kill this dangerous man.[87]

Other growing hotbeds of emergencies were to be found in Ethiopia where tensions with newly independent Eritrea simmered. Burundi and Rwanda were in a civil conflict between Hutus and Tutsis since 1990. A shaky truce prevailed in Angola. Warring factions in Mozambique had just months before signed the peace accords which had been mediated by the Italian government, the archbishop of Beira and the Community of Sant' Egidio of Trastevere, Rome.

West and Central Africa did not fare any better. Since 1990, sustained conflict in the Mano River basin has spread across borders and engulfed the region in a severe humanitarian crisis. Charles Taylor, a protégée of Libyan dictator, Col. Mu'ammar al-Qadhafi,

---

[87] Later in 1993, 120 commandos and Army Rangers were dropped into the heart of Mogadishu to go after Aidid. Two of the US Black Hawk helicopters were shot down. Surrounded by Somali militia, a fierce firefight left American troops trapped who fought for their lives. Eighteen American men were left dead, 70 wounded. Dead American airmen were dragged through the streets for all to see on TV. A humiliated America withdrew from Somalia.

CHAPTER 8: GHOSTBUSTERS OF WEST AND CENTRAL AFRICA

seized power in Liberia spread terror throughout Sierra Leone, Côte d'Ivoire and Guinea. It was now hard to believe that Guinea, Liberia and Sierra Leone had been pioneering a customs and economic union as early as 1973, the Mano River Union, to improve living standards in the sub-region. Had the Union succeeded it might well have prevented the conflict that was to follow. Then I stressed some of the factors of prevention: constructing a strong economy anchored in an equitable society; building peace and reconciliation through peace education after conflict, to prevent a simmering conflict from erupting again; construct a society of justice for all. In closing my presentation I predicted that the process of building democracy in Africa would most likely lead to much more bloodshed than we had witnessed so far. Was that worth it or should democracy slow down until Africa was really ready for it and it might be built from the bottom up? Democracy at the community level would require higher levels of education and participation, a process of a generation or two. One hates to be right in predictions like these. But unfortunately that was the case.

As usual I was included in the rapporteur group for the final report, this time with Martin Mogwanja and Deborah Comini. Deborah was one of the up and coming young economists in Richard Jolly's entourage. Deborah was from Brescia. A hard worker, she was also a soft, sentimental and poetic person. She was a cat person where everything and all else was about cats. I saw her back in New York. She knew the classics well; I forgot what prompted her then to suggest that I should read the love poems of Catullus. I still have to do that one day. We corresponded with each other for quite some time, even after my retirement when she was heading up the office in Macedonia, and later Nicaragua and Mongolia.

Towards the end of my assignment in the West and Central Africa Region I made trips to two very troubled countries whose wars were only just beginning. Liberia was cut in half most of the time, with Monrovia consistently under siege. Rebels continuously destroyed the White Plains waterworks; and each time Unicef dutifully rehabilitated them. Water trucks delivered water to the UN compound almost on a daily basis. The entrance for trucks was extremely steep and I thought that there might easily be one toppling over one day. I visited the Lutheran church with a Christian NGO. The church had fresh paint of a lively green and yellow colour. Six hundred women and children had taken refuge there just six months before and had been shot in cold blood by Charles Taylor's henchmen. The church was not yet used again as it was waiting for the renewal of its consecration. An eerie feeling got hold of me. I remained silent for many minutes, shuddering from repugnance.

We lived on the UN compound with groups assigned to rather fashionable and comfortable houses. One day Representative Carl Tintsman told me how Charles Taylor and his cronies in Gbarnga, capital of Bong County, had taken a Dutch Unicef consultant hostage north east of Monrovia. It was the base for Charles Taylor's National Patriotic Front of Liberia. He was hidden in a closet for several weeks and came out seriously traumatized. "But I told him", the representative said in closing his story, "that at least he was now media material". In Unicef we were always hungry for a good human interest story and for sure, the Monrovia office had one now.

In Monrovia, I worked with programme officer Esther Guluma in strengthening her child protection programme, in particular children in war. In the absence of a government counterpart, we worked exclusively with two very competent national NGOs that were already supported by Unicef in vocational training and literacy programmes for former child soldiers, street and working children. I visited a re-education centre for former child soldiers with her. The place looked more like a prison than a formative experience. I made a small speech to the children and threw it open to questions from them. One boy complained that they did not know what was happening on the other side of the wall. They wished for communication with family, several had parents in Monrovia. I proposed that Unicef give them a shortwave radio so that they

CHAPTER 8: GHOSTBUSTERS OF WEST AND CENTRAL AFRICA

could at least listen to the news on BBC Africa. I also suggested soccer matches as a link to the community outside. On Saturday I returned with Esther armed with a crate of Coca Cola. I played with them in their weekly soccer match. It was a rough but fair and honest game. I did not hold out long in the humid heat. They joined me soon for our post-match drinks. They were children alright, but budding adulthood already shone through.

Neighbouring Sierra Leone had been in war for two years. The office had invited me to work with the team on a child protection programme in times of war. At arrival I was informed that the 28-year-old President had declared three national holidays in the same week: the first anniversary of him taking power in a coup; Independence Day; and an extra official day to have a long weekend. To keep me busy the office arranged for a field trip to Kadema in the east. At one point our Toyota got two back to back flats. The driver disappeared with both tyres to get them repaired in the "nearest" village. Josephine, the junior communication officer and I found ourselves deep in the jungle near rebel held territory waiting for several hours, getting by on just water and biscuits. Strangely enough I never panicked and nor did she, but I was greatly relieved when the driver finally returned. We had just enough time to visit a mine, and watched youngsters looking for "blood" diamonds in the quarries and the river.

In 1993 the government of Nigeria was in the process of moving the capital from Lagos to the newly built city of Abuja. The government wanted to show off its construction achievements to date and requested Unicef that the Mid-Term Review be held in Abuja. The town was then going up fast, with construction sites working 24 hours, seven days a week. At night building sites were floodlit to pre-empt looting of materials. We stayed at the brand new Hilton Hotel with its lavish bedrooms of marble walls and oversized mirrors. I was with Ibrahima Fall, then Chief of Africa Desk, and Jane Hailey, Deputy Regional Director. I vividly remember The Minister of Planning in his opening speech heaping praise on Uganda, the first foreign embassy to move from Lagos to Abuja.

Its embassy was then still under construction. Weeks later I heard on the BBC that the Ugandan High Commissioner had vanished with three million dollars in cash. The theft had been uncovered by an internal audit at the Ministry of Foreign Affairs. Somehow the BBC's Africa service got hold of the story.

We witnessed the results of the first democratic presidential election in Nigeria since the 1983 military coup. When polls had closed, there were strong indications that the Muslim candidate from the North would be declared the winner. There were many jubilant supporters in the large reception area of our hotel, who were visibly excited. The next day I could feel a strange and tense atmosphere. Gone was the upbeat mood; suppressed anger reigned instead. I asked some who were in the elevator with me what the matter was. The results had just been announced and the Southern candidate Abiola was "declared the winner".[88] Another issue in those days was the census that had come out several weeks before and would have a direct bearing on Unicef's work: the country was declared to have now 94 million inhabitants instead of 120 million reported previously. In the past, figures were inflated to boost aid. This now meant that all our ratios such as child mortality and school enrolment had to be recalculated. Our programme review, based on false data, had become a pretty useless exercise! But were these new data now the right ones?

Just before going on home leave, Shob Jhie called me from Maputo. Would I be interested to be his number two? The country was in a post war reconstruction phase and the country programme was the fifth largest in the world.[89] A Swedish colleague with strong ties to the Swedish government would be the other deputy. Cecilia Gjerdrum had just a few years in Unicef behind

---

[88] The elections were later annulled by military ruler Ibrahim Babangida, leading to a crisis that ended with Sani Abacha heading a coup later in the year; Abacha died in his bath in 1998, a corrupt man who had stashed away millions of dollars in European banks in just five years.
[89] India was the largest Unicef office, followed by Pakistan, Indonesia, Bangladesh and Mozambique.

CHAPTER 8: GHOSTBUSTERS OF WEST AND CENTRAL AFRICA

her, with one rather harrowing experience in Angola. She had been evacuated in a hurry and was waiting at the Nairobi Regional Office for reassignment. Because of Cecilia's relative inexperience and the importance of Mozambique for Unicef, Shob convinced HQ to approve a second deputy post to be filled by an experienced planning and programme person. In any event, there was more than enough work for two.

Under the circumstances I could only be appointed by Executive Order – nothing unusual I dare say now – but this time there was an added novelty: Shob created this post especially for me – and got away with it.

Chapter 9: "A luta continua"

The door of the small conference room was slightly ajar, but I could just about see that the place was packed. This was going to be my new "home" in Maputo for the next three or four years. What was waiting for me this time around? I simply knew almost no one in this office. I felt certainly a bit apprehensive: at Unicef a new kid on the block is always intensely scrutinized.

Barely 18 hours before I had boarded the Boeing 767 of Linhas Aéreas de Moçambique at Charles de Gaulle airport. The cabin crew dressed in a brownish, boring outfit, looking like a holdover from the sombre Marxist days. The airline video on security was an opportunity to practice my nascent Portuguese. The national government newspaper *Noticias* ran an article with a photo of President Chissano opening an extension of a railway track in Inhambane. I was excited to be working on the opposite side of the African continent: from the Atlantic to the Indian Ocean, *"from the Rovuma to the Maputo"*. That was the slogan Samora Machel used when he returned to Maputo in a one-month triumphant trek, from the River Rovuma on the border with Tanzania to the River Maputo. During the journey, he addressed crowds in Nampula, Quelimane and Beira, where Frelimo had no presence during the independence struggle nor even all along the civil war years that followed.

Hours later the rising sun gave me a glimpse of the dense rain forest of Zaire; the dry lands of Zambia and Zimbabwe waiting eagerly for the rains; and the green hills of South Africa gently rolling into one another. From there we finally turned leftward into the Southern tip of Mozambique. To my surprise Shob was waiting for me after customs. I knew he would normally never do that. He took me to Polana, the splendid hotel built by the Portuguese coloniser in 1922, my home for the first weeks; he

CHAPTER 9: "A LUTA CONTINUA"

briefed me over lunch; and then took me straight to the office, that Thursday afternoon, the 11th of November 1993 to be introduced at a staff meeting.

Shob announced that seven nuns had perished that morning in Panda district of Inhambane province, when their pick-up truck landed on an anti-tank mine. Unicef worked with their Mission in one of the area-based projects. At the crack of dawn they had gone out in their pick-up truck with one of the nuns at the wheel, to deliver seeds and tools to a community to prepare for the new season. I thought, this then is the Mozambique I have come to. It was then a country in a tense post-war phase with a million landmines simmering underground,[90] where on average some 15 people were killed every week, many of them children; and where thousands were maimed for life. In fact the old war was not letting go that easily.

Barely a few days later we received the visit of Dr Gwendolyn Baker, the newly appointed President of the US National Committee for Unicef. She was a well-known educationalist in New York. In fact, Dr Baker was a pioneer in promoting multicultural education during a time when there were very few black teachers in the public schools. I accompanied her on much of her programme. She struck me as a very respectful and engaged personage. I asked if she had seen Mr Grant recently, and she said yes indeed, right after her appointment. As a matter of fact he had strongly suggested her to visit Mozambique on her first field trip to Africa.[91] Grant himself had plans to visit the country in 1994.

I accompanied Dr Baker on a courtesy visit to Graça Machel along with Gabriel Pereira, personal assistant to the Unicef

---

[90] Two million landmines was the official estimate at the time, but nobody knew for sure of course. When Mozambique declared itself free of "landmines" in 2015 only 177,000 landmines had been cleared.
[91] In an interview with the University of Michigan, Dr. Baker called her involvement with Unicef, "the frosting on the cake," as she was now in a position to take her work to the global stage.

Representative. Gabriel had been a youth leader in Frelimo during the Samora Machel years and he knew of course Mrs Machel well. The widow of the late president Samora Machel had been Minister of Education in the 1980s at a young age. Her office was modest: I remember simple furniture including a small sofa where Gabriel and I were enduring a severe squeeze. Coming both from education, the two women had much in common. Dr Baker recalled her lifelong passion in promoting multicultural education in New York. Mrs Machel recalled the suffering of children affected by the long war in Mozambique. Hundreds of schools were destroyed, and then rebuilt – only to be destroyed again. Thousands of child soldiers were in the process of being demobilised. An entire generation was lost for school unless some sort of catching up could be done for the lucky ones. Graça clearly "owned" this topic. About this time the United Nations General Assembly passed a resolution recommending that Graça Machel be appointed to lead a major global UN study on "Children affected by war". Secretary-General Boutros Boutros-Ghali appointed her a few months later.

As Shob had gone off to Nairobi for the regional representatives' meeting, I joined Dr Baker at her audience with President Joaquim Chissano. I found Chissano a rather modern man coming as he did from the Marxist era. I remember the President saying in truly Kennedy-esque fashion that he wanted his people to do things for themselves, not always be waiting for the government. He recalled how he himself had cut bricks for the missionary school where his father was a teacher at the time.

Well before my arrival, the representative had found irregularities in programme management and operations; and he wished me to double-check. One day Shob handed me a file called *Circo da Paz* and said, "Read this and tell me what you think of it". By the tone of his voice I could tell what he meant. He had sniffed trouble.

Circo da Paz was the pet project of the Information Section. It was a travelling "circus for peace" of young people, using art, drama, and song and dance in local communities as illustration to advocate tolerance and respect for cultural diversity. Apart from a lack of focus with too many activities and no specific desired results or follow-up, millions of *meticais*[92] travelled with the circus and were dropped all over this large country without the least accountability. Up country there were hardly any banks in those days, so carrying cash was not at all uncommon. But accounting for it seemed far away and in between. Then the activities seemed more like a string of parties and events rather than a serious development project with impact and a long view.

I recommended suspending the activities with immediate effect; to re-assess the project with our Information Section; and to recall the project leaders to Maputo to give us their own assessment and recommendations. Finally I recommended designing without delay a new peace education project that would no longer be run by Information, but by the area-based programme of Irene Galamba. A small working group would try to make it into an attractive project for multi-year funding by National Committees.

Just at the time when I came on board, a Unicef Toyota Landcruiser stolen six months earlier had been found at the home of one of our drivers. Clearly someone in the office had given him away. A complication was that this driver lived with his lover, a secretary in the Information Section. The senior management committee handed me a *cadeau empoissonné* by appointing me to lead the investigation. Both staff members were fired. Cleaning out irregularities earned management the occasional death threat, but these stopped in later years, when appreciation of our efforts began to take hold.

A couple of years later there was a grave incident involving two Unicef drivers. One of our drivers was involved in a car chase in the early morning hours. Driving his car at great speed, he was shooting from the window with a pistol in the air threatening a policeman. He had bought the gun from another Unicef driver. Trade in small arms in Maputo was a serious issue. UN personnel

---

[92] The metical is the currency of Mozambique.

are of course forbidden to carry arms – peacekeeping staff of course exempted. The pair were immediately suspended. The outlook was very bleak for both. Shob carried out the investigation on his own; and decided to issue only a letter of reprimand. I will never forget the handwritten letter from one of the drivers to Shob. A more severe punishment would have ruined his family. The good man, a super driver and a very pleasant person – was in tears with happiness and stayed out of trouble from then on. It showed to me Shob's compassion for naïve but honest people who are in trouble – and his judgement when they could and should be saved.

In order to integrate myself fully in my relations with the government, it was all-important to speak Portuguese fluently as soon as possible. Professor Barbosa of Eduardo Mondlane University became my private teacher. He was an older man to whom I am forever grateful to have more or less mastered the sometimes for me awkward pronunciation. But how Barbosa hammered that into my poor brain! Teaching me how to pronounce the syllable "ão", he would lower chin on chest, close his eyes and utter: "nãããooh" whereby his long nose started folding upwards, his whole face taking on an angry look. Try it, dear reader, it works! For two months I endured this peculiar way of learning a language from this otherwise soft-spoken and kind Professor. With a minimum of linguistic baggage I was then judged fit to go to Lisbon and follow the private course at the *Centro de Línguas*.

I called my mother telling her I would fly up to Holland from Lisbon after the first week and spend a weekend with her. Twenty hours later the dreaded call came: My mother had passed away after much suffering from emphysema. I was the last of the family to have spoken with her. The funeral was set three days later, leaving me insufficient time to arrive on time. This haunts me to this very day.

My main teacher at the *Centro de Línguas* was Ana. She was pregnant with her first child. Her oversized woolly sweaters left ample room for the baby; shades of green went best with her dark hair and eyes. Ana taught me in the morning, and in the afternoon another teacher would take over. All of them were women. Every week I would get a new afternoon teacher – she said it was a way to get me used to different accents – but Ana was my permanent guide. In the evening I did my homework for two hours, for a total of eight hours of Portuguese, every day for four weeks.

Still there was time to go out and enjoy the town. One evening I watched "Tout Lisboa" at the Fundação Gulbenkian. The famous Dutch recorder player Frans Brüggen was conducting a Brandenburg concerto. Then, after a dismally boring Kyrie Eleison of Mozart's Requiem, a peculiar thought crossed my mind: why can't religious music be played once in a while with a bit of beat and bravura. I thought then and there that Frans Brüggen should stick to his recorder and baroque orchestra, his biggest musical achievement in my estimation. Once out on the dark rainy streets of Lisboa I strolled among the chestnut roasting stalls. Roasted chestnuts seemed to me what *patates frites* are to the Belgian and the Dutchman: the street meal *"par excellence"*. Lisbon's women are petite, mostly not very pretty, but endowed with lovely thick hair of a chestnut colour. I found the city's architecture rather grand and pompous in some places, but then quite simple in others; many houses hundreds of years old were ruins, begging for restoration. I can still dream away about the quiet, pleasant, and in those days a bit provincial atmosphere of Lisbon. The steep hills connecting the *bairro alto* and the *baixa* made for spectacular tram rides.

After one month I was ready to take the language exam at level two and scored 87 out of 100. Ana strongly suggested that I should stay on for one more week and then, she assured me, I would be ready to take the level three exam. She was very confident that I would pass that too. I was tempted to do just that, but new responsibilities "lay in wait" for me back in Maputo; and I was eager to face them head on.

In those days Mozambique ranked as the fifth largest Unicef country programme in the world – after India, Pakistan, Indonesia and Bangladesh. I had oversight for the health, CEDC, emergency and area-based programmes. In addition I covered programme planning, monitoring and evaluation. My Swedish colleague Cecilia, the second deputy, got education, water, hygiene and sanitation and operations. The chief of HR reported directly to the representative. Shob chaired a restricted senior management group. Its members were his two deputies, the Operations Officer and the HR officer. These were often highly confidential deliberations. Sometimes funny things happened in that meeting. One day I had to take an urgent phone call and left the room. When I came back the original of a most confidential document had disappeared from my stack of papers. I glanced sideways to my right and saw it sticking out from under the papers of the Operations Officer. Embarrassed I whispered, "I am afraid that's my copy".

Shob and I both had an aversion to routine, recurrent meetings. In effect, in the beginning he did not even bother to organise a routine Monday morning meeting to kick off the week. We only met all together when there were urgent matters at hand that everyone needed to be aware of. For the rest there were enough communication channels for easy access and problem solving. Shob's door was always open, mine too. But staff clamoured for regularity and in the end he caved in – but then passed that responsibility on to me! I kept my meetings to an absolute minimum and I would also inform colleagues how long a meeting was estimated to last – and would end it well before its scheduled ending as soon as the opportunity arose to do so.

After West Africa I had had my fill of running or participating in regional workshops and events. I just preferred to stay put in Mozambique and get to know the country in depth. I only attended one regional workshop, the one on emergency preparedness and response. Emergencies were on the rise in Africa; and I thought that this training might well come in handy somewhere, some day. The venue of Lokichokio on Kenya's border with Southern Sudan was most appropriate. It was the tent camp of Operation Lifeline Sudan.

CHAPTER 9: "A LUTA CONTINUA"

I had been present in New York when Jim Grant and the WFP Director James Ingram[93] jointly launched this huge emergency relief supply operation in 1989 in the presence of Secretary-General Pérez de Cuéllar. There was no doubt that Jim Grant who chaired, overshadowed that event. It was the time of Southern Sudan's struggle for independence. OLS had set up a base camp for food and medicine drops into South Sudan. The mission was to bring aid over the border to the largely Christian Dinka population and other ethnic groups. The North-South route from Khartoum was infested with bandits holding up relief convoys. Every morning at six I heard the planes take off and return to base not long thereafter. Jim Grant's Corridors of Peace in Colombia and El Salvador had inspired the Lifeline and somehow Khartoum had decided to go along.

It was a most luxurious way of camping. In the base camp we sleep in large, individual tents, outfitted with comfortable beds and showers. The cook is Indian. My Indian colleague Adi Patel from Unicef Chimoio is right at home here.[94] He chats daily with the chef about the next dish. One of the "field exercises" is to visit a refugee camp and see psycho-social therapy in action. Child psychiatrist Magne Raundalen from Bergen, Norway, a resource person in the workshop, gives a demonstration how he gains the trust of severely traumatized former child soldiers. He has them make drawings on what they had seen in war; and so, having gained their "confidence", asks them questions. Watching the scene as curious onlookers, many of us feel ill at ease, as this is a "one-off demonstration" for which these poor kids are being used. A clear case of development tourism. In giving feedback in the workshop, we return to diplomatic niceties on this "field trip" but that changes nothing of our inner feelings. Just to say that this did not stop me from hiring Raundalen as a consultant in Maputo.

---

[93] James Ingram was the first Australian to head a United Nations agency.
[94] Adi had family in Pennsylvania. Once he gave me a photo of a street sign near his family that read "Mohrville". Back in my banking days I had once come across that sign myself, while driving a rental car through thick mist on the way to a client at seven in the morning.

He developed most useful guidelines for us on how to treat post-traumatic stress in children.

One of my first field visits was planned to the area-based projects in Inhambane. I accompanied Irene Galamba and Juanita Vasquez, who was going to leave Mozambique for good. She was going to say her goodbyes to her project counterparts and I tagged along on the chartered propeller-driven plane the office had chartered from a private South African company. Until then I had always liked small planes as one flies at low altitude and is able to see infinitely more on the ground. Little did I know that this time around our view would be far closer up than I had ever witnessed before.

Apart from the pilot and the flight attendant there are only the three of us. Half an hour into the air with our first cup of coffee and orange juice barely behind us, the two-engine plane begins to wobble. If anything, the jerking movement is only getting worse. Smoke comes out of the left engine, which is on my side. The South African pilot announces drily that one of the engines is on fire; that he will try to return to Maputo as Vilanculos was too far still; and that he will fly very low over the beaches in case we have to make a crash landing. I grab Juanita's arm and hold on to her all the way. Our pilot desperately tries to stabilise the aircraft. Somehow he is able to extinguish the fire but the propeller was of course disabled. It seems a miracle that we make it back on one engine. Once safely on the ground, the pilot tells us we have been lucky not to have had to land on the beach. Most of the beaches around Maputo were still heavily mined in those days and the chances of hitting one were high. Then he tells us laconically, "we will not fly this afternoon". The three of us break into a nervous laugh. Returning to the office after lunch, Shob says: "I thought you had gone up north?" And I say meekly: "not today, we almost had to make a crash landing on one of the beaches". I return to my office in a daze, taking up the workload; and soon forgetting how close we had been to death.

CHAPTER 9: "A LUTA CONTINUA"

"Giving peace a chance"

Taking it all around, my first full year in the country, 1994, turned out to be an eventful, at times quite agitated and tense year. With the ink on the Rome peace accords hardly dry, this was going to be the year of the first democratic presidential election. Elections for parliament would take place at the same time. Six months earlier Nelson Mandela had been sworn in as the first freely elected president of South Africa signalling the end of Apartheid. Overnight this meant a sea change in South African-Mozambican relations. Mozambique was finally liberated from foreign destabilisation. Now peace had a real chance.

Almost two years before, reconciliation between the government, Frente de Libertação de Moçambique (Frelimo) and the guerrilla movement, Resistência Nacional de Moçambique (Renamo), had become a fact. The venue was the Community of Sant'Egidio in the Trastevere section of Rome. Sant'Egidio had been studying war and poverty for some time, concluding that they are increasingly intimately linked. In the words of the Community itself: *"War is the 'mother of every poverty', destroyer of the humanitarian commitment for the future of entire populations; civil war in which members of the same population no longer recognise each other as brothers"*. In Mozambique there seemed to be no exit for the twins of war and poverty; but the two warring factions were tired and exhausted; there was no victor in sight; the country was at risk of breaking up into a North and a South; and that was in nobody's interest. Negotiations lasted for 27 months and were mediated by Sant'Egidio and Mgr. Jaime Gonçalves, the Bishop of Beira and a close friend of the community, who had the trust of the two warring factions. On the 4th of October 1992, President Joaquim Chissano and the leader of Renamo, Afonso Dhlakama, signed, thus ending the 16-year conflict. Along with other UN agencies Unicef attended the signing ceremony.

A UN peacekeeping force (ONUMOZ) was put in place to ensure that the elections could be held in a calm and peaceful environment. That was not an easy task. There were incidents of violence, many perpetrated by disgruntled soldiers who had not been paid for months. Other complaints were that the process of demobilisation and reintegration was slow. Towards the election date things got hotter. Soldiers were looting shops in Matola with the help of a tank. Another time they set heaps of loose asphalt on fire that were meant to repair the road to Nelspruit in South Africa, where we shopped for food supplies on weekends. I was in the midst of this trouble but luckily UNOMOZ was on the scene and quickly waved me through.

Some three months before the election, the IMF came with some well-timed good news: GNP had grown some 19% in 1993, a phenomenal figure that masked the fact that most investments favoured the Southern half of the country. Back in 1987 the government had launched the economic recovery programme *PRE* (*Programa de Reabilitação Económica*) that dictated massive cost cutting, curbing of inflation and privatisation of state owned firms. In just a few years some 500 state-owned firms had been sold to the private sector. The social effects of *PRE* were devastating: by 1989 some 35,000 people were laid off. Three Mozambicans out of five were living in absolute poverty, with levels reaching far higher in the North. This North-South divide would haunt those in power for many years to come. Right from the beginning, the challenge for the government was how to turn Mozambique into an equitable and united nation. In effect the marginalisation of their people was the clarion call for the Renamo in the Northern provinces, where it continues to retain a political stronghold to this very day. The chronic balance of payments deficit increased sovereign debt to unsustainable levels. Foreign debt was five times GNP. By 1995 some 60% of the state budget was financed by donors.

Seven hours before polls opened, Dhlakama pulled a fast one on the entire country: while the country was sleeping he announced that Renamo would boycott the election because the Election Commission could not guarantee him a fair election. When people woke up to the news the following morning, there was total

CHAPTER 9: "A LUTA CONTINUA"

confusion. The population in rural areas people had of course no clue of what was going on in the capital and had already begun to vote. In the midst of it all, Saad Houry had just arrived for a programme support mission. Walking together to the office we passed the residence that the government had made available to Dhlakama. That morning there was much commotion. We peered through the fence and noticed some aides of Dhlakama, UN staff and diplomats running all over the place, no doubt trying to salvage an impossible situation. Hours later Renamo came out with a statement insisting on a seven day postponement of the election. In the end an extra day of voting was added to make up for confusion and lost time.

The popular incumbent president obtained 53% against 33% for his opponent, with the remainder going to smaller candidates. For Parliament the outcome was far closer. Frelimo failed to win an outright majority and won just one seat more than the opposition. Renamo won most of the Northern provinces with the exception of Cabo Delgado. That is the province where the Frelimo movement had invaded from its base in Tanzania in 1962 under the leadership of Eduardo Mondlane. The election had cost the hefty sum of 70 million dollars, and was almost entirely funded by the UN and bilateral donors. In December the cabinet was formed without Renamo ministers. Pascoal Mocumbi went from Foreign Affairs to become Prime Minister; Health Minister Leonardo Simão went to Foreign Affairs; and a brilliant young man, Tomaz Salomão, was appointed Minister of Planning and Finance, with Luisa Diogo from the World Bank as his Deputy Minister. For the next years Mozambique would remain under a one-party government with the country still in a North-South divide. The argument I heard for not having a government of national unity was that Renamo "lacked the depth to govern".

ONUMOZ took credit for the success of Mozambique's process towards democracy. Its chief Aldo Ayello commented at the time *"I don't believe Dhlakama is an angel. But I look to his real interests. He will try to get what he can... The relatively small amount of money needed for the trust fund was the insurance that everything else would work."* In fact, the agreement was to a large extent only possible because part of the deal was for Afonso Dhlakama to get an incentive of $300,000 a month. The statement implied that although Dhlakama did not achieve political power, much of the success could be attributed to the fact that he was effectively paid off by the UN[95]. No real political concessions here, the power of money alone was sufficient to make the deal work.

I knew Ayello from my time in Geneva when he headed up the small UNDP office there. He was an exceedingly well-dressed man. I found him then a rather pompous and conceited man. Ayello was outspoken and that did not help the peace process. The government of Mozambique found him abrasive and disrespectful.

ONUMOZ was responsible for demobilisation, with the International Organisation of Migration providing transport of demobilised soldiers back to their communities. Nine out of ten soldiers wished to be demobilised in return for food, one-time cash, clothing and a tool kit; thousands were former child soldiers; but capacities of the UN and IOM to deal with it were vastly insufficient. Unicef joined hands with the International Committee of the Red Cross to settle children without parents into their families and communities. Another problem was that the Rome accords were too general, which resulted in much stalling in the peace process. But in early 1995, with peace apparently holding, the UN peacekeeping troops were withdrawn. But that did not mean that Mozambique was now suddenly safe.

The situation remained tense and one could feel it almost daily. Local terrorism was rampant. One evening the Piri-Piri restaurant, popular with expats, was attacked and several people died. Nobody from Unicef was present at the time. Bandits were roaming around the country. One day the army and the police

---

[95] The Trust Fund was established to transform Renamo from guerilla force to a political party .

were fighting one another in Machava, which left several dead. Many areas were still no-go until long after the elections. The road to Xai-Xai was often closed for a number of days. For field trips official authorisation was still routinely required throughout my assignment. Natural disasters added greatly to food insecurity. Cyclones are common leading to flooding. I drove through Central Mozambique after one cyclone had hit there, witnessing thatched rooftops sticking out above the flooded fields. I saw Beira flooded several times. In 1995 it was the opposite: the Southern provinces suffered a severe drought.

One evening I got a call from our French emergency programme officer Jean-Claude Legrand who was in charge of Unicef staff security. In the confusion he spoke English, sounding tense: "Baudouin, there is trubble in town; did you 'ear the shots? The populations run all over town". I calmed him down, saying that a Portuguese Bank was celebrating its centennial in Mozambique with a grandiose dinner at Hotel Polana. These shots then must surely be fireworks. But it was a lapse in security that the international community had not been forewarned, let alone the population. Better still: the fireworks should never have been allowed under the tense circumstances in the first place. The incident showed that literally everyone, including our own staff, remained on edge.

Another time, Shob's wife Marinette drove me home after dinner and we got lost near the presidential palace. Suddenly we saw young soldiers of the presidential guard running down the hill with AK 47's pointed at the car. Marinette slammed on the brakes. Of course we had no identification on us. Luckily the diplomatic number plates saved us.

Implementing a post emergency country programme
Much of my time was devoted to programme planning, implementation and monitoring of the country programme. A few times a year I led progress reviews of the on-going implementation. We would gather in the conference room with the Section Chiefs and

the project officers and review the eight programmes with their projects and activities. It was based on a tracking system that Shob had elaborated with a small team in New York. I found it stressful to time-manage these meetings. Sometimes it was hard to figure out whether money that had been passed on to government had been translated in an actual activity. Outstanding advances to government were a constant nightmare. The review was often more financial than activity-oriented. Field visits that could substantiate on-going activities were often far away and in between. Except for the water and sanitation, children in difficult circumstances and area-based projects in rural areas, most other programmes such as health and education were carried out at central level.

Some projects had a very large number of activities. Impact and results leading to set goal that was linked to a sector programme was often floating in a vacuum. Some colleagues were very verbose, severely taxing my patience. I would then start to arrange my folders and put them on a neat pile in front of me. I would then whisper to Cecilia, "I am packing". More than once in these meetings I suffered in silence, until patience gave way to frantic paper shuffling. A soft voice would then whisper in my ear, "are you packing?"

A few months before the election, a small group of us travelled to Xai-Xai for a three-day retreat to thrash out a revamped peace education project to replace *Circo da Paz*. Susan, an intern student from MIT, wrote the project outline with me as a basis for our work at hand; there was Saad Houry, now on a leave of absence but consulting once in a while, who had seen peace education at work in Lebanon. Youth camps for peace had been particularly successful there. Irene Galamba was there for her input on community participation. Peace education was going to be part of her area-based programme. We had colleagues from health and education, where peace education had useful channels of communication like school curriculum and social mobilisation.

We built our peace education project in accordance with Unicef policy guidelines. Unicef had considerable global experience in prevention and resolution of conflict. In several post-conflict countries, such as Lebanon and El Salvador, activities would normally include summer camps, multi-cultural education in schools. For Unicef peace education promotes ways to bring about change of behaviour among children and adults to prevent, resolve and to create conditions that are conducive to peace.[96] In this effort the school environment is an important channel for peace building, for example in outreach to children out of school through sports; through voluntary support to families in need with literacy or household chores; and links to other schools and culturally diverse communities. Children's camps have successfully brought together young people from various religious beliefs. Most disciplines of the school curriculum lend themselves very well for teaching respect and understanding of diverse cultures. Through media training with journalists, Unicef tried to strengthen peace and reconciliation content on radio and TV.

Two months after the peace education project had been defined and budgeted, Irene suddenly died on the plane that returned her and her husband from home leave in Portugal. When Shob called me at our farm – I had just gone on home leave – I could hear his voice choke. He had great respect for Irene as a person and leader of her complicated but well run area-based programme section. Immediately upon returning from leave I went to see her husband António. He was heartbroken and together we wept. Over dinner he told me the story, a few months earlier Irene had fallen off her horse and had developed a blood clot in her leg that had gone unnoticed. During the long plane trip back home the blood clot travelled up to her brain and the stroke killed her.

Barely one month later young Inácio of Finance Section suddenly died after lunch in the office. Rumours began to circulate among staff that bad spirits had invaded the premises. I then proposed to take the entire office on a two-day retreat in Swaziland, whose deeper purpose was to be far away from the workspace, and

---

[96] Abridged definition of Unicef Programme Division, 1999.

mourn together as a team. We were lucky to have Saad around, whose calm presence helped us a lot in these terrible circumstances.

The project soon began to attract attention from donors. After kicking off the activities with general resources, we succeeded in obtaining a $5 million multi-year grant from the German Unicef Committee. Manuela Kikilius had come to Mozambique beforehand to see our peace building activities in action. A journalist from the Aachener Zeitung accompanied her, and wrote an article for the *Weihnachten Aktion* that the committee had developed with several German newspapers. The campaign raised considerable funds.[97]

After a year or so the Canadians noticed the project and wanted to come in as well, which could have doubled the size of the project. Regretfully the Canadian Committee, which worked often in partnership with the Canadian International Development Agency (CIDA), tried to dictate how we should restructure the programme. Their increasingly detailed conditions were impossible to stomach. The discussions with Canada were endless. In the end I suggested Shob to call his close friend Tony Kennedy, Director of Programme Funding, and have him explain to the donor that although Unicef Maputo would of course listen to counsel, Unicef could not simply surrender its prerogative of programming to a donor, lock stock and barrel. That was the line in the sand. Besides, the Germans were there first and they were happy with the way things were going. Kennedy fully agreed and added that he had already noticed an upsurge of meddling by donors as to how Unicef should structures programmes and projects. Shob and I willingly let go of a potentially large contribution.

Life of children in the street of Maputo

Our country programme had several projects for street and working children. Perhaps Dutchman René Boezaard had found

---

[97] The braintrust of the Christmas campaign was young Special Events officer Dieter Pool.

the most novel project approach. Boezaard ran a refuge for street and working children, at the time Maputo counted some 450 children who lived in the street, some 50 of them were girls. Boezaard had come to Mozambique from Defence for Children International in Brazil. He was now ready to begin for himself. It did not take him long to find an old building and fix it up as a shelter. He himself went into the street and started talking to the children about their problems. Several started coming to his shelter by themselves. Mouth to mouth street communication did the rest. The group grew to some 70 children from as young as nine to 17 years. By doing odd jobs they contributed to some of the running cost of their "home". Vita Stern from a Dutch radio programme for schools did an interview with Boezaard. She noticed a well-stocked pantry with rice and millet; lots of chickens roaming around free; ten goats for milk consumption; some 200 chicks to sell for raising chickens; and a neat classroom with wooden benches. The Boezaard School went to sixth grade. On weekends some of the interns spent time with their families but returned at night to the refuge. They had simply grown too independent and that made reintegration in the family impossible.[98]

Boezaard did far more. He organized that the children could get a meal at the market. He put together a football team with a trainer who came three times a week, three hours a session. There were film shows in the evening. In general he created an environment of friendship and camaraderie. There was a teacher who taught them Portuguese and maths. Boezaard co-opted A. to teach English to the street girls in the Botanical garden. She used the Garden's gazebo as a "multigrade" classroom. In an interview with Vita Stern, A. recalls: *"I am teaching some street children who are beaten up mentally; learning English for them is to 'become American', to identify with America. They have no identity of their own anymore, no tradition. Often the teaching is quite crazy: they put on frames without glasses, or snorkel masks they found somewhere and act things out; they throw stuff to each other*

---

[98] Dutch educational radio programme, Vita Stern, Radio 4, 1995.

during class, sit under the bench. This acting out inspires me to make English sentences around their 'theatre'; and then they laugh their heads off. You could call it improvised teaching, applied to the situation of the moment. The most important is togetherness, affection and something to learn on the side". Boezaard's Portuguese teacher pointed out that street children are hard to teach. Things happening around them quickly distract them. They are short-tempered and impatient. Girls are harder to teach, he finds. Girls as young as nine sleep at the market and make money as prostitutes for food and drugs. Some of them had already been seven years on the street.

One day A. ran into a 14-year-old boy who was making merry-go-rounds from wires at the WFP compound near the Indian Ocean. Surely the *Feira Popular* had had an influence on him. A. taught Julião how to make bicycles and improve on their shapes and sizes, adding a colour or two for freshness and originality. Very soon Julião started coming to our house almost every day. On days he was not selling, he worked on our front porch making bicycles. Hamidou gave him lunch. The boy started making little figures, sometimes as backpackers complete with rucksack on the back. A. found lots of people to sell his work. Marianne de Mul, wife of UNDP chief Erick de Mul, bought seven bikes when her husband was reassigned to Afghanistan. We ourselves still have a whole collection of them at home. In any event João made good money with it during the two or three years of turning out bikes. As we have seen, getting income-generating project off the ground for children was nothing new to A. In Abidjan the Tuareg kids made good money with decorating key rings and Bic ball pens with coloured plastic wires. Cards painted by the children with Tuareg scenes of the desert were also much in demand. On the International Day of the Child A. joined Medecins du Monde at an event with street kids who painted a mural on a wall at the *mercado central*. A. organised Julião to come along to try to sell his bicycles. He sold many that day. Afterwards she took him on a walking tour pointing to houses of friends where he could sell his bicycles once we would have left for good.

CHAPTER 9: "A LUTA CONTINUA"

Hurdles to build an equitable nation state based on rights
Perhaps the greatest challenge for Mozambique was and still is to build an equitable one-nation state. Its provinces are geographically and culturally far apart with the capital tucked away in the far South. How could all 16 million inhabitants feel "Mozambican?" There surely was a problem of national identity. Once I travelled with Prime Minister Mocumbi to Niassa, where he addressed a town meeting in Portuguese. Nobody would have understood Mocumbi if he had spoken in Chopi, a dialect of Tsonga, his maternal language of the South. His words were translated in Chiyão, a Bantu language spoken in Lichinga. If you lived in Maputo you could see real progress, mostly in construction that generated ad-hoc jobs, but no long-term employment. Three out of five people there were living below the poverty line. Educational opportunities were still very limited, especially after primary school. In fact, one could not always hide behind the war as the only cause for poverty in Mozambique. At independence 95% of the population could not read or write. Then the war killed in the bud whatever modest development, notably in health and education, was beginning to be achieved.

There was also the legacy of the colonial era. In return for the riches they got from the country, the Portuguese developed little and left little behind. Perhaps the colonists will be best remembered for their skills in designing Lourenço Marques just like Georges-Eugène Haussmann is remembered for Paris.[99] For me the most spectacular *Avenida* is Kenneth Kaunda with its slow descent towards the Indian Ocean. The Sommerschield section of town with its jacarandas, acacias and whitewashed houses reminds one of a well-to-do Portuguese suburb. We rented a three-story house on Rua Dom Afonso Enriques off Avenida do Zimbabwe, where the Unicef office still is. Bougainvillea gives Maputo a Mediterranean flavour. The Portuguese had a knack for choosing

---

[99] Hausmann was Prefect of the Seine Department. He was chosen by Emperor Napoleon III to carry out a massive programme of new boulevards, parks and public works in Paris in the latter part of the 19th century.

spectacular bays – whether in Lourenço Marques, Luanda, Vicente or small and cosy São Tomé. No doubt they suffered from *saudades* for their beloved Lisboa just by staring at the ocean. Likewise the Indian families from Goa who gathered each Sunday at the oceanfront to watch the sunset were no doubt thinking of their beloved land and kin back home.

Niassa 2000

Mozambique remained backward and undeveloped, especially in the rural areas where schools and health facilities were practically non-existent; and Niassa was no exception. Although at the start the Marxist government of Frelimo made remarkable progress in health and education against all odds, the economy itself suffered from lack of investment by the liberal economies of the West that sought friendlier outlets, such as in Côte d'Ivoire and Kenya. Then came the conflict between Renamo and Frelimo and geopolitical destabilisation. Who can win in such a context?

Perhaps I can single out one man who tried hard to unlock the North and make it part of a one-nation state. His name was Aires Bonifácio Baptista Aly, the then just appointed young and eager governor of Niassa. Aly was from the northern part of Niassa Province. This man beamed optimism with a good dose of charisma and had definitely other plans.

Early on in his first term, Aly invited a group of us donors to a consultation in Lichinga to map out a development agenda for the Province with goals to be reached by the year 2000. Lichinga made a deep impression on me, if only for its jacarandas that were then in full bloom. These were the healthiest jacarandas I have ever seen; and yet they were rooted in dry ground on a dusty plain. It was perhaps symbolic for Niassa: if you have willpower to make it, anything goes – even under harsh circumstances. Here was a city about the furthest away from the capital than any other town in Mozambique. And yet there was a young aspect to the town. There was a promising huge banner announcing the event: *Niassa 2000*.

CHAPTER 9: "A LUTA CONTINUA"

This was a forward-looking workshop to debate where Niassa could and should be in the year 2000. There was no doubt that Aly was the dynamic focal point of the meeting. I thought then and there that he probably had a great political future. He was enthusiastic, sharp, and never lost sight of his goal. He aimed at a good outcome of the meeting on which he could go to work with solid partners for the good of his province. The meeting struck me as refreshing and very well put together. Young people in the organisation seemed totally energised.

On the other hand the population, marginalised and poor since time immemorial, had dubbed the meeting *"Niassa dois contos"*. This was either a misread, desperation or dry humour at its best. *"Dois contos"* was the negligible equivalent of 2,000 meticais, no more than a dollar or less at the time; it was to express in veiled terms that they expected nothing from the central government – in spite of their local son now being their Governor. An old man taking the floor during the workshop was especially vocal when he exclaimed: "We do not want your gates and fences on our homes or alarms in cars, if that entails development. Stay with those development gadgets and your thieves and development back in Maputo". I wondered indeed what the local people were thinking when I ceremoniously planted a tiny Jacaranda in a prepared hole. Development tourism? Would it grow up high and healthy as a symbolic tree of life like the jacarandas in bloom around us?

Prime Minister Mocumbi has come for the event, along with his grey-haired and reflective Minister of Environment, Bernardo Ferraz. The PM strikes me as a modest and almost humble man with a sense of humour and even naughtiness; he certainly likes to make fun of people in public. On the margin of the workshop we visit a village of former soldiers. Gloria Kodzwa and I suffer from the Prime Minister's humour at first hand. When introducing us both, he adds, almost as an afterthought: "at Unicef they always come in twos..." Such a comment can have many meanings. When introducing his entourage, he refers to the grey hair of

Minister Ferraz as "someone who has been around"; the young Minister of Mining, not grey, gets it in another way: "he still has his black hair, he is a new minister". Then he turns to me, I was waiting for it, and I quickly cover my scalp. The villagers laugh: they understood before PM did. But I am not off the hook. As a former Minister of Health, Mocumbi then talks about the importance of good nutrition. He points to me and says: "you should all eat well, like him, why do you think he is tall". In fact we notice many stunted children in this village. Several are coughing, no doubt affected by acute respiratory infection. Goiter, a sign of iodine deficiency, is very noticeable among some of the women.

The main seat next to the PM is reserved for an old thin man in a grey suit with an equally thin stick to go with the build of his frame. Former soldier as he is, I study his erect body and rumpled face – a human relic from the struggle against the Portuguese. As the sun is setting the convoy speeds away to the airport. A cloud of dust envelopes the waving villagers until they are out of sight.

Mocumbi flies back with us to Maputo. A good politician, he works the aisle taking all his time. He stops at every row of seats for a chitchat, refers to today's recommendation by Unicef for a salt iodisation drive in the North that would include local testing. Mocumbi warns that testing of salt for iodisation may scare the local population that have strong cultural and mystical beliefs. And he shows us how. Puts salt on a piece of paper, lets a drop of water fall on it, and it turns red. This means that this salt is iodised. But the population associates red with blood and will therefore never consume it. So, he concludes, salt iodisation testing equipment may be of no use in Niassa. His general point is that the UN should study local cultural beliefs and traditions before launching such an initiative.

By 1995 imports outpaced exports ten to one, resulting in a chronic deficit that required continued massive assistance from the IMF and World Bank. It was at this time that tensions rose between the government and the Bretton Woods institutions. One hot issue during my time and afterwards was the cashew industry. Smallholder farmers were responsible for about 95% of total raw nut marketed production and some one million rural households (40% of the rural population) made a living off cashew trees. As one of the conditions for further lending, the World Bank made it a condition that the Mozambican government should liberalise the cashew sector. It recommended that the government drop the requirement that traders sell raw nuts to Mozambican industries and simultaneously lower export tariffs on raw nuts. The government clearly wanted Mozambique to close inefficient plants and only export raw beans, especially to India, its biggest cashew-trading partner. After initial resistance – in those days Mozambique was one of a few very poor African countries to stand up against its "benefactor" – the government had no choice but to cave in. By 1997, most factories had closed and about 10,000 jobs were lost.

Relations with the IMF did not fare much better. The population could simply not endure any further the austerity measures; thousands had no means of any kind. Angry food riots broke out in Matola and other outlying areas of Maputo. But at the end of 1995 Mozambique reached a new three-year agreement with the IMF. Upon returning home Minister Salomão informed the press that the IMF had declared, "Mozambique is on track".[100] But in effect Mozambique was still a long way off from structural adjustment with realistic growth prospects for jobs and purchasing power. *"Adjustment with a human face"* had definitely not reached Mozambique's shores yet. Later on, for some time to come still, poverty reduction strategies on the continent continued paying mostly lip service to the principle of protection of the most vulnerable.

Death of Jim Grant

On the 31st of January 1995 we got the stunning news that Jim Grant had passed away. On the second day of Christmas he had

---

[100] *Mozambique – Economy: Crawling out of the rut*, Interpress Services, January 1996.

fallen into a coma at home and was hospitalised. He had been felled after an almost two year battle with cancer. Unicef offices throughout the world opened a Book of Condolences. Gabriel oversaw the setting of this at the office entrance. He placed a large photo of Grant on the front desk together with a bouquet of white roses. For two days he and I took turns to stand motionless for hours behind the desk, assisting government, members of parliament, the diplomatic community, civil society and international NGOs to sign, often accompanied with some words of appreciation and respect. The first one to appear was Foreign Minister Leonardo Simão, who had known Mr Grant since when he had been Minister of Health. It was not easy to stand there for hours on end. In fact it was my own choice never to use the chair. Gabriel did the same.

What kept me going were my thoughts of this great man, who had transformed Unicef almost singlehandedly into the lead agency for children, and sustained it through sheer willpower and determination. Children were always foremost in his mind. Shortly before passing away, Grant called President Clinton, pleading with him to sign the Convention. He finally did so, but the Republican-held Congress never ratified.

Grant simply had a way of getting people "on board". Using immunization for all children as his *cutting edge* as he called it, to improve primary healthcare systems and delivery, he could do almost anything in the end without being opposed. Gradually his passing gave rise to two types of Unicef staff: those who had known Jim Grant and those who had not. I often thought about my own, very swift transformation from banker to Unicef aid worker since my interview with him almost 10 years before. His inspiration for me had much to do with it. Perhaps I simply did not want to fail him.

Jim and Ethel Grant had a style of their own. Every morning prior to the first Executive Board session of the day, they hosted a breakfast in the "Roof House", their penthouse apartment on

38th Street. I remember a rather informal setting with some 30 people from all over the world sitting and standing around in the living room. The apartment was very light with windows almost from ceiling to floor. Ethel was a caring woman making sure that we were well taken care off. The ultimate treat for me was the abundance of strawberries topped off generously with snow-white Crème de Chantilly. It was the last time I saw her. One year later, during a visit to the Taj Mahal with her husband and Jim's close friend John Rhode, Ethel was struck down by a massive heart attack.[101]

Mozambique and the international donor community

In March 1995 Shob dispatched me to the World Bank led consultative group meeting[102] for Mozambique in Paris, I spoke on behalf of Unicef and outlined our funding plans for the country. Bilateral donors were outbidding one another as if there was no tomorrow. Italy raised an arm: 100 million dollars, without any specific allocations, other than saying that a portion of this aid would flow through the Unicef and other UN agencies in Maputo. My ears perked up: by 1995 our own funding gone had gone down with the end of the emergency, so new funding from Italy would therefore be most welcome.

In the following year an Italian aid mission arrived in Maputo, and then every four months or so thereafter. They always faithfully included Unicef. Getting fed up after three "empty-handed" visits from COOP Italiana, I asked Shob if he could take care of the next one. He did, then realised what I had felt. In our time Unicef in Mozambique never did see any funding from Italy. Even Brazil, thus far not so active in Africa pledged a considerable amount in Paris, a breakthrough of sorts. But here also, details of allocations were scant. With over one billion dollars pledged, the

---

[101] Adam Fifield gives a harrowing decription in *A Mighty Purpose: How Jim Grant sold the world on saving its children*.
[102] A World Bank led pledging conference for developing countries that brings the international donor community together with a specific country.

meeting was declared a success. Everybody left in a joyful and upbeat mood. What choice did we donors have? Donations, debt forgiveness and extension of new credits were easy to come by, but long-term job-creating investments seemed elusive. Austerity was always the watchword. Meanwhile sovereign debt was piling up further, with the largely illiterate and poor population not seeing any productive benefits for them.

After the meeting I felt a bit frustrated in that I had learned little about what projects some of these donors were going to donate to and why. And then an idea came into my head: we at Unicef needed to profile the multi and bilateral donors in Mozambique over a period of time. What were the trends and levels of contributions, but especially also the type of projects funded? Could they be linked to specific business interests of the donor? Whose aid was in effect tied aid and whose was not? Could a specific profile of donors in Mozambique be a way to avoid misunderstanding and duplication among donors and even give less "sexy" projects a better chance? Could it be a "marketing" tool for project presentation for UN agencies and NGOs that entirely depend on contributions from donors? Would the donors themselves judge a *Profile of Donors* useful? First I did some "market research" among the embassies and the response was very encouraging. Then the idea was born: create a *Profile of Donors in Mozambique* as a reference for improving aid coordination aid to Mozambique and leveraging of funds for children.

It was only appropriate to take 1987 as the starting year for the *Profile*: just months after Chissano had been sworn in as Mozambique's second president, the government invited the Bretton Woods institutions in 1987 to assist with a structural adjustment programme. It was called the *Programa da Reabilitação Económica (PRE)*, front-runner of what later was to become the strategy for poverty reduction. That year was the turning point in Mozambique's relations with the West. But *PRE* was far removed from the Unicef notion of adjusting *with a human face*. Michael Cross gives a vivid example: *"In PRE there*

CHAPTER 9: "A LUTA CONTINUA"

was an attempt to rationalise the Ministry of Education. The first victim was technical education. Technical schools degenerated; and interest in technical schools disappeared. The second victim was literacy and adult education; this was the worst hit victim of structural adjustment. The World Bank had a devastating impact".[103]

I hired a young consultant to kick-start the process of the *Profile of Donors*. Rosa did important legwork with the embassies, but was not senior enough to access the higher levels and get confidential information faster. I began to approach my counterparts at the embassies. Many were most responsive. One collateral benefit was that the exercise suddenly had made attending cocktail receptions very worthwhile. I did most of my business there and it was by far the best place to lobby for the success we needed. Embassies became "fired up" and even began to write their own narratives to accompany data and trends.

Each donor country chapter was divided in two parts: one covered bilateral assistance to Mozambique and the other direct contributions to Unicef Mozambique. A problem developed with France, because it had never contributed directly to Unicef programmes in Mozambique.

One evening my friend and neighbour Jean-Claude Barais of Agence française de Développement (AfD) dropped by for a drink after work as he often did. He was up in arms, he had learned that France was not going to be in the *Profile*. He pleaded with me and I kept egging him on. In the end I caved in but insisted that he try his best to get at least a token contribution from his government, even if it was just in the form of a pledge for now. I could deal with that later. The deal never came through: Barais was reassigned shortly thereafter. The *Profile* was a very useful present for dinner invitations. I took one copy to a dinner at the residence of the new UNDP Representative, Belgian Emmanuel de Casterlee.

---

[103] *An unfilled promise: transforming schools in Mozambique*, Michael Cross.

His English wife was "into" canaries. Two small cages were swinging right above the dining table, while the birds were chirping enthusiastically, almost as background music. Two hours of this ordeal began to seriously affect my nerves. NGOs were some of the ardent takers of the *Profile*, using it to analyse potential partners on funding trends and thematic priorities. The last time I looked up the *Profile* on the Internet, it had made it to the US Library of Congress, where it was no doubt gathering dust.

At the Social Summit: Serving on a panel on children affected by war

The second part of the mission to Europe was to serve on a panel on children affected by war at the 1995 World Summit for Social Development in Copenhagen. I focused on landmines and children with disabilities in Mozambique. I spoke about the one million landmines still to be unearthed; the weekly fatal casualties with most being children; and how Unicef rural projects had come to a standstill in mined areas. My seat was next to the chairperson, Nils Thedin. I knew I was in the presence of a great man, who had done much for Unicef. Thedin was the first Chairman of the newly created Swedish Committee in 1954. From 1970 to 1972 he had been Chairman of the Unicef Board. His first relief work experience came during the Spanish Civil War when he worked with the International Committee for Assistance for Child Refugees in Barcelona[104]. I noticed my former boss Victor Soler-Sala sitting high up in the amphitheatre with Peter Ustinov and Richard Jolly. The latter would soon lose his battle to succeed Jim Grant.

I presented the case of Mozambique. Other panellists were from Bosnia, Angola and Cambodia. It was the very beginning of the "road to Ottawa" and Unicef in Mozambique was going to be very much part of that.[105] At the end of my intervention I made a plea that the United Nations should hire far more people with disabilities than the organisation did at the time. In fact there were

---

[104] *The Children and the Nations*, Maggie Black, page 228.
[105] The process that led to the signing of the UN Convention banning the production, stocking, laying of landmines in November 1997, see Chapter 10.

many types of posts that people with disabilities could easily do: secretary, assistant, receptionist and so on. As soon as I had uttered these words I felt the "foot in my mouth". As the panel disbanded, an elegant English lady in a wheelchair accosted me: "Mr Mohr, surely people with disabilities can do more than being a doorman or a secretary; surely you remember Franklin Roosevelt, who was in a wheelchair, and yet he became President of the United States". *Touché*, I thought. I deeply apologised to her for this enormous gaffe and said she was entirely right. She remained magnanimous and friendly all the same. But I have never forgotten her comment.

A champion for civil society

I was always keen on strengthening national organisations and associations, to make them more independent from government and international donors. Unlocking the North's civil society for its autonomous participation in development seemed to me a crucial issue for Mozambique.

The democratization process, begun in 1992 with the peace accords, led to freedom of association in Mozambique as enshrined in the new constitution. Through the various programmes of international donors and UN agencies to improve "good" governance, local NGOs began to be involved as project implementing agencies. But the bulk of UN funding was still channelled in those days through the international NGOs rather than local organizations.

Being so far away from the central government, I thought – perhaps naively so – that civil society organisations in the North might eventually stand a better chance for autonomous decision making together with Unicef. In any event they definitely had the advantage of being far closer to the rural population than the central government. A study for Unesco on governance and civil society in Mozambique concluded that autonomy from the State could often constitute a countervailing force to government. It was argued that NGOs can even be a stepping-stone towards the creation of a viable democratic civil society.[106] Mozambican civil society in that sense had hardly left the starting blocks. But who knows, perhaps the "renaissance" Governor Aly of Niassa might turn out to be a visionary of truly decentralised government working hand in hand with civil society one day.

One day in the town of Nampula I moderated a focus group with local civil society organisations. My objective was to see where the NGOs could be instrumental in implementing some of the Unicef projects in the area; and the NGOs were looking to Unicef for guidance. The health and education sectors, but also child protection and agriculture were strongly represented at this meeting. After a general presentation on Unicef's work – we already constructed boreholes and latrines with local brigades in Nampula – I identified areas of potential collaboration. I then opened up the debate, essentially advocating for two issues. The first one was to find ways to make these NGOs stronger and a bit less dependent on donor money. It was all-important to engage in some local fundraising however small, in cash or in kind. A project would essentially have to be running at least for a year before the NGO should approach an external donor. Only then would the NGO have something to show for.

The second issue was that most of the associations present in Nampula were essentially a one-man operation. I proposed that they consider looking for ways to merge with like-minded local NGOs or other civil society organisations. The congregation clearly did not like this last idea. They obviously all wanted to retain control. Not wishing to labour the point, I launched the idea of a civil society umbrella organisation that could represent NGOs and other civil society organisations. International NGOs would be invited to join and to become a "mentor" of one or several local associations. Members would elect a

---

[106] *UNESCO: Governance, Civil Society and NGOs in Mozambique*, Stefano Bellucci, 2002.

CHAPTER 9: "A LUTA CONTINUA"

secretary-general for overall coordination. The umbrella organisation would be a clearinghouse for information sharing, joint programming and harmonisation of policies affecting children. It would provide the NGOs with one voice vis-à-vis the government in national policy affecting children, and this could be particularly useful in advocacy for child-focused budgets. This proposal was very well received. Unfortunately the time remaining in my assignment was insufficient to actually support its implementation. All I could do was to advocate for the creation of such an umbrella organisation at almost every public speaking engagement until the end of my assignment[107].

Official engagements

Perhaps the most memorable official event I ever attended in all my Unicef years was the ten-year anniversary commemoration of the death of Samora Machel, Mozambique's first president. On the morning of 19 October 1986, Machel left Maputo for a summit in Mbala, Zambia, with President Kaunda of Zambia and President dos Santos of Angola. The strategy of the Front Line States was to move against Mobutu of Zaïre and Banda of Malawi in an attempt to end their support for UNITA and Renamo, who they regarded as South African surrogates.

Machel would never see his beloved country again. Minutes before landing the plane crashed mysteriously on the approach to Maputo airport, killing the president along with several cabinet ministers and other officials. Nine survived. The weather forecast for the flight had been favourable. Although the case was reopened several times, the investigation resolved nothing. One theory has it that a beacon guiding planes into Maputo airport had been misplaced on purpose, causing the plane to crash into a mountain.

---

[107] In 2007 civil society organisations – 10 national and 10 international – founded *the Liga das ONGs em Moçambique (JOINT) to promote cooperation and exchange of information between its members*.

Ten traumatic years on, Heads of State and Heads of Government, principally from the SADC[108] countries, cabinet ministers, members of the National Assembly, the diplomatic community and representatives of civil society assembled at the National Monument dedicated to Mozambique's Heroes. Dhlakama was noticeably absent. 1986 must have seemed like yesterday to most of those present and indeed, to the whole nation. The Monument contains the tombs of Samora Machel, Eduardo Mondlane and other heroes fallen in the struggle.

As is usual, the diplomatic corps had arrived at the monument well before the Heads of State and government. Nelson Mandela, since two years president of a liberated South Africa was the last to arrive. Jailed from 1964 to 1990, he had of course never known Machel personally. Although he walked with a brisk pace, Mandela appeared to do that with some difficulty. Only once did one of the two white South Afrikaners in charge of his security steady him ever so briefly. Mandela settled on a spot that was barely a few metres away from where I was standing. He stood erect and completely still – totally unsupported all this time. There was still a bit of the soldier in him, but the face belied a soft and compassionate side. There was something extraordinary in feeling his presence from so close by. If I can express it so, I felt some sort of "radiation" right then and there.

President Chissano led the procession followed by Nelson Mandela and the other heads of state. There were perhaps 20 steps or so going down to a large space. It was cool inside. The plastered walls were lined with tombstones of the fallen heroes. It all gave me an eerie feeling. I could understand that for any Mozambican who had been in the Frelimo struggle, this might be a very trying moment. In any event, the people moved very slowly. The ones I could see in front of Machel's tombstone took their time. As the diplomatic corps went in, some of the foreign guests

---

[108] The Southern African Development Community is an inter-governmental organization with its headquarters in Gaborone, Botswana.

CHAPTER 9: "A LUTA CONTINUA"

and national dignitaries were coming out. Now it was their turn to wait for us under a burning sun that did not bode well for the rest of the day. I looked forward to escaping soon the extreme heat of the day that was surely to come. I estimated that the speeches would end in a couple of hours. But that was not to be.

There were many chairs lined up in long rows. Several rows back were reserved for the international donor community. We could just about see the backs of the heads of state and government sitting in the first row together with President Chissano and the cabinet. There was King Mswati III of Swaziland and his 22-year-old new wife, whose face disappeared under an oversized pink top hat. President dos Santos of Angola, a big man who towered over almost everyone. Dos Santos spoke of the common struggles that cemented a bond between Angola and Mozambique. Both countries had encountered destabilisation by South Africa. All praised Samora Machel for his leadership, intelligence and inspiration for his people to work hard towards common goals. Nelson Mandela bestowed on Samora Machel posthumously the highest award that can be awarded to foreigners for their contribution to the people of South Africa.

Speech followed speech while the sun was climbing to its zenith. It all lasted for many hours. Some snacks, water and soft drinks were on sale behind us. Several foreigners had already left. I was bent on staying until the end, but began to think that I was trapped in a health hazard. Choosing health over diplomacy, I sneaked out at 7 pm. I thought that Machel, who was known for addressing crowds utterly unbound by time, might have found nothing unusual with the protracted ceremony.

Unicef as lead agency for children is of course in the forefront to celebrate the annual Days of the Child with the government. There are two of them: the International Day of the Child on 1st June and the International Day of the African Child on 16th June. The latter day had been chosen in memory of the children killed by South African police in the 1976 massacre of Soweto. The

International Day of the Child was adopted by the United Nations General Assembly in the closing months of the 1979 International Year of the Child.

I had barely comely back from the Portuguese language course in 1994 or I had to make a speech in Portuguese before thousands of people assembled in a stadium of Maputo on the occasion of the International Day of the Child. There was President Chissano himself; Minister of Foreign Affairs Pascoal Mucumbi; and then Minister of Health Leonardo Simão. A former Unicef staff member from Brazil, now a communication consultant, had written the Unicef speech. He coached me in delivering it and straightened out pronunciation errors. Some words I could never get straight. I wrote those phonetically in the margin to utter them as best as I could. Dominique Buff of the Red Cross thought I had mastered Portuguese long ago! Unfortunately with the end of the emergency phase ending, ICRC[109] was wrapping up and Dominique was leaving. I lost a golfing buddy, but we remained friends.

Every year I participated in celebrations of the African Day of the Child. One time the main event was organised in Xai-Xai. I spoke off the cuff on child rights, and emphasized the obligations that go with it: parents have an obligation to keep their children in school; going to school is also an obligation for children themselves; "parents have an obligation to first care for the health of their child at home as best they can, so as not to overburden the health centre unnecessarily: we can build health posts, but you can help prevent diseases at home". These sound bites made it to TVM in the evening news. Some kids were taking part in a dancing competition. A little boy won first prize: a *bolsa* for the *Escola de Dança*. A girl asked me for a dance on the stage in the middle of the sandy soccer field. Another girl moved towards the stage gently dragging the Minister of Health off our stand. The governor came next. And so the three of us trotted in single file to the stage, cheered on by hundreds of kids. I felt an awkward sense of

---

[109] International Committee of the Red Cross.

CHAPTER 9: "A LUTA CONTINUA"

pre-arranged orchestration. There were hundreds of children making dancing movements but not really coming on stage. I whispered to my dancing partner: *"não pode convidar todas as crianças para dançar connosco?"*[110] She was shy and said nothing.

Next thing I know, we are back on the stand and the bandleader invites all the children to come on stage; the Governor hesitating, evoking a question of security, but finally waving an approving hand. A sight to see: the TVM cameraman jumping on a long table to get a good shot; hundreds of children streaming on stage and breaking loose in a wild dancing feast. Finally it *is* a party, if ever so briefly. For a moment I feel like having "conspired" with these children to give them a good time.[111]

Another piece of officialdom was to sign condolence registers. A relic from the Marxist days, Mozambique was one of very few African countries to entertain relations with the Democratic People's Republic of Korea. Ever since I was a ten-year-old, I had keenly followed the war between North and South Korea. After the invasion of the South by North Korean troops, the Security Council voted to send a UN force to the South. The Russians had walked out in protest just before the vote. That was a fatal mistake, as they otherwise could have exercised their veto. Dutch soldiers were fighting courageously alongside Americans, British, Canadians and Turks. From a young age I listened to the news on Dutch radio. I still remember a commentator saying that the Turks were the fiercest and the most feared.

Until I met Shob, I had never met anyone from Korea. Shob was a retired colonel of the army. He had gotten a scholarship from his Ministry of Defence to study in France and train French youth in judo in Paris. Shob for one did not believe in any North-South reconciliation, calling the North Vietnamese brainwashed and the

---

[110] "Can you not invite all the children to dance with us?"
[111] When Roald Dahl, the master of story telling for children, was once asked what his great secret was with children who liked his stories so much, he replied: "conspiracy".

political establishment insane. Then one day in June 1994, Kim Il Sung died after a reign of some 30 years. Shob was conveniently out of town. I silently cursed him. So I had to go to the North Korean embassy to sign the register of condolences. I had a super strong aversion in going there. I tried to get out of it, but with each passing day Gabriel insisted that I go, adding that it would only be a very brief affair. I kept him on tenterhooks, opting to go at the very last minute of the very last day when the signing was about to be closed.

Arriving at a villa that begs for multiple coats of white paint, I walk the short pathway up to the front door. There is no official outside to accompany me, no diplomats, and no one else to offer condolences to. I wonder if anyone had come to sign. I knock at the door and a junior diplomat opens the door, gesturing me to follow him. There's a table and he sits down. Beckons me to sit down in the opposite chair; no words exchanged; I think how I should sign, with some text like "Unicef will miss the great leader" or perhaps "Unicef mourns the loss of". I desperately want to peek back a page or two to see who else had signed, but decide that would be bad taste. I decide to just sign my name for Unicef and head straight for the door. He panics: "No, no, come this way". I follow the man to a large room where a gigantic portrait of his great leader hangs. He motions me where to stand. I study the man who is standing in a starkly painted surrealistic countryside setting. Coming outside in the cool July air of winter, a feeling of liberation of this oppressive atmosphere, this jail-like environment, sends shudders through my spine. Sometime later Unicef opened a liaison office in Pyongyang to deal with the famine emergency. Our EPI officer Osvaldo Legon, who had been looking for reassignment for some time, was selected to head it up. A national of socialist-friendly Cuba, he was the right choice. At least Shob had a hand in one issue that concerned the DPRK.

The *crème de la crème* event was National Independence Day. It began with a review of the Independence Parade of the military and communities marching beyond a stand. The diplomatic community sat with the national dignitaries on the reviewing stand. After the speeches, those invited would drive to the Presidential Palace for the annual garden party given by President Chissano.

From the 20th anniversary on that Sunday, 25th of June 1995 onwards, I became a *habitué*. The celebration looked very much like a British affair: well-kept lawn among impressive trees; round tables with spotless white table cloths; women in light dresses strolling under elegant straw hats of summer; yellowish low sunlight filtering through the tall trees making for long shadows; and winter temperatures in the low twenties taking care of the rest.

The President was an amiable man. His eyes were small, alert and perhaps even a trifle "naughty". His trademark was a small pointy beard hanging down from the chin only. I remember him walking among the round tables, relaxed and taking all his time to discuss this or that business or just putting in a nice word here and there. There were always the heroes of the revolution: Minister of Development Cooperation Jacinto Veloso, the white Portuguese born and raised in Lourenço Marques, who deserted the *Força Aérea Portuguesa* in 1963, flying a plane to Dar-es-Salaam to join Frelimo; the poet and painter Malangatana, who illustrated the struggle. I met him towards the end of a period when he painted harsh scenes of people's suffering in the civil war. An obituary in Johannesburg expressed it like this: *"the pictures seemed to say, we won one battle, but a luta continua"*; there was always Marcelino dos Santos, who once served as Vice President of Frelimo under Samora Machel in the early days; the journalist Carlos Cardoso, another Portuguese-Mozambican who joined Frelimo before independence; and many others.

Food and drink were plentiful as if there was no tomorrow, temporarily moving ideas of equitable development far from our minds. The party only ended when the sun was about to set. It was here that I befriended Mokhtar, the Polisario Representative. Mokhtar was our neighbour on Rua Dom Afonso Enriques in

Sommerschield. His living room was typically Moresque, with long sofas lining the walls. He taught us a lot about life in the refugee camps just inside Algeria on the border with his country; the history of the Spanish colonist; and their never-ending struggle for independence.

Social life in Maputo

I hosted a good many official dinners at home. As always, the dinners among friends were the most fun. One day I arranged a dinner for some 20 friends and Unicef colleagues. A. was away in Abidjan at the time. An extra table was set. There was Helmut Rau, the amiable German ambassador and his Scottish wife Sheila; Max Deneu who ran the rehabilitation centre for mine victims in Maputo and his wife Pascale; Ariane Zwahlen, who headed up Terre des Hommes; Theo, the French-Moroccan who led the street sign project for Maputo and his beautiful wife Maria; our neighbour Eric, gendarme at the French embassy and his Portuguese wife Maria. There were many other French guests, along with Tiburcio of Unesco and UNDP's Deputy Akhbar.

This turns out to be a chaotic dinner. After the copious entrée of gambas and a white fleur du Cap– Hamidou had found a cheap source of gambas at Katembe just across the bay – guests already get ready to move around. In fact most walk over from our rather formal long black marble table the very informal wooden one where some people seemed to have the best laughs. In fact, that table doubled beyond capacity.

Some people who cancelled show up. Hamidou has proven improvisation skills, bringing in a third table. Meanwhile the newly arrived guests are scouting all over the house to find more chairs. The whole house is now upside down. Some people spill over to easy sofas and chairs, bringing their food with them. The marble table is demoted to side table for bottles of wine and leftovers. There is an *empregada* who Hamidou had contracted as extra help in the kitchen. I for one have no idea who she is and where he had found her. I ask him what her name is, but he does

CHAPTER 9: "A LUTA CONTINUA"

not know. Sometimes it's better not to ask... The empregada is rather good looking. I am not sure if she spends much time in the kitchen, because many of the guests warm up to her and keep her engaged. I start wondering about Hamidou's oversight qualities – or rather lack thereof. No wonder that many mistake her for one of the guests. The woman plays the part, delivering warm *beijinhos* to every arriving and leaving guest.

Another time, I hosted a dinner for some 30 participants at a UNDP and Unicef seminar on sustainable human development. I had led the session on poverty and ways of reducing inequality. A funny thing happened before dinner as the guests were having a drink. Hamidou is in charge of managing the kitchen crew. At some point I lose sight of him and look all over the place for him. And here is Mr Hamidou, chatting amiably at one of the tables with the newly appointed Minister of Environment, Bernardo Ferraz. Ferraz speaks fluent French, has a soft spot for Burkina Faso, in particular for its late president Thomas Sankara whom he had known personally. After studying the pair from afar, I feel sorry to interrupt their animated conversation and restore Hamidou's service to the event. Hamidou was always totally at ease with authority and did not look up to it. In fact, *il s'en fichait pas mal.*[112]

The French consul was a woman from Martinique called Maggie, who lived on our street. She was a lively woman, always ready for a party. In fact she regularly threw dinner parties in her garden that would turn into a disco as the clock ticked the hours away. Her favourite song was *Hey Margherita!* It played over and over again till the early morning hours. Both A. and Nadim were in town at least for one of these parties. I still see all these fists going up untiringly in the air, singing along this brain-impregnating refrain. Hamidou was barman along with someone's Beninois houseboy, who drank one beer after another. Well before four am the Christian barman from Benin had abandoned his post and was

---

[112] "He couldn't care less".

found fast asleep under the bar. Hamidou the Muslim remained alert and polite, and continued to serve alcohol stoically to the merry guests.

Coming from West Africa, Hamidou was very popular with the Francophone community, who liked it that he spoke French. Maggie and other French expats asked him to come and help at big French dinners. In fact Hamidou had a knack for languages. He spoke rather good Portuguese, just by picking it up from the street. He learned English on trips to Swaziland and South Africa. His friend, a cook from Ghana, did the rest.

A. was more often away now, spending time with Nadim in Abidjan where he had taken a job. Hamidou no longer went on trips with the family as our "bodyguard" as he used to do, to places like the Zimbabwe ruins or Lusaka. Hamidou had found other, most useful activities besides cooking and cleaning. I encouraged that, as I wanted him to make as much cash as possible before returning to Burkina Faso for good. He bought himself a Canon camera for 50 dollars at the *mercado de ladrões*[113]. He began to take pictures of guards standing proudly in front of the main gate, often dressed in special clothes for the photo-op and sold them for a dollar a piece. A new street scene photographer did not go unnoticed in Maputo in those days. A Portuguese family living across from us asked him to be the official photographer of their daughter's wedding. I gave him driving lessons, and he learned fast. During my home leave he took advantage of my absence and drove my car – it had CD number plates - through Maputo with his friends in it. Shob had seen him do it. I was mad and reprimanded him severely.

Hamidou had the instinct of a businessman. When I left for a brief holiday in Abidjan to see the family, he gave me a huge empty suitcase. If I could please bring back *pagne* and *boubous*. His cousin

---

[113] "The market of thieves".

CHAPTER 9: "A LUTA CONTINUA"

Aruna would do the shopping. If I only had known what I had gotten myself into. I brought back a very heavy suitcase. There was overweight to be paid. I could not get it over my heart to take it off Hamidou's pay. He fetched me from the airport and we go straight to Natasha and her friend. I had no clue where and how Hamidou had befriended these two hard Russian women. Sometimes you don't want to know. Natasha is a trader in clothing. I still see her throwing the clothes onto the king-size bed just by holding one side of the suitcase open. A fierce trading session gets under way. She is tough as nails. Hamidou too never caves in. He is simply fed up. We leave with the heavy, still full suitcase. Not surprisingly he fell out with the girls later. In the end he sold the entire contents very slowly, but made a hefty profit at two and a half times the cost; and kept an elegant *boubou* for himself. For him it had been worth waiting for.

After three years I was ready for reassignment. I felt I had done it all. Very timely, just after the Mid-Term Review, the Chief of Human Resources in New York called me. He invited me to come to New York to discuss my "options". In one way I was elated. On the other hand I had no clue of his motives for this rather suspect invitation. I had lobbied far and wide for jobs, including the deputy positions at the Division of Information and the Programme Funding Office. I came back from New York totally disappointed. Some people were obviously working behind the scenes to retire me early. Surangkana who worked at HR said my interview with Lennart "had not gone well". How could she know? Lennart had said to me I should strengthen "participatory management" skills. Was that a clue? People at HQ who would have rooted for me – not in the least Jim Grant – were no longer around.

One more year in Maputo seemed to be in the cards. That was too long to imagine. My work was surely going to be repetitive and routine. But then "passion" woke me up, giving me a "second wind." The job of demining Mozambique was not finished; the panel in Copenhagen had made that clear. In an interview with the Sunday paper *Domingos* I had audaciously declared that Unicef in Mozambique would support demining activities in localities where we had area-based projects. Demining was totally beyond Unicef's mandate, but now that I committed for Unicef, I had to deliver. The *"Road to Ottawa"* opened up before my eyes.

Chapter 10: De-mining: preparing the ground for development

On a Monday morning in June 1997 I arrived at the French school in Maputo well before its students. I thus had ample time to put on display the assortment of landmines that I had carefully kept a careful vigil over at home. They belonged to the UNDP Demining Centre in Moamba that had given them to me on loan as illustration for my talk. This was the project of Pascale, a teacher and the wife of Max Deneu. Max ran a prosthesis production and rehabilitation facility for amputees in Maputo for the British charity POWER[114]. Unicef supported his project. Pascale, a lively and expansive person, was an aspiring actress who had put together an amateur theatre group in Maputo. One day she wanted to cast me for one of the grey-haired roles in Chekhov's *The Cherry Orchard*; but regretfully I would be absent from Maputo when the play would be staged.

Just months before, at a *vernissage* at the Franco-Mozambican Cultural Centre, Pascale had introduced me to Mireille, the headmistress of the French school. After taking in together some paintings of the celebrated artist, the three of us settled down outside with a glass of white wine. Mireille complained that her students were very much living in a protective cocoon, totally ignorant of the world around them. She asked if I could perhaps give a talk about Unicef. I told her Unicef was involved in de-mining in rural areas where we had routine project activities, which was highly unusual because it was outside our mandate. The idea caught on. One week later we met again and the school project was born. In fact the children were going to design a mine-awareness campaign of their own making.

---

[114] Prosthetics and Orthotics World Education & Research.

The opening session had been reserved for me and lasted all morning. On the classroom wall there were posters on mine awareness and advocacy. The art teacher of the school had made a particularly ingenious poster: It had a photo of a bird with an impressive wingspan, flying over a tree. It was a barn owl, which the French call a *chouette*. The copywriting was simply brilliant: At the top of the poster it read: *"C'est chouette la vie"*[115]; and then below: *"Pourquoi se miner?"* This was a double-entendre as this means simultaneously: "why mine ourselves" and "why undermine ourselves"; and then the punch line: *"Ottawa, ça nous concerne tous"*[116]. Ottawa was the upcoming venue for the signing of the Treaty on the banning of landmines. The poster's text and photo had been placed in a large circle, so that a lapel button could easily be made from it. I later introduced the art teacher to the Canadian embassy and proposed that her poster be reproduced for the Ottawa Conference.

Slowly the children start to trickle in. The atmosphere is relaxed: summer recess had just begun, but the seniors had opted to embark on a two-week project to study landmines. I give them first time to look around at the display of the different types of mines. Realising the seriousness of the issue, their interest is intense. Pascale had surely given them a good briefing beforehand. They sit down in a semicircle, and several have to sit on the floor for lack of chairs. It is all delightfully informal.

I began my presentation by sketching the situation of unexploded devices in Mozambique. At that time there were wild guesses of an estimated one to two million unexploded objects. Anti-personnel blast mines were the most common type, typically deployed on the surface (hidden by leaves, branches and rocks) or buried just centimetres underground. There were mines attached to a wire nearby to fool the passer-by. Stepping on the "tripwire" was enough to detonate the mine. The heavier fragmentation mines

---

[115] "Life is beautiful".
[116] "Ottawa is everybody's business".

CHAPTER 10: DE-MINING: PREPARING THE GROUND FOR DEVELOPMENT

spew on explosion metal parts over a large area severely wounding innocent bystanders. Large anti-tank mines could wipe out a truck or even a tank. Landmines laid in Mozambique came from all corners of the world, including China, the former USSR, South Africa, Italy and France. Renamo got its mines from South Africa. French landmines were a relic of the Algeria war. Instead of destroying the French stockpile that it had inherited from the former colonial power, the government of Algeria opted to keep them. These mines ended up in Mozambique. In 1993 they were discovered in an army depot in Quelimane[117]. French mines often had a plastic casing that made them undetectable. The lightest pressure would explode them. This type of mine was registered as a *"mine antipersonnel à détection volontaire, modèle 1959."* Only the French language lends itself for such elegant euphemism, even for such weapons of mass destruction.

I explained to the students the dangerous work done by sappers, who crawl over large mined areas, a few centimetres at the time, holding metal detectors just above the ground. That work required the highest concentration. There existed now also mechanical demining. A German agronomist named Krohn had invented a kind of panzer vehicle by transforming a tractor that could explode mines without the driver getting hurt. It was being used in the heavily mined district of Moamba. In a 1996 interview with Deutsche Welle, Krohn complained that the United Nations peacekeepers seemed to prefer manual mining – calling this a "mystified scientific approach"[118]. Under an agreement with the German and Mozambican governments, Krohn's vehicle destroyed some 20,000 mines on 150 ha of agricultural land around Moamba in the province of Maputo. The contract was renewed several times. During the long rainy season, the immensely heavy Krohn truck remained idle, which added to its operating cost. Krohn ran out of funds fast. Not one organisation offered to buy his expensive trucks, which could be had for half a million dollars.

---

[117] Bertrand Legendre, *Le Monde*, 17 Janvier 1996.
[118] Interview with *Deutsche Welle*, English service, 1996.

It was not only humans who got killed or wounded. Precious livestock on which whole families depended was often wiped out, but of course no statistics were kept on that. That reminded me about a story Richard Jolly once told us in New York when he debriefed a group of us upon returning from Afghanistan. The year was 1989 and the Russians had just left for good. The population had found a new idea to deal with the old Russian-laid landmines: sending flocks of goats across the plains.

I give the students statistics on victims of landmines in Mozambique and other countries; I give them a sense what it is like to walk through a mine field; I explain the process of the *"Road to Ottawa";* I point out that Unicef had no other choice than to support demining, at least around our own rural-based activities. I am proud to say that Unicef now has a fully integrated de-mining programme consisting of mine-awareness campaigns in schools and communities (with Handicap International); de-mining (with Mine Tech); support to rehabilitation of mine victims (with POWER); and, through our traditional rural area-based projects, support to women to start again cultivating the now de-mined land. All along the two weeks, UNDP, POWER, Handicap International and other organisations come to lead sessions pertaining to their work.

Two weeks later I attend the closing of the workshop. Many parents and siblings are present. I am in awe: drawings of mine explosions and victims are lining the walls; the children have written stories about the atrocities; and they enact a mine-awareness play on children encountering landmines. They had written that themselves, surely with a little help from Pascale.

Only a few months before his death, Jim Grant had called for a total ban on landmines in a speech to the Third Committee of the UN General Assembly.[119] My own motivation to get Unicef

---

[119] *A Mighty Purpose: How Jim Grant sold the World on savings its Children,* Adam Fifield.

CHAPTER 10: DE-MINING: PREPARING THE GROUND FOR DEVELOPMENT

involved had begun at the 1995 Copenhagen Social Summit, where I served on a panel on Children affected by War. I recalled the traumatic experiences of children with landmines. In Mozambique there were still hundreds of children dying in landmine explosions each year; others got maimed for life.

I had often seen for myself that sometimes Unicef area-based activities could not advance as they were in or near mined areas. In public settings I began to make the point that Unicef should support de-mining, in particular around its project areas. That thought never left me. Clearing Unicef project areas of landmines might also give a powerful message in international fora. Unicef was already actively involved with NGOs and schools in building mine-awareness; in giving support to the amputee rehabilitation centre in Maputo run by the British organization POWER; and actively advocated with its NGO allies the prohibition of the production, stockpiling and sale of landmines. Physical de-mining, totally outside Unicef's mandate, would make the final point: getting rid of landmines was everybody's business in any case, in whatever shape or form, mandate or no mandate; It was a wake-up call for "all hands on deck now" – even if the effort might seem against all odds.

The break-through came when the Sunday paper *Domingo* requested an interview with me. To be interviewed by the national media was routine for me. But this time it was different. I saw my chance and grabbed it. Most of the interview was dedicated to my new passion: getting rid of landmines and getting Unicef to be part of it. On that Sunday 3rd December 1995 the headline said it all: *Unicef vai envolver-se na desminagem, diz Boudewijn Mohr, representante em Moçambique*[120]. A large photo of a rather concerned-looking me accompanied the story. I was literally in shock to read back the words I had spoken just days before. I had told journalist Miguel Ramos that for the first time in its almost

---

[120] "Unicef is going to take on demining", interview with Ramos Miguel, Domingo, 3rd of December 1995.

50-year history, Unicef was going to be directly involved in de-mining operations, and Mozambique was going to be the first country in the world where this would happen. I had already asked Halo Trust, a British private sector firm to do a cost analysis of de-mining at an identified, specific Unicef programme site. HALO had recently trained two platoons[121] of sappers and was working with them in Zambézia. I had approached some donors and the Australian embassy held out the possibility of funding early on. In the country programme exercise for 1996 we had already begun to make budgetary provisions for demining in rural development projects. Meanwhile Unicef signed an agreement with Handicap International for linking its de-mining project with a national mine-awareness campaign. We already were clearly on the move – it was just that we had no money! I was beginning to feel as a Unicef pioneer from the past, when everything was possible, as long as you took the bull by the horns.

I was a bit apprehensive that this story might be seen at Headquarters. Unicef could not engage in mine clearance. Would Programme Division intervene and say no? I did not want HQ to stop it, now that we were so tantalisingly close. And what would Shob say, he was after all the Representative, not me. The following morning I walked into his office, first thing as usual. From behind his desk, this man of few words simply says, *"Well done, go ahead"*. I could have hugged him there and then.

The real nightmare was only beginning now. De-mining was very costly. How would the Mozambican government deal with this idea? Would they object if we perhaps would have to siphon off some funds from other commitments? Could HALO lend us a platoon or two of well-trained sappers who could begin clearing mines as soon as possible? Where would Unicef find funding for a project that had nothing to do with our mandate for children? And then the incredible happened.

---

[121] A platoon consists of 45 men.

CHAPTER 10: DE-MINING: PREPARING THE GROUND FOR DEVELOPMENT

Through our work on the *Profile of Donors* – then about to be published – I had forged excellent working relations with several of the embassies. Shortly after the interview with *Domingo* my Danish counterpart called me. He said Copenhagen had emergency leftover funds from 1995 that needed to be used urgently. Otherwise they would be lost. Instead of handing the funds over to the *Comissão Nacional de Desminagem*, the Danes proposed to make a direct contribution to the Unicef de-mining project! Would I accept? The amount was a whopping 360,000 US $. The *Profile of Donors* was clearly beginning to pay off! I was greatly moved.

We found a platoon of Zimbabweans through a demining company from Zimbabwe, *Mine Tech*, who had already de-miners on the ground in Mozambique. Some of them were former soldiers who had laid these mines ten years before; and they sometimes remembered where they themselves had hidden them.

I received a comprehensive briefing from UNDP and the National De-mining Commission. In fact I took that briefing twice. As Nadim and A. were going to join me on one of the outings, they also needed to be briefed beforehand, and I went with them for a second time.

The UNDP Demining Coordinator showed an almost life-size map that illustrated the worst mined areas in Mozambique. ONUMOZ had started to accelerate mine clearance during the 1994 elections, at first training hundreds of sappers, but logistical back up was still missing. HALO Trust did a survey of the worst mined areas of Inhambane and Zambézia. In Maputo Province there was a 100 km ring of mined roads around Moamba, only 60 km from the capital. The Cahora Bassa dam, which provides electricity to a large part of the country, was heavily mined. So were other infrastructures such as waterworks and pumps. We were told that, should no more mines be laid, the problem could be defeated in 15 to 20 years. Meanwhile mines continued to kill. Just days before our briefing a little girl had picked up a mine near Matola and took it to a nearby market. There it exploded, killing eleven people and injuring twenty-two. A harrowing illustration of the "after-war" that Mozambique was still facing. The Coordinator said pointedly, "The war isn't over until all mines are gone."

We learned that mine detection was difficult in areas where soil has a high metal content; also, manufacturers constantly tried to make mine detection equipment more effective, making them less detectable. When ONUMOZ left, UNDP inherited the de-mining project along with Department of Humanitarian Affairs (DHA). The UN supported the Mozambican government in creating the *Comissão Nacional de Desminagem*. There was an inter-ministerial group chaired by the Foreign Minister. Governors and other local authorities, NGOs and the private sector coordinated implementation. UNDP had already trained 600 former combatants as *sapadores*. Norwegian People's Action (NPA) had a large training programme for de-miners in Tete, Zambézia and Cabo Delgado.

We were told that most mine accidents with sappers happen on Fridays between 9 and 10 a.m.; and Mondays between 6.30 a.m. and 1.30 p.m. There's less concentration then as their thoughts are with the upcoming weekend; on Mondays it's exchanging the weekend stories that distracts them. They work in pairs for twenty minutes, then rest briefly and begin again. Sappers work continuously until lunchtime when the work is finished for the day; working again after lunch might distract and risk loss of concentration. Sappers are between 18 and 24 years old and earn approximately 1,000 US $ per month. Their families are beneficiaries of a modest life insurance.[122]

Living and working in a minefield as a sapper was something I wanted to learn more about. In July 1996 I travelled up north to take a look for myself. I was lucky to have Jorge Lampião with me. Jorge was Unicef project officer at our Chimoio office in Manica Province, which he called home. Jorge had just taken over

---

[122] Notes on demining briefing at UNDP, Nadim B. Mohr, March 1996.

CHAPTER 10: DE-MINING: PREPARING THE GROUND FOR DEVELOPMENT

the office from Adi Patel. I could not have had a better guide. He spent most of his time far away from the office – the field was his *champ de bataille*. He loved cooking; his *Provençal* shrimp dish was reputed all the way down to Maputo. Shob wanted him badly on the Maputo team but he resisted the pressure and remained "home". From a story I wrote at that time for Unicef[123], this is what he and I experienced when visiting a base camp for de-miners:

"The land cruiser travels the sandy roads through baobab forest and low bush until the base camp is finally reached. Several de-miners in bright orange fatigues are huddled around the campfire drinking tea after a hard day's work. Trained not to speak during working hours to enhance their concentration, they seem to be a silent bunch all around. Presently, some are going about rearranging their tents, which have become unsettled on the rain-washed ground. Others are hanging up clothes on a makeshift wash line. Meanwhile, a soft rain is falling and mist is moving in fast. At five o'clock in the afternoon, the night has come in from the cold.

"In complete darkness and soon a driving rain, the journey continues for barely one kilometre until we reach our destination, a locality in the district of Machaze, a cluster of thatched settlements, living space for 7,000 people. Machipanda, near Vila de Manica on the border with Zimbabwe, is mined on the northern and western approaches and further to the south on the fringes of the path leading to a lake.

"In the stillness of the night, this landmine-imprisoned village is not without sounds altogether. Under a huge tent, a group of Italians are preparing their evening meal, the flames of the fire giving them a spooky appearance. A small generator is purring softly nearby. The newly arrived Pakistani contract workers are pitching their tents. A dog is barking in the distance.

---

[123] *"Preparing the Ground: De-mining for development"*, Boudewijn Mohr, July 1996 (unpublished).

"We camp out at the school for the night. I pitch my camping bed in the stockroom among stacks of school materials donated by Unicef. A torrential rain hits the undulated roof mercilessly all night long in a symphony of raindrops with different sounds. In the distance, a Baptist group from Brazil is singing religious songs till late into the night.

"The next morning the village comes to life. The Italians are repairing the foundation of their water tower, which has suffered from last night's rains. The Baptists are saying farewell to some local officials at the school. The Pakistanis, looking more like Afghan guerrillas, are preparing tea and smoking Hooka through a complicated pipe system that rests on the ground. Their leader makes me an irresistible offer: 'Take wisdom, have tea'. Kakuzo Okakura's century-old 'The Book of Tea', could not have said it better than this.

"The foreign contract workers are here to repair the pylons of the Cahora Bassa power lines to South Africa, which, once completed, will give a much-needed boost to Mozambique's export earnings. With tents and trucks all around the village, there is a sense of migration here, as if Machipanda were a 19th century gold mining town, to be left desolate before long. But simply nothing is farther from the truth: for over a year, good things are happening to this community.

"UNHCR contracted GTZ[124] to build a four-classroom school and a health post and to drill a borehole, which instilled much needed life in this community. According to the president of the locality, the results were already showing: although waterborne diseases and sexually transmitted diseases persisted, overall mortality rates were showing a downward trend.

"Perhaps inspired by this visible progress, the women have organized themselves with the help of a local trader, who donated seed

---

[124] Gesellschaft für Technische Zusammenarbeit.

CHAPTER 10: DE-MINING: PREPARING THE GROUND FOR DEVELOPMENT

money to start a soap-making and sewing business. Greatly encouraged, the women are now planting vegetable gardens on a fertile stretch of land bordering the lake. With the best corn and sorghum harvest in years coupled with the gradual, natural reconstitution of livestock to a current level of 400 cows, there is a sense of optimism here. The president of the locality even has plans to build cabins along the lake for tourists wishing to take in a view of the hippos and crocodiles.

"Jorge Lampião explains why Unicef is interested in starting to work in the remote district of Machaze. 'With the UNHCR phase now complete, we are preparing the ground to assist the community here in converging these activities such as rebuilding of livestock and horticulture'. To guarantee the safety of future projects, Unicef has contracted the Zimbabwean de-mining company Mine Tech to clear landmines around the village, returning the land to grazing animals.

"Indeed, de-mining is a sine qua non for starting development assistance in rural areas in Mozambique. As Shob Jhie, Unicef Representative in Mozambique, explains: 'De-mining is an inevitable component of country programme assistance'.

"Initially begun with a grant from the Danish government, the strategy is to ask private companies which are under contract with bilateral donors and already operating in Unicef project areas to clear mines for free. As a first, Halo Trust, funded by the British Overseas Development Assistance (ODA) de-mined for Unicef free of charge in Ile district in Zambézia province. Norwegian People's Trust, commissioned by the governments of Norway, Denmark and Australia, has offered to de-mine for free in Sofala's heavily mined Búzi district, site of a Unicef-supported water-drilling programme.

"In 1987 José Sithole, then 26 years old, laid three boxes of antipersonnel mines, for a total of 90, on the approaches to Machipanda, host to a Frelimo army post at the time. Would he

mine ever again? 'Now that I realize that the problem remains after the war is over, I would refuse to use them', he states categorically, adding that each time he hears a mine explosion, he feels sorry for what happened. Perhaps to forever free himself of a psychological burden, he would like to become involved in mine clearance himself. Thanks to José, who warned the population of mine locations, only one man has been killed by a mine incident. Three donkeys, two cows and two goats were less fortunate. Even a tree felled by a storm hit and exploded a mine.

"The sapper creeps slowly forward. At each 'reading' by the detector, he stops and uses the small shovel, digging carefully. It was in this way that Philip Matya, 19 years old, found his first anti-tank mine one year ago after having just joined the Zimbabwe Mine Tech team in Machaze district. 'When I found it, I was just very happy', he says, adding: 'One cannot afford to be afraid for fear of losing concentration'. In Mabsisinga he found his second one, this time an anti-personnel mine. At the end of the day, Philip writes in his diary about the day's events. How does he feel to be the 'baby' on the team? And his unexpected, very positive reply: 'As the youngest, the older ones tell me about life'.

"Not all is that easy or routine. Team leader Paul Billie, explains: 'Some become homesick and lose concentration. We then give them a day off and counsel them. One can see when a de-miner suddenly becomes scared. Then we discuss and deal with it'. But Billie has his own anxieties. 'What if something goes wrong now, what would I do?' he often asks himself. Something did go wrong: two months later I got the news that Billie had stepped on a landmine and had lost his foot. He blamed it on having momentarily lost his concentration. Several months later he was reportedly back with his platoon, directing the operations as before.

"With hundreds of years of colonialism followed by many years of war, Mozambique is a wounded nation left with the scars of a million landmines. From the first mine explosion in 1965 in Cobue, Niassa province, until today landmines have claimed more

CHAPTER 10: DE-MINING: PREPARING THE GROUND FOR DEVELOPMENT

than 10,000 victims. According to Handicap International, an estimated twenty people step on a landmine every month in Mozambique. Sixty per cent of them die because they lack access to health services. There are 2,000 areas in the country identified as having been mined, with the exact number of mines unknown. Landmines can be cleared but only laboriously and at enormous expense. Trained workers have to probe the soil inch by inch. One person can clear only 25 to 50 square meters per day. These weapons cost as little as three dollars to manufacture, but can cost up to 1,000 each to clear.

"For someone to go into de-mining seems sometimes linked to the destiny of one's country. Perhaps the young Mozambican sapador expressed it to me best of all: 'Não tenho medo; fui formado para isso; estou a libertar o meu país'.[125]*"*

One day I accompanied *Le Monde* journalist Bertrand Legendre on a visit to a large mined area on the South African border. As the gateway to the capital, Namaacha had seen its share of the war. Nadim and A., now fully briefed on landmines, came along. Together we trotted along on a very narrow path marked by a protective makeshift fence on either side. Signs with a skull and bones on a red background warned visitors to stay on the path at all times: *Perigoso Minas! Emina!* And in the local language: *Xibulukwa! Dzophulika!* People walked in single file, in complete silence. Partly that was out of fear; and partly it was so as not to lose concentration. We saw mines still sitting in a hole that had only just been uncovered. The nature around us still bore scars of intense fighting with cut-off branches and neglected cashew trees; the area seemed deprived of life and normal routines. It gives one an eerie feeling to walk through a minefield. Death or serious injury is just meters away. There are tense feelings all around you, and you can feel them. One expects something to happen and it does not. It does not? Well, that day something did happen that made us scared.

---

[125] "I'm not afraid; I was trained for this; I am liberating my country".

When she disappears over the steep hill, I become apprehensive. Somehow A. had accelerated the pace to join a group ahead of us. Meanwhile Legendre, Nadim and I stick together. Suddenly we hear a deafening explosion: a landmine! It comes from the direction where A. has gone. We cannot run after her as any commotion could unsettle the situation. We are in a total state of utter anxiety. Our tour through the minefields continues as before, with the guide leading us slowly back to the base camp. There we wait another 15 minutes in nail-biting expectation. We fear the worst. Here now appears A. over the same hill *si de rien n'était*. It so happened that Sir David Steel, British MP for the Lib-Dems and member of the Armed Services Committee was on an official mission to the country. He had requested that a mine be exploded in front of his eyes. No one has thought of giving our party advance warning.

The "road to Ottawa" was by now in full swing. In March 1997 Graça Machel opened an international conference of NGOs in Maputo. As expected she made a passionate plea to prohibit landmines. Jody Williams was there for the International Coalition for the Banning of Landmines (ICBL). She sketched the progress the movement had made and urged us on to make Ottawa a success. Several NGOs presented their work. Of course all of them were preaching to the converted.

We were elated that Mozambique had been selected by New York for the shoot on location of a film produced and directed by David Feingold. His movie, produced in cooperation with Unicef Maputo, was called *"Small targets: children and landmines in Mozambique"*. HQ was funding it. I came along on a few shoots. I witnessed a staged explosion from nearby. David told us to cover our ears tight, as we might otherwise become permanently deaf. I attended a shoot at a school where the teacher was engaged in an animated mine-awareness session. Max Deneu was interviewed at the POWER amputee rehab centre. At a demining site Jean-Claude Legrand rightfully made the point that mine clearance is an issue of child protection. If we did not do that, then all Unicef's efforts in education, health and water and sanitation would make

CHAPTER 10: DE-MINING: PREPARING THE GROUND FOR DEVELOPMENT

no sense at all. Unicef Executive Director Carol Bellamy confirmed this in an interview with Feingold: *"It's completely natural that Unicef should be in de-mining"* – an endorsement for our audacity that filled my heart.

Small Targets featured at the signing ceremony of the Ottawa Treaty the following December, where 122 countries signed. Over 80% of all countries ratified it. Jody Williams and the International Coalition for the Banning of Landmines (ICBL) received the Nobel Peace prize that same year. Unfortunately the laying of landmines has not stopped[126].

Summer was now approaching fast and leaving for good was becoming a reality. The last days spent at any duty station are always rather emotional. I thought back on the years spent here, the highs and the lows; the people I had been close to and would probably never see again. My involvement with the "Road to Ottawa" had come to an end. Others would carry the torch in trying to rid this world of landmines once and for all.

Last impressions of Mozambique

Nacala was the last town on the coast I got to see. A stunningly beautiful bay, colours of the sea shifting from light green to grey to dark blue with the moving clouds and intermittent sun; simple coloured fishing boats coming ashore; two men carrying a heavyweight marlin across the beach, each one of them holding on either side, with the sheer weight slightly curving the spine of the fish. Our small Unicef group huddles with local authorities under a *paillotte*. I cannot resist leaving my place and walk slowly on to the beach. It is another way of saying my goodbyes. In less than two months I would be leaving Mozambique for good. And I keep wondering about the future of this beautiful but still so wounded country.

---

[126] On 17 September 2015, Mozambique was declared free of land mines after the last of some nearly 171,000 had been cleared over a 20-year period. That was considerably less than the number of 1–2 million estimated back in the 1990s.

Light rain begins to fall in the small stadium across from the *Feira Popular*. This was the old *Benfica* football club of Maputo, now called *Clube Desportivo*. René Boezaard's soccer boys had recently been integrated in the club. For the last time I see a match of theirs, this time in their new stadium. Boezaard is beaming with pride. After a long season of playing soccer, the field was more sand than grass. But that does not deter the "Boezaard Boys". Used to a sandy pitch as playing field at home, they play their hearts out until they only narrowly lose. But losing was not the issue. Soccer gave them recognition in other communities. In a land once freed of explosives, there was going to be hope for a better life.

At the last minute I decide to take Hamidou one more time to America. It would be sentimental to have him with us at the farm at this juncture to reminisce about our adventures of eight years in Côte d'Ivoire and Mozambique. He is not joining us for the third and last assignment in Africa, but going home to his family, who needs him badly. This was how I proposed the idea to him: *"Hamidou, tu m'avais demandé si je peux t'acheter un pair de chaussures en Amérique; je crois ça serait mieux si tu les achètes toi-même, qu'est ce que tu en penses?"* and his surprising, beautiful answer: *"Personne refuse d'aller en Amérique"*.

Chapter 11: Two pearls in the ocean

In the dark night of a new moon, the TAP plane took us low over the dark waters of the ocean towards São Tomé Island. On the approach only a couple of lights were visible belonging to vessels sitting offshore. Then in the far distance red dots of light serving as a beacon for planes appeared on a disproportionally big building: this was the nerve centre of the "Voice of America". VOA moved here in 1989 when civil war broke out in Liberia. The VOA site was a mysterious place. Its installations were mostly top secret. The Americans shied away from the expats at cafés and discos. Apart from radio broadcasting, the structure seemed to hide major listening capabilities in the sub-region and possibly beyond. It was an ugly reminder of America's omnipresence in the world that even a tiny island nation could not escape.

Now flying just a few metres above water, a runway sticking way out into the ocean appeared before our eyes. A driving rain was hitting the plane. In "making landfall", the pilot slammed hard on the brakes as if the runway was too short for this plane.

Walking some hundred metres to the small terminal, a warm tropical shower welcomed us. A Unicef driver was waiting for us at the conveyor belt. Inside it was a crowded affair. There must have been over a hundred people there who were waiting for consultants, colleagues or family. Airport staff had their hands full. Baggage handlers earned good money. Their load was voluminous because passengers brought extra stuff that was not readily available on the island, mainly clothes, electronics, food and drink.

In those days the plane arrived on Sundays. Hundreds of spectators were waiting outside for family and friends who had spent time in Portugal. For others it was just a weekend outing.[127] People were barbecuing on small, improvised fires. Most had come walking from town. It really looked like one big party. Enriched with these very first impressions of my new duty station, A. and I settled into Hotel Miramar, the best hotel in town. German manager Herr Manfred welcomed us. He gave me a personal safe at the desk that he let me keep all along my assignment at no cost. Miramar and its *Café Passante* on the oceanfront were to become my second home.

The first time I had heard of the name of São Tomé and Principe was in 1991 in Nairobi at the All Africa Representatives' meeting. I was checking out country nameplates and there it was. I asked the then Resident Project Officer where exactly São Tomé and Principe was located on the map of Africa. It is precisely 674 nautical miles to the north east of Angola. In those days São Tomé was a sub-office of Unicef Luanda for historical and political reasons. When Unicef Angola joined the Unicef East and Southern Africa Region, São Tomé and Principe moved with it. In terms of Unicef's way of organizing its regions, this was an anomaly that started me thinking. São Tomé and Angola were brothers in arms during the struggle for independence. They are part of the Lusophone group of countries in Africa that form a strong bond.

No one thought that I would accept the assignment. Surely they thought that I could do more for Unicef than running an office that was barely larger than the number of *empregados* I was going to hire at home. Some called it "following Mario Soares in exile".[128] But in fact the job came for me at the right time. I was rather exhausted from four years of constant travel in West and Central Africa and another four years in Mozambique that went

---

[127] When the weekly flight later changed to Thursday, the crowds were just as big as before.

[128] The socialist leader opposing the Salazar dictatorship was exiled to São Tomé and Principe from 1968 to 1970. He was subsequently exiled in France until his return to Portugal in 1974. Soares was President of Portugal from 1986 to 1996.

CHAPTER 11: TWO PEARLS IN THE OCEAN

through a tense post-conflict situation during my time. I could do with letting go off some steam, while at the same time quietly building a Unicef team that could handle a country programme the children of São Tomé and Principe deserved.

A not so glorious history

In fact I could not have been posted to a more beautiful country, although it has a rather depressing history, as we shall see. São Tomé and Principe is the second smallest country in Africa after the Seychelles. The islands are part of an inactive volcanic range in the Gulf of Guinea situated some 200 nautical miles off the north west coast of Gabon. The equator lies at the southern tip of São Tomé Island, and crosses over the tiny island of Rôlas. A favourite Sunday outing there is to swim across the equator, an exhilarating feeling I can attest! Rôlas was still a fishermen's place in my day – some 400 people lived there – but they were later chased off the island to make room for a Portuguese owned holiday resort.

From the 16th century onwards, under the whip of the Portuguese colonizer, slaves cleared whole tracts of tropical rainforest to make room for plantations. As such the *roça* remains a symbol of slavery to this very day. With a constant need for more labour, traders brought thousands of slaves from other Portuguese colonies, principally Cape Verde and Angola. By the mid-1500s the islands for a while became Africa's largest exporter of sugar, later replaced by coffee and cocoa for which the rich volcanic soils proved well suited. When slavery was abolished in 1876, forced labour took over until abolished at independence a century later. An international outcry of labour conditions and the beginning of a cocoa boycott led the colonisers to introduce a "token" wage. Forced migration and intermarriage led to a gradual loss of identity for Cape Verdians, Angolans and the local population. Even during my time, the elite still principally looked towards Angola, Cape Verde and Portugal and had little affinity with the Anglophone and Francophone countries on the African continent.

The *roças* opened up the islands' development through a network of railways, roads and ports, cutting through rocky summits and steep valleys. The islands have several micro climates. For example the climate and soil at *Monte Café* at 670m altitude was particularly well suited for the cultivation of Arabica coffee. One of the oldest plantations, it became the largest coffee producer of the two islands early on.[129] It was one of the tourist places to go to with friends from overseas. A tour of the facilities showed how coffee was cultivated, produced and stored. In 1908, São Tomé became briefly the world's largest producer of cocoa, still the country's most important crop. Sporadic labour unrest culminated in 1953 with an outbreak of riots in which several hundred workers were killed in a clash with their Portuguese rulers on São Tomé Island. The "Batepá Massacre" is commemorated every year.

Another large *roça* is *Agostinho Neto*. Founded in 1865 as *Rio do Ouro*, it was one of largest and most advanced plantation of the whole archipelago. At one time it had a population of around 2,500. After independence, it was renamed in memory of the Angola's first president for his support to São Tomé and Principe, not in the least for supplying oil at below market price. I vividly remember its grand entrance with some of its tall regal palm trees still standing. One could still see some tracks of the former railway that used to transport cacao and coffee to the coast through an inaccessible landscape, a distance of some 68 km. Finally realising that health of its workers was important, the Portuguese built a first-class hospital there in the 1920s. Even the urban elite of São Tomé town preferred to come here for treatment. In my time it was a rather pitiful sight to see. It was no longer a hospital, just empty space. The long hallways were completely deserted. Only a small health post remained. One is surrounded by curious, half-naked children. Many have blown-up bellies and discoloured hair, all signs of malnutrition. This was desperate poverty of the worst kind. But as a national monument to the country, the *Roça Agostinho Neto* is portrayed on the 5,000 Dobra note.

---

[129] *"Roças de São Tomé e Príncipe"*, Duarte Pape, Rodrigo Rebelo de Andrade, Revista Monumentos n.32, Décembre 2011.

CHAPTER 11: TWO PEARLS IN THE OCEAN

I loved the smaller *roças*. With the backdrop of mountains rising up behind, this made for an intimate feeling. They were almost like tiny hamlets, with pigs, chickens and *cabritos* roaming around in the wild. On walking trips it was always a surprise to suddenly come upon a clearing and admire these hidden treasures. Children would come running to you. There was *Bombaïm*, high up in the mountains towards Pico de São Tomé. *Vista Alegre* was a richer *dependencia* of the Roça *Santa Margarida*. In most *roças* living conditions in the barrack-style *dependencias* were appalling. Typically each family shared a single room of some 10m². Overcrowding must have been worse now than in the past when contract workers did not have their families with them. Kitchens were mostly outdoors and shared.[130]

Living conditions were not much different at *Roça Manuel Mora*: dilapidated houses overgrown with moss; pigs and chickens running around; and young girls doing the wash in the stream. Surrounded by canyons, it is stunningly beautiful, were it not for its extreme poverty. *Manuel Mora* lies on the way to the *Pico de Sao Tome*, at 2,000 metres the highest peak. Unicef driver Jorge and I went to pick up Nadim, who had just climbed the Pico with Sarah, a young British intern who worked at the EU office. Before arriving at *Manuel Mora,* one had to drive through a very narrow passage lined with steep rocks. Our driver Jorge recalled that slaves had to cut out the rocks by hand on both sides. Hundreds perished here under extremely harsh conditions. The short passage of just a few hundred metres took us half an hour to get through. Jorge always told me a lot about the history, he simply loved his country. He was one of the finest men I have come across in São Tomé. I greatly encouraged him to apply for the permanent post of UNDP driver of the UNDP and get on with his career. I was very sad to lose him, but happy for him.

Taking up my post

There was a long stretch of hallway before arriving at my office. The long wall had some poorly made posters on children. There

---

[130] CCA, Anthony Hodges for UN São Tomé, 1998.

was a badly framed Unicef mission statement of ten points – like the ten commandments – so as not to forget. On the way I peeked into a small "dishevelled" library that begged for a thorough revamping. I always attached great importance to Unicef libraries, no matter how small, where students could consult historic documents. I am happy to say that after Noemia's reorganisation, students of the *Lyceu* came to consult our documents. Over the years, Unicef field libraries went largely out of style and in the process many data of great historic value were lost worldwide. In some countries Unicef wisely transferred historic documents to universities.

My team was waiting in what was going to be my office for several years. The building was a monstrosity of modern red brick, not at all adapted to the sweet environment of the island. The building, going by the name of "United Nations House" was definitely oversized compared to the number of the agencies and their activities. Since 1995 Unicef was under one roof with the other UN agencies in São Tomé. Common premises were very much in vogue in those days. As to my office, the space looked more suitable for a Wall Street banker than for a Unicef head of office, to whom not even ten staff reported.

Marian Boonzaaijer as officer-in-charge did the hand-over.[131] Alberto Neto, the one and only national officer, was clearly the senior of the national team. The rest were general service (GS). After the introductions, we went around the table and looked at some of the current issues at hand. Alberto had invited regional Education adviser Ana Obura to come and assist in strengthening his programme. That impressed me. I already knew Ana from Nairobi and I had a high regard for her. She was instrumental in convincing Unicef of the stimulation aspects of the child-to-child approach in schools. The child-to-child approach was especially relevant in school health: children themselves play an important role in improving health and hygiene in schools and even in their

---

[131] Boonzaaijer was a Junior Professional Officer, funded by the Netherlands.

communities by bringing the message home.[132] Noemia Santos was programme assistant. Osvaldo, another programme assistant, ran the health programme. Manuel Pontifice was a finance assistant without an operations officer.

After this initial briefing, driver Diamantino gave A. and me a tour of São Tomé and its outlying villages. The first thing I noticed were these old colonial houses, many rather dilapidated and crying for restoration. There was one on the marginal that had an impressive, round window. Nadim later wished to restore that peculiar house to its old beauty. Many were shop houses, with families living upstairs. We saw one rather big shop house that sold kitchen stuff, appliances, and so on. There was an outdoor staircase leading to the offices where one could write a US cheque and get cash Dobras in return. That shop house became my "bank". We saw the covered market, which had abundant fruits, vegetables, pork and fish. Pork was about the only meat available. Arriving at the port my maritime fantasies started to flow. There were three small vessels waiting to be unloaded. I thought of the book *Cargo ship Travel* by Hugo Verlomme, a French novelist who travelled extensively on liners and cargo vessels. It was a most appropriate gift from Nadim before I left for my new duty station. I was now bent on checking out vessels that were going to call on São Tomé.

One of my first actions was to thoroughly improve the office environment. Most of it was very basic. For example I had a big blackboard made in Libreville to track field trips, flight arrivals and departures and the name of the driver. There were also decorative considerations. One afternoon while rearranging the library with Noemia I hit upon seven large colour reproductions of old and very detailed Portuguese maps of São Tomé and Principe. I felt like a stone mason finding a treasure behind a wall. Miraculously the maps had survived the onslaught of documents and books leaning

---

[132] The *Dokter* programme in Indonesia was a good example of the child to child approach.

against them. I took them to the US during home leave, returned them framed and hung them in the hallway side by side. Each one was stunningly beautiful.

None of my predecessors had ever taken the trouble to take the team away from the office. Early on I organised a two-day office retreat at Santana Beach Resort. In a relaxed setting we discussed current issues at hand and perspectives. We stayed overnight in individual cabins. We had a fabulous lobster dinner. I think the retreat achieved the essential thing: It set the tone for working together in a more relaxed, and yet professional way.

Finding a good house was of course high priority. The head of the national oil company, José Barbosa, was looking for someone to rent his just completed house. It was on a hill with a bird's eye view of the ocean. Barbosa's was a clean and comfortable two-bedroom bungalow with a decent bathroom and a large kitchen. An L-shaped balcony lined the side of the house. I made it a habit to rise early and read documents there while having a leisurely breakfast on papaya and mango. There were many houses under construction at *Campo do Milho* and some had been abandoned for lack of money. The uncompleted house of our absentee neighbour had turned into a ruin overgrown with shrubs and weeds, a landmark for the most colourful birds.

The garden was virgin territory for A. It had to be planted from scratch. If you wanted to make a garden, you would look for somebody like Duki. Duki had initiative, drive and energy to burn. He planted bougainvillea and hibiscus; grew shrubs and trees from twigs cut at friends' houses and nursed them in plastic bags until ready for planting. The islands are a paradise for bird-watchers and our garden was no exception. In the springtime small brownish birds descended on the trees with the yellow flowers, making hanging nests. They would enter through a hole underneath to feed the little ones. The ultimate chance was to spot the grey parrot with its red tail in the wild. These birds were poached illegally for the pet trade, making them vulnerable to

CHAPTER 11: TWO PEARLS IN THE OCEAN

becoming extinct. I for one only "spotted" them at the market or at someone's home.

One day Duki asked me if I could help him get his driver's licence. He passed the exam in no time at all. Then he left for Portugal and never came back. Given the chance many young São Toméans left for good, while keeping preparations for their departure a deep secret. When I learned of his disappearance I smiled. At least Duki came to Lisbon with a driver's licence in his pocket. So he was much more valuable now. Then we got his brother Zé to replace him.

Safety is a constant concern at any duty station. Once there was a serious breach of security at my house. I had two excellent guards; at least that was what I thought. Idalécio and Danilo were in their late twenties, charming guys. They were strong. They alternated their days and came on duty from 6 pm to 6 am. Both loved football and played it too. I often invited them to watch an important match. Danilo knew much about strategy and could predict to whom the ball would be passed next; like someone telling you a film before it happens. Sometimes that took the fun out of it, but I admired him for it anyway.

One day Zé tipped me off that both had a habit of going home at around two o'clock in the morning. Zé felt an obligation to tell me for security's sake. So one night at the proposed hour my alarm clock went off. It was definitely an eerie feeling: under a full moon I searched with a flashlight around the house in that ghost neighbourhood of unfinished houses on *Campo do Milho*. No one. I had literally caught my guard off guard! The next night I did the same, and again no one around. Then I fired both of them on the spot. Inside I felt very sorry, because I liked them very much. Danilo was rounded up three weeks later by an army patrol looking for fit young men to enlist in the 300 man-strong army. I must say the army had made an excellent catch, because Danilo was very strong indeed.

I was asking around to replace them. Someone recommended the guard of the European Union representative. Neil Crumbie had just retired. I was told beforehand that there was only one problem, Fernando was afflicted by polio and could only walk on one leg. I said, if he worked for the EU, he could certainly work for me. When Fernando came for the interview he sustained himself on a rather long cane with a curved handle. I asked if he knew of a second guard, and he proposed to do the job alone for double the money; and he would come every day. I immediately accepted. Fernando was unbelievable. He usually came well before 6 pm. At night you could hear the ticking of his cane on the pavement. One did not need to check if he was there or not: he never missed a beat. He used his cane to scale the wall, preferring to enter that way rather than using the main gate.

First encounter with the Island of Principe

Field trips of course brought Unicef staff and government in touch with reality on the ground. They are essential in planning the country programme. In the United Nations jargon "going to the field" or making a "field trip" meant going to the districts and see projects and assess the situation from up close. São Tomé and Principe was still a very rural country in my day and as such one had the feeling to be permanently "in the field". Where could one see pigs roaming around freely on the beach?

From day one, the Island of Principe held a special fascination for me. I was keen to "make landfall" there as soon as possible. Our Health Programme Assistant Osvaldo took me there. I thought it was important that A. could familiarise herself with the second "Pearl in the ocean" early on, so she came along.

At that time Air São Tomé and Príncipe operated a Twin Otter plane, its one and only aircraft, flown by Portuguese pilots. It served the two islands and neighbouring Gabon. Coming into Principe the plane flew low with mountains close to the left and the right, until we reached a clearing on a plateau and landed safely. Fascinating as it was, it looked scary enough. Portuguese pilots rotated from Portugal to fly the plane and routinely trained new arrivals who would be on duty the following three months.

CHAPTER 11: TWO PEARLS IN THE OCEAN

Incidentally, these pilots did a brisk business in buying cases of whisky at the duty free shop at Leon Mba Airport and selling them at a handsome profit in São Tome town. This sometimes resulted in serious delays. Meanwhile we passengers waited restlessly in the terminal while the crew was doing their leisurely shopping. On those days the aisle would be packed with lots of cases stacked up on one another, a total hazard in case of an emergency.[133]

Not even a thousand people lived on Principe Island. Buildings were half in ruins with pinkish or yellowish colours covered by moist and moss. The hospital in Santo António was poorly equipped. There was a constant shortage of drugs and vaccines. In the maternity ward pregnant women about to deliver sat on metal beds with makeshift mattresses. Patients were supposed to bring their own. Mattresses belonging to the hospital had been stolen long ago.

At the hottest time of the day we drove a bit of a distance to visit a *roça*. At the foot of a short but steep hill our driver stopped, could not go any further and would wait for us there. After 30 minutes or so of climbing over rocks we reached a tucked away settlement. The health post was dilapidated, dirty and without drugs. If there had been something resembling a crèche or a classroom I do not remember it.

At the end of the first day Osvaldo took us to a lookout where one had a steep view on *Praia Banana*, so named because of its shape and yellowish colour of the sands. One had to walk through a palm forest before getting to the beach. We held our heads with both hands, as it was the season for coconuts to drop. One would definitely not survive a hit. At around that time a Dutch couple were staying with us, they were train drivers who had been camping just days before on this very beach. They told us stories of the life of a train driver, not as glamorous as it seems. Seeing

---

[133] The plane crashed in 2006 on a training flight of the coast of São Tomé near Ana Chaves killing all four on board; the airline subsequently folded.

accidents and suicides on the rails cause severe traumatic stress. While swimming, their tent was robbed of literally everything, camera, money, credit cards and all. So we invited them to stay with us until their holidays were over.

Running the country programme

The Country Programme of Cooperation I inherited was of course tiny in comparison to what I was used to. But that was not an issue for me. In effect, as we had no project officers other than in education, I was fully involved in all aspects of programme implementation and I was thus, in addition to my representational duties, fully occupied. The problem lay in the very limited capacities of the Unicef office. In 1993 the programme budget ceiling "ballooned" to three quarters of a million dollars for which the then two-man office was ill equipped. The first national officer post (for education) was not created until 1997, the year I came on board. In spite of a weak staffing structure the country programme comprised all traditional programmes of Unicef, including information and communication. Meanwhile, before my time, only general service staff were added, and they were mostly on temporary contracts.

A Unicef supported country programme is anchored in a Basic Service Agreement with the government that spells out responsibilities of the two partners. The programme is planned and implemented jointly with the government, our principal partner. Unless the country is in a state of emergency such as a civil war, planning is done on a five-year basis to coincide with medium term cycle of the government. The United Nations agencies on the ground harmonise programme cycles so as to arrive at one UN development framework. Besides Unicef, only UNDP, WHO and the World Food Programme (WFP) were on the ground in São Tomé. UNFPA was represented by UNDP.

Under the health programme Unicef supplied essential drugs and vaccines to the government. In 1998, 60% of all children under five had been immunised against the six contagious diseases, such as polio, measles, whooping cough, diphtheria and others.

CHAPTER 11: TWO PEARLS IN THE OCEAN

In collaboration with *Nueva Fronteira*, an Italian NGO from Milan, Unicef supported training of community health workers and social mobilisation. A national NGO, Zatona-Adil, an offshoot of World Vision, also came on board for the effort. So did Cruz Vermelha with health and hygiene education. Community health became the watchword for accelerating health care through establishment of health posts equipped with basic drugs and staffed with a community health worker through a financial cost sharing scheme and supported by a local health committee. The problem was that stock-outs were common and of course poor people could not pay.

At the ministry I worked well with National Director Dr Lima. He was a very engaged man who wanted to do far more than he could, given the limited capacities of the government. I enjoyed the field visits with him and learned much from him over time over time. On the 24th of December 1998 he dropped by the house for a drink, Dr Lima was building a house near us and he had been checking out progress on the site that afternoon. He told me that he had just been appointed that same afternoon Minister of Health in the new cabinet of Prime Minister Guilherme Posser da Costa. I was very pleased for him, but also for Unicef. Our drink reinforced an already excellent relationship between the minister and myself. I switched to calling him *"Excellencia"* and the new minister continued with addressing me as *"Señor Representante"*. We found this both perfectly normal.

One day Dr Lima invited me to come and visit the training centre for female nurses in São Tomé town. The institution was trying to survive on a skimpy budget and he was eager to maintain and revive it. But the ministry had no budget to hire them after graduation. Even the next graduating class could not be hired. I then did something that was a no-no in Unicef. I signed an agreement with the Ministry of Health: the government would continue to be responsible for the training; and upon graduation, Unicef would pay newly graduates their salaries for three years. After that the government would hire them.

Early on I was focused on "professionalising" the Unicef country programme exercise. I instituted internal reviews of programme implementation; these were periodically reviewed with government and other partners; and at the end of each year we pulled this together in an end-of-year review with all stakeholders present. Unicef was also instrumental in pushing for a Common Country Analysis of the UN country team. We contracted international consultant Tony Hodges[134], whom I had met in Luanda where he had authored the Unicef Situation Analysis.

Unicef and the Government conducted the first ever Mid-Term Review, a routine exercise in most countries. The venue was the *Palacio dos Congressos*, a Marxist style building constructed by the Chinese in the 1980s[135]. Gabriel Pereira came from Maputo to assist with the exercise. It was an inspiring exercise for everyone. Mid-Term Reviews are a one-time-only opportunity to review lessons learned and make mid-way corrections for the remaining years in the programme cycle. Our MTR recommended to extend community health to half of the population through training community health workers and provision of the most essential drugs; to advance education for girls through 6th grade; and to formulate a project for children who are not in school and get them back on track specifically through accelerated education and vocational training; with clean drinking water sources getting scarce as a result of a fast growing population, protection of water sources and improving hygiene in the *roças* was crucial to fight malaria, the prime killer disease.

Gabriel's presence greatly enhanced Unicef's professional standing in the country. He was often invited to dinner by government colleagues eager to get news about Mozambique. He got an invitation to the Independence Day festivities in his own right. I still see us sitting together on the reviewing stand, watching the colourful

---

[134] Hodges, Anthony Common Country Analysis São Tomé and Principe
[135] Naturally at that time the marxist government of Pinta da Costa maintained diplomatic relations with communist China; with a new political wind blowing in the 1990s, Taiwan opened an embassy instead.

parade of associations of women and proud inhabitants of the *roças*. Everyone greeted Gabriel as if he had been longer in São Tomé than me. He loved his charming hotel *"Residencia Avenida"*. We often had lunch there – a mix of simple Portuguese and Santomean food – to prepare for the afternoon sessions.

One evening I arranged a dinner with Minister of Health Dr Lima and Gabriel. I also invited the interim director of the *Instituto Camões*, a young woman who had come from Lisbon to get the Institute up and running. The Portuguese Prime Minister, António Gutteres, had opened this Portuguese Cultural Centre just a few months before. I remember him as a friendly-looking man in his late forties with a quiet disposition. Sipping afterwards a *Laurentina*[136] on the Marginal with Gabriel, we heard on BBC World Service that John F. Kennedy Junior's plane had crashed off the Connecticut coast. I just I stared for a brief moment at the dark, threatening waters of that same Atlantic Ocean where he had perished just hours before, thousands of miles North West from here.

The state of children in São Tomé
Not long before independence the Portuguese had practically eliminated malaria. They were keen on cleaning up the environment, a major factor in malaria control. They would fine people in São Tomé town who were found to have stagnant water around. Banana trees, which hold stagnant water in their big leaves, were banned in urban areas. But discipline waned with independence and sanitary conditions in overcrowded *bairros* worsened fast. And so malaria returned with a vengeance. To make matters worse, the comprehensive malaria control programme supported by the World Bank in the early 1990s failed miserably: swamps were drained to kill the vectors but the mosquitoes simply moved elsewhere; indoor DDT spraying could not be sustained; and bed nets became a monofocal supply approach without the essential support of social marketing.

---

[136] The excellent local brew.

Italy was funding a research project to study behaviour of mosquitoes. When I visited the project, two Italians were dissecting mosquitoes and looking for clues. I could not help laughing when he demonstrated the technique of catching them with a net on a long pole like *Mijnheer Prikkebeen* in the Swiss children's story[137] and put them in a jar. One of them would sit for hours with one leg exposed. He was looking to find the percentage of mosquitoes that were carrying the vector causing malaria. I believe it was one in three. He noted what time of the day they would try to bite him most. On another score, the "Roll Back Malaria" public-private partnership, an initiative by WHO and Unicef taken in 1999, did much to reduce the incidence of malaria-related mortality and morbidity in sub-Saharan Africa. São Tomé and Principe was no exception.

Diarrhoea and acute respiratory infections occurred frequently in children. It was about strengthening prevention and control measures such as these, but also about catching the symptoms of disease and malnutrition early at an early stage. Parents were mobilised in community sessions to improve care at home based on simple practices, such as hand washing with soap, exclusive breastfeeding for six months, making children sleep under a bed net and administering oral rehydration salts to fight diarrhoea. Tiziano Pisoni's *Nueva Fronteira* and the national NGO *Zatona-Adil* were instrumental in what Unicef called "social mobilisation".

São Tomé e Principe was one of the countries selected to be part of a global study on micronutrient deficiency funded by the Netherlands. Several African and Asian countries had already been selected. For sure, I had a hand in getting São Tomé in, knowing that this would

---

[137] *Mijnheer Prikkebeen* is a famous 19th century adventure story for Dutch children. It is based on a Swiss story by Swiss Rodophe Töpffer, (1799–1846), and was reworked by Dutchman Johan Gouverneur. It is considered the first comic strip anywhere. Prikkebeen means "thin-legged" ("spillenbeen" is another word for it in Dutch). His favorite pastime is catching butterflies for his impressive collection with a net on a long stick; in 1943 my father, Ben Mohr, well known for his graphic designs, reworked the Töpffer illustrations for the Dutch edition of 1943, published by Ad Donker of Rotterdam.

lead to greater visibility and donor funding for this little known country. Besides, a study of this kind was long overdue here. The global study focused on anaemia, Vitamin A and Iodine Deficiency, all major problems here.

Anaemia still is an important nutritional disorder worldwide. If that situation could not be reversed in São Tomé and Principe, it would lead to a permanent decline in productivity and family incomes, and that would significantly increase poverty. Anaemia deficiency was most alarming in the *roças* where poverty was chronic. It affected children and pregnant women alike. Nine out of ten women were found to have anaemia. It is a major cause of contracting malaria; and often leads to low weight for new-borns. Both phenomena were on the rise. In São Tomé half the population suffered from iodine deficiency. Unicef promoted legislation that only iodised salt could be imported. The research team encountered many large families, with eight to ten people living under one roof. Food security was fragile on the islands. Local foodstuffs such as manioc and *fruta de pão* were not enough to feed the population. The country relied heavily on imports of rice, beans, sugar, cornflower and wheat. But poor people could simply not afford it. Stunting was rising dramatically: one third of children under five were found to be of low height for their age.

Cycles of most primary schools in rural areas stopped at fourth grade. Girls then dropped out far more than boys. To go to a full cycle primary school would require very long walks every day, making them vulnerable to harassment and worse. Adolescent girls were often needed at home. Following a study on the situation of girls' education, the government and Unicef prepared a donor proposal for a comprehensive education project for girls to achieve 6th grade. Being a small island nation I thought early on that São Tomé could be attractive to donors, especially to some of our smaller National Committees. But I thought it was not useful to submit any half-baked proposals until the quality of our projects would improve. And this seemed to be the case now. We now had a strong tandem in two national officers (NO- level C), Idalécio Neves in Health and Alberto Neto in Education.

Unicef supported construction of fifth and sixth grade classrooms in faraway Porto Allegre. There were other ways to keep girls in school, such as improving access to school supplies and facilitating latrines especially for them. Prolonged teacher strikes plagued the sector, simply because teachers were not paid for long periods of time. As they were powerless, many teachers quit to look for money elsewhere. Half of the teachers had no training to be one. *Roças* closed schools as teachers quit. The adult literacy programme collapsed. On the Island of Principe, Unicef started experimental vegetable gardens at schools.

Another important study looked at the problem of child labour. It was carried out with the International Labour Organisation under the leadership of Alda Bandeira, a former Minister of Foreign Affairs. Child labour was a growing phenomenon in São Tomé. Boys as young as ten cut stones for construction; were apprentice as metal workers and car mechanics; and did heavy labour on the plantations. These activities were all considered hazardous and were targeted for elimination by an ILO Convention. I remember that researchers ran into a wall in an attempt to extract information from employers who hired them as apprentices at minimal or no pay at all. These learning periods could last a long time and sometimes began to suspiciously resemble a form of forced labour. Girls worked in households for long hours and were vulnerable in other ways. Many of them were school dropouts or simply had never seen the inside of a classroom. Other surveys revealed that in spite of being endowed with abundant water sources, water quality was rapidly deteriorating. Only about a quarter of the population lived under more or less acceptable conditions of hygiene.

A national umbrella organisation of civil society organisations in the making

Implementation of Unicef activities is not possible without the involvement of national and international NGOs, in particular in community development. Choosing "strategic" partnerships is essential. NGOs and youth associations look to Unicef as the lead agency for children. In São Tomé we were lucky to partner with

CHAPTER 11: TWO PEARLS IN THE OCEAN

Nueva Frontiera and *Zatona-Adil* in rural community development. We supported sports activities of a youth association on the island of Principe. With the *Associaçao dos Deficientes* we focused on vocational training for girls with deficiencies, such as tailoring. My guard Fernando was its treasurer. At the end of my assignment, the director of the Association made me an honorary member of his organisation.

In my day, national non-governmental organisations and associations were mostly weak in Africa. Truly independent they were not. Their leaders often came from government. Unicef tried to support local NGOs that had a proven track record in implementing viable projects. This way they would be capable to help implement Unicef activities, especially those that had a focus on community development and participation. The international NGOs on the ground had a much stronger resource base and thus had a more independent voice. But I knew of a way that could make São Toméan civil society stronger; and just weeks before my assignment was coming to an end, I moved on it.

I organised a seminar with the objective of launching a national umbrella organisation of NGOs just as I had tried in Nampula before. The UN conference room was packed with government, NGOs and the international donor community. In my presentation I mentioned that Mozambique and the Gambia already had such an umbrella organisation that could well inspire us. Under the leadership of an executive director the network would represent its members in advocacy with the government, for example in pro-poor, pro-child budgeting; act as a clearing house for sharing information on matters of common interest; promote joint projects; promote a "buddy" or adoption system for stronger NGOs to partner with weaker ones; and promote and help organise mergers of small NGOs. The umbrella organisation might do much to alleviate suspicion between government and civil society; with growing democracy there was now more chance to achieve this; and that might one day lead to a new form of *contrato social* between government and civil society to accelerate development for children and women. An animated discussion followed and the proposal was adopted by acclamation. Not long after I had left, I learned that the framework had indeed gotten off the ground with multi-year funding from USAID.

"Taking São Tomé and Principe under my arm and going west"

During my first year, ideas had begun to get into my head where São Tomé should be in Unicef's organisation in Africa. Being part of Nairobi Regional Office made no sense at all. It all began with a mission to our area office in Luanda. Surely there were historical ties between São Tomé and Angola, but that was not sufficient reason to have a Unicef link between the two countries. Besides, Angola was torn apart by an endless civil war. Our colleagues in Luanda lived in some type of fortress with a very high level of insecurity. They had their hands full with the emergency. As a result São Tomé could not expect to receive support missions from there, whereas the whole idea was to empower our isolated colleagues in São Tomé in programme and operations.

Clearly the island nation would be much better off strengthening links with Unicef country offices in West and Central Africa. In fact, back in 1984 when Unicef established a liaison office, São Tomé was overseen from an Area Office in Brazzaville. When Luanda became a full representative office in 1985, São Tomé was attached as a sub-office. Returning São Tomé and Principe to the region where it had come from was therefore not at all a far-fetched idea.

My chance came on a Sunday in November 1998 in Nairobi. On the sidelines of the Regional Management Team meeting, the executive director met with all representatives one on one. On that Sunday it was my turn to meet her. Just before going in, I paced room 331 at the Serena Hotel looking at my three-page proposal one more time. This was the first time I would meet Carol Bellamy in person.

CHAPTER 11: TWO PEARLS IN THE OCEAN

She opened the door of her suite and said, "Hi Boudewijn, raise any subject you want to raise". She pronounces my first name – constantly massacred in spelling and speech all along my career – surprisingly correctly. I said I had come with a proposal to regroup some small countries in West Africa to make for better programme implementation and management. I initially foresaw a grouping of Cameroon, Gabon, Equatorial Guinea and São Tomé and Principe. These countries could mutually strengthen their capacities in the exchange of programme planning and operations experts. Like the other three countries São Tomé should come under the umbrella of the West and Central Africa region, even if this meant delinking it from Angola. Bellamy was looking for fresh ideas to streamline Unicef and she encouraged me that I should further review with the regional office in Nairobi the practicability of this idea. Although the issue was not on the agenda of this meeting, I informally launched my lobbying the same evening at a buffet dinner for all representatives at the residence of the regional director Urban Jonsson. I vividly remember his mother, who was in her late eighties. I spent almost all my time that evening with her, fascinated as I was by her depth of thought.

My proposal was approved a few months later at the Nairobi representatives meeting in March 1999. Regional director Urban Jonsson reacted rather curtly in plenary. Using few words he said something like, "Boudewijn will take São Tomé under his arm tomorrow to Abidjan. Of course Rima will still have to agree to this." From then on things moved fast.

I still remember "crashing" the meeting of representatives in Abidjan barely a few days later. I saw many familiar faces. Rima Salah had just arrived to take up her post of regional director. Jean Dricot whom I knew from my orientation trip to Vietnam in 1986 had just been appointed regional planning officer. Hervé Peries had come over from Nouakchott; and deputy regional director Martin Mogwanja was waiting for his agrément in Kinshasa. In some ways I had come "home". Rima was enthusiastic and would go for the necessary approvals from Headquarters. São Tomé would initially report directly to the regional director as a country office in its own right until a possible grouping of small country offices in the Gulf of Guinea had been created.

In July the regional director asked me to become the regional focal point for the task force on small country offices (SCO) with the mandate to study the situation of six small country offices in the region: Cape Verde, Gambia, Guinea Bissau in West Africa and Equatorial Guinea, Gabon and São Tomé and Principe in Central Africa. I gladly accepted the assignment. It was the beginning of a renewed but different involvement with the West and Central Africa Region: as special adviser and resource person to the regional director.

Reform of the United Nations in the field locations

Incoming Secretary-General Kofi Anan had placed reform of the United Nations high on the agenda. In the spirit of creating one United Nations team in field locations, the UN agencies met routinely and often. Joint programming and common services between agencies became "en vogue" but the effort did not succeed. Sometimes a post would be shared, such as the one created for information and communication in São Tomé. The cost of common premises was a constant concern. Running costs of the building spiralled out of whack. The joint internet connection organised by UNDP for the agencies functioned poorly. In the end I called Chris Larsson of IT in New York to help me install our own cable system. He came, saw and conquered. He ordered a whole new system from Copenhagen for Unicef alone, with which we could upgrade. He hired a São Toméan, Aguinaldo Salvaterra, whom he trained to do the cabling. It was low-cost and super efficient for its time. In fact the other agencies were rather envious of it. Salva became a good friend of the family. He later obtained a long-term local contract with the Swedish Internet provider Bahnhof to find customers for the "st" (short for São Tomé) domain that Bahnhof had acquired.

In several ways the collaboration with the sister agencies worked well. Cécile Molinier was an active coordinator of the team. She was open for ideas. The UN team developed terms of reference for an international consultant to develop a UN website for São Tomé. As the Internet was still very new, Cecile asked me if Nadim would be available to construct the UN site. The year before Nadim had trained journalists at Radio Nacional in Internet news-gathering. It had been fun to drive to work together in the black and red Suzuki that he had rented for his stay. I looked forward to doing that again.

Nadim did the website layout for the UN country team. Each agency supplied photos and text. I supplied him with text for the Unicef site. It had pages on São Tomé's history, the Unicef team and the country programme of cooperation; and a page called "Perspectives" that was in effect a prognosis of future plans and strategies. For example we projected to create with the government a National Commission for Children and Youth that should be the protector of children's rights. Another one was called "Newsreel", an original name given by Nadim for a page where journalists would contribute feature articles paid for by Unicef. We commissioned the first two articles to Ambrósio Quaresma, an excellent journalist, who was suffering professionally and financially because of his opposition to the government. I specifically liked his concise feature article on child labour that was becoming a widespread problem. Our São Tomé website was among the first of Unicef country offices in Africa.

Partnering with the media

Like in most African countries, Radio Nacional and TVS news were principally a mouthpiece for government and donors; and were therefore predictably monotonous and boring. One young woman ran a TV programme for children and wished to link up with Unicef. I thought the programme lacked spark. It consisted mostly of amateurish singing, dancing and winning prizes. I suggested doing a weekly educational feature, people who might have made something interesting, or could tell something about the history of São Tomé. I gave the example of a daily five-minute clip aired just before the CBS evening news with Walter Cronkite.

It was called *On the Road with Charles Kuralt*. Kuralt was a round and easy-going American in his fifties, who interviewed special characters doing extraordinary things in remote places in America that no one had ever heard of. It gave children and their parents dreams, ideas and it challenged them. Short but sweet. São Tomé surely had original talents hidden somewhere; and I offered to fund this through our education programme. But the woman showed no interest, preferring to continue the easy way. *Leve-leve* as the São Toméans call it, "take it easy".

In terms of national news, not much was happening in São Tomé. Up until 1985 there were newsletters appearing with some regularity on walls, tracts as we might call them. There was no daily newspaper, so the population relied on radio and TV. *Noticias São Tomé e Príncipe* had been founded as a weekly reaching a circulation of 900 by 1995. The UN team began to publish a UN newsletter. People who could read had nothing or next to nothing to read on a daily basis. The Island of Principe had even less access to reading material. All hope was now vested in gaining access to Internet.

Gigi of TVS was one of two presenters of the *telejornal*. That Sunday I thought I had a scoop for his evening news. It happened like this. At breakfast on the back balcony I noticed parachutists being dropped over the airport. I jumped in the Toyota Landcruiser to watch them come down. It turned out to be a simple training exercise. A young man came to me and pointed out a white unmarked plane. He said that the plane had landed at 2 in the morning and had hit one of the two switched off floodlights that then crashed down on its left wing. It was totally bent. Glass everywhere. So the pilot had miscalculated the distance of the floodlight pole! The plane looked like a total loss. It might soon be rusting into oblivion in the adjacent field of the old Biafra propeller driven cargo Constellations, the last of its kind before the jet age[138]. This was then one of the mysterious planes I had heard so

---

[138] These Canadian cargo planes had been diverted in 1968 to São Tomé during the Biafra war; Portugal never returned them. Meanwhile the salty air had destroyed them.

much about. Such planes would land at the darkened airport when ground personnel had long left for home. On the way back I stopped for coffee and croissants at *Passante*. Gigi at the wheel of the TVS Suzuki raced by and I waved him to stop. I said, "Go to the airport, there's a story for you." Without further ado, they sped off. Mysteriously, the event was the great, absent item of the evening news.

Another major news item was the theft of Unicef essential drugs at the port. I was appalled that anyone would rob the poor people of the *roças* of essential drugs. Would I please come to the TV station? Gigi would like to interview me on this. I was all fired up to vent my anger and showed it too. Of course the drugs were never found.

School trips to Unicef

Education in the formal schools could be very boring for children. It was mostly about reading, writing and maths. To give them some good time and learn in a different way, we began to organise school trips to Unicef. These visits are among my best memories. My team loved every minute of it. TVS came to cover it. At one time we invited the primary school of Porto Allegre, a town on the southern tip of the island. We were building fifth and sixth grade classrooms there. Unicef had chartered a bus to fetch them. Most of the 30 children or so, between eight and twelve years old, had never been to São Tomé town, which was just 30 km away. Although the road had been partially resurfaced, whole stretches were still very bad. It took the bus close to an hour and a half to make the journey.

The children are excited when they arrive with their chaperons at around nine o'clock in the morning, no doubt after a fascinating and noisy bus ride. They are received with a snack and a *sumo de laranja*. This way they quickly feel at ease. We divide the group in two. Fifteen come to my office and sit at the big round table. My session is on the history and activities of Unicef, I try to explain that in the simplest of terms. The children listen attentively. I keep it short and then some ask questions. That day it is the turn of

Alberto to talk about Unicef and education. Another day it will be Idalécio talking about Unicef and health and nutrition. After half an hour my group trots off to Alberto's office; and his group files into my office.

After the sessions we invite the children to sit on the floor in a semi-circle. It so happens that we have just received the Portuguese version of *"Sara"*, an animated cartoon film series under the Sara Communication Initiative sponsored by Unicef in East Africa. The series originated in South Asia with the girl Meena after whom Sara was modelled. The stories promote child rights, in particular girls' education. Constraints such as early marriage and girls' domestic workload are skilfully mixed in with the exploits of Sara and her friends. In addition to the radio series, the initiative developed animated films, comic books and audiocassettes. This instalment is about Sara who wants to go to school, is enrolled but later taken out of school by her father to help with household chores. The video has a lot of lightness in this otherwise serious issue. I can still hear the laughs and giggles of these children. But they really explode with joy when we hand out copies of the comic book relating the same story they have just watched.

At the end I have one more surprise in store for them: a tour in their bus through São Tomé. I happily join in this outing. We go all over town to show them the places of interest. I keep the presidential palace to the last. They stand at the low wall staring at the pink colonial building. I explain that this is the nerve centre, the "seat of power" of their country. A couple of boys are ready to climb over the wall. From there the bus returns to Porto Allegre. Never will I forget the waving of some sixty hands of children who might forever remember this day, each one of them in their own way.

Life on the waves
No story about São Tomé and Principe is complete without one's own personal story of "life on the waves". Daydreaming about cargo ship travel as a passenger, I kept looking at ships that were waiting offshore to unload merchandise. The port was way too

CHAPTER 11: TWO PEARLS IN THE OCEAN

small for big vessels. One day I got word from customs that I could visit a ship that was registered under the Liberian flag and had a Ukrainian crew. I took A. along with me. We had to hurry as the vessel was sailing for Lisbon after midnight. The problem was that same evening we had a dinner engagement at the UNDP residence with Cecile Molinier, the resident representative. It was of the essence to be back in time. After informing Nadim who happened to be in town, we sped off in a tugboat. When reaching the huge freighter I climbed the long rope ladder first, to show A. that there was no danger. But the dark waters looked menacing enough. I came up on deck and waited anxiously for her. Suddenly I saw two hands appear above the railing. Other hands grabbed her and then she, in her long skirt, proudly walked on to the deck. The captain, quite under the weather already, invited us to join him at the captain's table for vodka and salami. Here is how Nadim tells it in a letter to a friend dated 17 April 1998:

"Interesting things have been happening here, Annette and Boudewijn almost being kidnapped by a Ukrainian ship. Boudewijn was attempting to feed his love of ships and decided to board a cargo ship that is lying offshore here. I was to join but due to a previous engagement I decided there was not enough time; and what a good decision that was. The captain was a rough Ukrainian, the ex-Soviet type, who seemed to have trouble keeping his shirt closed. They were to leave after fifteen minutes to a dinner at the UNDP res rep's house. Fortunately I got there early to explain over a beer that Annette and Boudewijn may be a little tardy. No one realised how tardy they actually would be. The only people onshore who had any idea that something was wrong were the dinner guests.

"My parents sat at this time at the captain's table sipping vodka and eating rolled up salami. By that time I had moved from the bar to the French restaurant conversing with my dinner guests. We had no clue that the couple were still stranded on the boat out there on the sea. At about half past eleven I arrived home and commented to the guard how funny it was that the youngest

person in the house should be the first to arrive home. Meanwhile the jolly Ukrainian captain assured that they were doing everything to get the tug boat back, heaping much blame on the Santomean people for being incompetent... In reality however, the tugboat had already returned a few times. Finally Boudewijn lost his patience and walked with Annette on deck. The tugboat was there. The captain's hopes to take them to Portugal were dashed. Annette and Boudewijn returned home at around the hour of 1 am. Awaking them this morning and asking them how the dinner was, neither of them could hold a straight face or hide their enthusiasm to tell the tale of being taken hostage by a Ukrainian ship".

I lived quite a few other stories about ships that called on São Tomé. One Saturday a cruise ship had dropped anchor at large. Rumour had it that many passengers would come and visit for a few hours. A sudden frenzy spread far and wide. Taxicabs were waiting in line; people were standing at the oceanfront, waiting for small motorboats to make it to the harbour. Suddenly hundreds of Germans flooded the capital. German became the language of choice. There must have been some three hundred Germans at least. One couple was asking us for directions. I offered to give them a tour and they gladly accepted. I hailed a very old and rusty cab. In fact I had never taken a taxi in São Tomé town. Our cab was filthy with holes in the floor; seats totally worn; windows stuck and so on. We toured a good part of the town and beyond. We had a coffee with them in *Passante* of course. And they loved it all. Meanwhile the shopkeepers, moneychangers and cafés made good money and taxis had plenty of rides, a boon for the weekend. It was the first and also the last time that I saw a cruise ship making landfall in São Tomé.

Another time, a Dutch friend called me from Amsterdam saying that one of his *bootjes* was on the way to São Tomé. Harry Heyst knew very well of my interest in cargo ship travel. One morning the agent called me. The captain had invited us to lunch that day. I dropped everything, invited A. to join me and she eagerly accepted, the Ukrainian adventure notwithstanding. This *bootje* was a small cargo ship and had seven passenger cabins. The captain was a friendly man of about 60, his round face reminded me of my father. He showed us a cabin that looked roomy and comfortable. Over lunch on some Dutch *broodjes* and a few *Grolsch* beers, I said I was retiring soon and was interested in making a long sea voyage; and could I have one of the cabins to write up memories of my past. He said that unfortunately he was soon to retire himself. So my chance went up in the air. I had found him the perfect captain to go with on a long voyage.

Another day the French navy called at São Tomé. The cruiser had just evacuated UN personnel, including Unicef staff, from Guinea Bissau at the time of an especially violent coup d'état. With the refugees, the "population" on board had swelled to some three hundred. We toured the ship from top to bottom. It was not very roomy to say the least. Hallways and stairs were narrow. I wondered how life had been on board with so many people. It worked out fine they said. Here's the secret: For the French having legroom is not the most important in life at sea... but food and drink is. Touring the kitchen, the officers introduced us to the cook who they called the "*chef*". That said it all, a sign of respect if there ever was one in such an overcrowded situation that they had just experienced. They praised him for never having run out of food and wines. Enjoying an excellent lunch, we could certainly attest to all that.

Then at one time Tiziano and Marie-Angela proposed to go sailing to Annobón Island with skipper Jon, a Spaniard who owned a 12-metre yacht. Nadim happened to be in São Tomé on a consultancy and joined for the fun. Annobón belongs to Equatorial Guinea and is the last of four volcanic islands with São Tomé, Principe and Bioko (capital Malabo) situated to its north. Annobón is a very isolated place with no more than 5,000 inhabitants. In those days it was known as a dump for toxic materials, perhaps it still is. It has an abundant supply of fish, fruits and vegetables. There is no regular shipping service to the rest of Equatorial Guinea, in fact this part of the Gulf is not known for crowded shipping lanes. Passing ships might call a few times a year at best to take fresh provisions. Jon decided to make landfall at the provincial capital San António de Pale on the north shore where the governor, whom he had forewarned, would issue us tourist visas.

We had already sailed with Jon several times and knew him to be an excellent skipper. The voyage would take some 36 hours one way depending on the winds. We only had five days to spare. The trip started off well. We left São Tomé harbour at 10 o'clock on the 1st June 1998, all of us in an upbeat mood. As usual the long mountain range was shrouded in low-lying clouds. First we sailed south east in a straight direction to our destination, then crisscrossing on the head winds. Being on a 12-metre yacht with endless water around you and no land insight made one feel small and irrelevant, no matter what.

We had plenty of provisions for the voyage. Maria-Angela had prepared small Italian pizzas for our aperitivo and hamburgers and grilled aubergines for dinner. The salty air had made us ravenous. Maria-Angela had been rather seasick and slept most of the day, so her making tapas and a warm meal was quite a feat. Nadim and I were visibly struggling with seasickness too. But soon we all adjusted to the ship's at times spastic movements. We started moving around with ever more ease. Reading was not possible; just light conversation or meditating until Jon would call for helping hands.

When night fell flying fish came for the leftovers. It was a beautiful sight to see, they never hit mast or sail. Birds of a brownish colour were sitting on waves as if on a branch of a tree hit by storm. Then the dolphins came, but just a moment before I had asked Nadim if he could find my glasses in the hold. You see, with my eyesight there's no point looking for glasses without glasses! He missed all the spectacular jumping and rushing of the dolphins and never forgave me!

CHAPTER 11: TWO PEARLS IN THE OCEAN

In the middle of the night we woke up to a big blast. The engine bellowed thick smoke, not far from where Nadim and I were sleeping. Strangely enough we were not at all afraid. I guess we were focused on the problem, not the danger. And this was after all a sailboat, supposed to sail and not to use the luxury of its engine. Jon acted fast, was already heading below deck, and tried to get the engine up again. But it had gone out for good, at least for this trip. So we hoisted the big sail in the dark and turned the boat around. Going back would be fast with the tail winds blowing from the south. Some 15 hours later the islet of Santana loomed through the mist, our first sighting of land since having left. Of course we were deeply disappointed not to have set foot on Annobón, but relieved to have made it back safely.

We sailed often with Jon on Sundays. At one time, Bettina and Claudio Corallo with their children Richarda, Nicolo and Amadeo were also in the party. Claudio was a most interesting Italian. He had come from Zaïre to São Tomé with his family to try his luck on cultivating cocoa here. In Eastern Zaïre he cultivated cocoa on large tracks of land not far from the Congo River. With the rebels of Laurent Kabila closing in on Kinshasa, navigation on the Congo River had become unsafe. With beans rotting on his plantation, Claudio gave up and went to try his luck in São Tomé. He started training a small group of São Toméans in helping him to terrace a hill of neglected cocoa plants and to plant new shoots. It was a labour of love to say the least. He treated his workers well. After a few years, his plantation began to flourish. He built a cocoa processing unit; "chocolate made in São Tomé". Through the honorary consul of São Tomé and Principe in Marseille, Claudio developed contacts with exclusive chocolate shops in Paris and Milan.

Passing *Ilha das Cabras* Jon pointed to foam spouting up in the air. Dolphins! Scores of them came to greet us, surfacing in pairs of two, three, four or even more! They moved fast in semicircles under water. Their colour under water was blue and silvery, and brownish when coming to the surface. There were hundreds of them jumping high up in the air the way you see them do it at Sea World. The children were jubilant. The dolphins huffed and puffed when they surfaced, sort of a "whiff" sound, as if to catch their breath. Baby dolphins jumped behind them. Seagulls followed them on their hunt for fish.

Claudio suddenly had an idea to go swimming among the dolphins. He went down in the strap first, and was then pulled by the boat. Sticking his head under water, he could hear their high-pitched sounds that are messages between them. The children followed, swam behind the boat and came back up with ease. They were ecstatic, because they had heard it too. When it was my turn, the dolphins had moved and the sounds with them. Then suddenly the winds picked up and the boat sped off, the distance to the yacht widening. I briefly panicked and thought the better of it. I pulled the line towards me to reach the stern, which was hard enough. Then I tried to come up to the step nearest to the water but failed. Claudio saw I was in trouble, did not hesitate for a moment, jumped in and told me to stand on his shoulders. He lowered his whole body and even put his head under water to give me an easy first step. I had to do it fast as he might tire out. I was deeply grateful for his swift action. Claudio most likely saved my life. Meanwhile far out in the distance the dolphins reappeared, playfully splashing their way to new catches.

Life on the beaches
If we were not on a sailboat, we would swim far out, away from the beaches. It was as the French say, *l'embarras du choix*, an embarrassment of the choices we had. All beaches are tiny, many tucked away. One beach could only be reached by driving through a hazardous stone road cutting through a swamp. Only a motorised canoe could reach *Ilha das Cabras. Cabras* consisted of two rocks with a beach in the middle. There was a challenging climb to the lighthouse from where one had a stunning view of the blue and green colours of the waters below. When the sea was quiet one could stay in the water and swim for long hours alongside the island's coastal line.

With our friends the Gourlaouens from Bretagne we travelled one day to a beach near Porto Allegre. Jorge was taking us there in a

CHAPTER 11: TWO PEARLS IN THE OCEAN

Landcruiser. On the way we came across a man in the middle of the woods carrying a plastic bag with lobsters sticking out. The man is looking for a customer. One problem: none of us have dobras. Then Bernard pulls out some dollars; the man asking how many dobras that is; Bernard counting fast like a teller at Société Générale; the lobster man satisfied; the lobsters alive and well. Further up the dirt road, a huge tree has fallen over the trail leading to *Praia da Inhame*, our final destination; Jorge trying to back out; back tyres spinning; car stuck in the mud; and now what? Jorge looking for the machete he always carries in the car just for bad luck of this kind; *"nunca aconteceu a mim"*, mumbling frustratedly to himself. Jorge going to walk to the nearest *roça*; the four of us now walk to the beach, not too far to go; Christiane putting the lobsters on a string in the water attached to a heavy stone; more time for the bottles of rosé to cool in the cooler; Jorge back after two hours, all sweaty and tired; cutting branches and putting them under the back tyres; Bernard and me to the front and pushing the car backwards; car finally moving! Finally we settle down on the beach while Jorge is flipping the lobsters on the fire; after all this he still has energy. We open the *rosé* and each one gets a lobster. Then another swim and home we go – before dusk and darkness get a chance to pose another problem. All this recorded on video and photos by the Bretons, to get in some more good laughs later.

We snorkelled often at *Lago Azul*, spotting a wide variety of fish. Tiziano and Maria-Angela would pass us in their utterly "patriotic" kayak: their oars were painted with the colours of the Italian flag! *Lago Azul* is a bay with depths of several kilometres in places. It is a great place for divers. One day swimming a bit too far out I suddenly heard an enormous splash behind me. It could have been a whale but also a shark. There were plenty of them near the coast and there were accidents. Just weeks before a shark had ventured into the mouth of Rio Grande River and had bitten off the arm of a community health worker. I was alone and scared. I literally swam for my life, never knowing whether I had been mistaken or not.

Others that use the beaches are marine turtles that come ashore to lay their eggs. In my time the European Union ran a *tartarugas marinhas* programme to save this endangered species. They paid São Toméan fishermen cash in return for each turtle caught in their nets. The conservationists would then tag them and put them out to sea again. Rumour had it that the fishermen knew rather precisely where the project had set the turtles free, caught them again and collected money again, "often for the same turtle".

Hiking in misty mountains

Hiking in inaccessible mountainous areas of tropical forest is something unforgettable. At an altitude of between 1,000 to 1,500 metres, it is warm, humid and misty up there, often sprinkled with a fine drizzle. Wild orchids twist themselves around brush and vines that grow against taller trees, making it hard to detect them. These outings are sometimes called "orchid spotting" walks. This is a paradise for botanists and conservationists, who come to study the flora and fauna from medicinal plants to butterflies and marine turtles.

That day we walked 30 km, everyone with a backpack loaded with water and food. One memorable moment was a steep decent and then reaching a large clearing of a grassy, very green round patch of land. This had been a crater that had filled up with water and grassy land over millions of years. The guide warned us to follow him in his footsteps. There were parts where one would sink way down into oblivion! We spotted our first orchids, tangled up in vines against brush and low growing trees. Their whiteness was an enormous contrast with the different shades of green all around them. Suddenly our guide stopped in his tracks. A big fat cobra was crossing our path, slithered his way up on a tree and rested on a branch for all of us to study him. This guide was simply excellent in pointing out hidden orchids, medicinal plants and organizing cobras!

The frenzy of a national sport

Soccer was the national sport of choice. Trained by a French manager, the national team had come a long way. One day there was an African Cup of Nations qualifying match between São Tomé and Sierra Leone. The small stadium was packed. Nadim and I had front row seats. It was an exciting and indeed historic match: São Tomé won 2–0, its first ever win in a qualifying match. The home crowd was at its best, cheering their team each time they had the ball.

Another time I got tickets for Zé, his friend Leila and Fernando and myself to see a local match with between Riboque and Bom Bom. Leila herself was a star on the local girls' team. Her brother Dede was a forward star on the national team. At stake was the championship of São Tomé and Principe. Bom Bom is a locality on Principe and Riboque a *barrio*[139] of São Tomé town, often a hotbed of troubles.

Soccer fields in São Tomé have no fences and people can walk about as they wish. When a dog comes on to the field, play is suspended. Instead of playing for the ball the players are now running to catch him, a funny sight to see. Some 15 minutes before the end the linesman flags Riboque for an offside goal and suddenly a brawl turns ugly: police escorting the referee and linesmen from the field; stones beginning to fly about; the three of us stealthily saving ourselves; and some supporters ending up in the hospital. Leila says that important matches always end up in fights. Checking the TV replay in the evening with Fernando, who is not at all a chauvinistic person, he confirms that his team Riboque had indeed rightfully scored. Such is the heat of soccer battles in São Tomé.

Marrying a Dutch couple

In June 2000 I received a phone call from a Dutch couple who had been due to marry in Principe the following day. All documents from Holland were in order, including a translation in Portuguese. All was ready from the Principe side, the church, the choir, the lunch and so on. All they needed was a validation of some documents from the honorary consul of the Netherlands. As the fax

---
[139] Neighbourhood.

from the consulate had never arrived, it was all over! I comforted them, and suggested they come on Monday. They seemed outwardly calm when they arrived at the office, but I perceived great anxiety. The worst was that back in Holland friends were about to throw a big wedding party for them. What if they came back unmarried? Time was of the essence. I picked up the phone.

"The consul just left", says the secretary dryly. I feel she might not be telling the truth. I dash off with Unicef driver Tete with the couple tailing us in their rental Suzuki. It turns out the honorary consul is sitting behind his desk. I tell him he does not seem to be doing his job in representing my country. He does not seem to care, but when I threaten to inform the Dutch embassy in Luanda, the tide turns. The consul begins to study the validity of the documents. Meanwhile I certify the Portuguese translation of the Dutch documents. And now we had to locate the registrar.

It was a clear day with a marvellous breeze – a day more fit for sailing with Jon than chasing a marriage certificate. The consul stops his car in front of a rusty gate; and starts clapping his hands. In São Tomé handclapping replaces doorbells, which are unreliable because of frequent power cuts. A dignified lady of about 50 appears in the driveway. While the consul is explaining, I put my hand on her arm, a sign of friendship in São Tomé. I consciously keep my hand there until we have a positive decision. The consul is long-winded. "Yes", the registrar could finally get a word in, "do what you plan to do, then come to the registry and I will make the document; wedding tomorrow."

In the evening I invited the couple to a "pre-wedding" dinner in Miramar. South African hotel hostess Beverly had made an elaborate arrangement of orange flowers, appropriately the colour of the Dutch House of Orange. There were only the three of us, but it was a real feast. They asked me there and then to be best man and witness all in one. I was definitely in the mood for a wedding.

The ceremony took place in a *casa de palha* decorated with palm leaves along the walls mixed in with flower arrangements to create

CHAPTER 11: TWO PEARLS IN THE OCEAN

a sense of intimacy. Meanwhile I was holding on to a box with the rings. Dona Hirondina asked for them. My great moment had come. I came up front and took Rob's finger and shoved it on. Clearly, I had lost touch with weddings a long time ago. "No oh no", she panicked, "the bride should do this". So Rob and I frantically pulled at the ring. It was a wonder that his finger survived! Ceremony over, everyone hugged. We trotted to our *dîner dinatoire*, the four witnesses and two hangers-on from the registrar's office. Beverley was a witness of course. It was a copious meal of lobsters and shrimp topped off by a big chocolate cake. I made a little speech thanking the Registrar and the consul for having this made possible pointing out that in my country one could not possibly marry in 24-hours. Hirondina told us that most young people here don't even bother to get married. In the evening alone again I watched from the terrace the TAP plane taking off to a moonlit sky. Rob and Tammy were off to a new *destino* with a story to tell.

São Toméans love parties for sure. I thought that perhaps the best annual festivity was São Tomé Day. It starts on the 21st of December and ends on Christmas Eve. It is a *feira popular* with little kiosks and food stalls assembled along the *Marginal* in no time at all. Even decent restaurant settings and dancing areas go up fast. All places are marked and assigned. All is decorated with palm leaves and flowers in honour of the great protector of fishermen. It's great to pass in the afternoon of the preceding day and see all the frantic activity of everyone constructing his site of commerce. One could shop simply for small Christmas presents or just eat, drink and dance well into the early morning hours. And then suddenly at Christmas Eve, everything goes silent. It takes less than a day to return the Marginal to its normal self as if nothing had happened. People sweeping and dumping leaves and rubbish in trucks. In half a day all is gone. When it comes to organising a party, São Toméans know how!

With A. leaving for our new pied-à-terre in Aix-en-Provence and Nadim to return to SOAS[140] to continue his masters, our farewells

---

[140] School of African and Oriental Studies in London.

to friends got under way early. Nadim and Salva organised a big party at the house on *Campo do Milho*. They had hired a DJ who came early to set up an impressive sound system. I feared the worst. Somehow word had gotten out that there was a party on *Campo do Milho*. No need for Facebook to get people to a party here: Two thirds of the guests are not even on the guest list. It all starts out calmly with Osvaldo Santos' trio playing their own songs from the balcony. Their first CD, *Ile de Chocolat*, funded by the São Tomé Consulate in Marseille, sells well that evening. After the food is devoured – there is no other word for it – the DJ turns up the sound system and the house starts to tremble. Zé and Leila tap beers and dole out wine as if there is no tomorrow. The living room turns into a disco packed with hot and sweaty moving bodies, Salva in the middle of it all, grinning with satisfaction. A quieter group, Claude Lonchampt, Alberto Neto, Bettina and others, holds out in the garden. In the early hours of the morning the party stops for lack of beer and spirits. People suddenly gone. A. and I calmly study the mess left behind.

Another time São Tomé Town was spruced up in expectation of the official visit by Portuguese president Jorge Sampaio to commemorate independence twenty-five years on. Streetlights had come to São Tomé earlier in the year. The *Parco Popular* got a facelift with small repairs and coats of white paint. A Portuguese tradition is to paint the bottom of tree trunks white. We never ask the trees how they feel about that. Women sweep the sands off the streets for days, something never seen before.

Meanwhile Alda Bandeira predicts a bleak period for São Tomé with people becoming increasingly restless. Many agree with her that another general strike is looming. Others doubt that because, "Partying in São Tomé comes first". The parade on the marginal is bigger than ever, with the 300-men army almost entirely on display along with military hardware. I am trying to spot Danilo. The *Correios* opens a memorable exhibit of old stamps issued since independence. Dignitaries receive an envelope with four commemorative stamps. I send mine off to our friend Bernard, who had looked here in vain for his extensive stamp collection. During a lunch at the Portuguese embassy I brief President Sampaio on Unicef's perception of the country's problems: poverty, inequality, illiteracy and governance. The President struck me as a modest, truly humble man who listened calmly and sympathetically. He seemed honestly concerned with the chronic poverty and inequality on the two islands.

Last months in São Tomé

I was now spending my last months in São Tomé alone. Most had left on home leave. Thoughts and images were rushing through my head, all at the same time. I tried to catch as many last minute images from *São Tomé* as I could. I went swimming at *Praia das Conças* one more time, picking up some shells to remember it by. At sunset I motored to Pantufe, along the oceanfront, past the *Palacio dos Congressos*, where we had held so many big meetings and workshops. I looked up to the wall sloping down from Pinta da Costa's invisible house remembering my courtesy visit. I ran into the red and black Suzuki that Nadim had hired to go to work when he trained journalists in Internet surfing. The *Marginal* was now lit up at night from the newly installed street lamps. Coming downhill from *Campo do Milho*, the view was stunning.

I joined Minister Lima one more time on a field trip, to inaugurate a health post in Bombaïm. At a graduation ceremony for the nurses – Unicef had supported their training and now guaranteed their job for the next three years – I watched the Minister hand out diplomas to cheers in the audience. I wiped away a tear of happiness for them. Minister Lima and his National Director Dr Claudina Augusto da Cruz organised a farewell drink for me at the Ministry along with their staff. He gave me a nice woodcarved box.

Meanwhile oil fever had hit the island. Drilling in the waters neighbouring Equatorial Guinea and Nigeria became a serious prospect when blocks were negotiated and signed up by Chevron and others. The downside was that the reserves lay at a depth of five to ten kilometres. The price of oil had to stay very high in order to make extraction worthwhile. But that window closed when prices started to fall.

At one of my last coffee breaks at *Passante*, I thought how important that oceanfront had been to me. I reminisced about the two sperm whales far out at sea I once had spotted from *Passante*, while sipping a coffee with Idalécio Neves. The happy splashing and spouting could be clearly seen. There were other memories. One day a gambling locale run by Corsicans opened right behind the terrace. The space belonged to Hotel Miramar. Gambling was very popular with São Toméans. I was quite upset that gambling had come to this poor island. One evening we saw a clearly distressed *empregada* leaving the gambling locale. Marie-France from Quebec who ran a clothing boutique next to it said the woman had lost all the household money, with which she was supposed to buy food at the market for her mistress.

With a Presidential election on the horizon, politics began to heat up. As Trovoada could not run, the race was wide open. Carlos Tiny had come back home from Mozambique to prepare his candidacy. I had known him there as the WHO representative. At the time Tiny had offered to rent his house to me. It was a stately mansion on a rock right above the surf and had never yet been lived in. It was too big and too expensive for us. Tiny threw a farewell lunch for me at his sister's house. He sounded me out for serving on his international advisory committee should he win. I said I would think about it but I could perhaps first help with modernising his campaign American-style. All this did not happen. Our paths did not cross again. Carlos Tiny only obtained 10% of the national vote and never ran again.

I went to say goodbye to Alda do Espirito Santo at her home. Alda was a hero of the fight for independence and a renowned poetess. She was in her mid-seventies. She gave me a copy of her anthology *Cancões do Mar*, sentimental poems about the sea, a bit like the Portuguese *fados*. All my duty stations had faced the ocean. This

CHAPTER 11: TWO PEARLS IN THE OCEAN

was not the first time I had been to her house. I found her a fascinating woman and listened with great interest to her concerns for the country's youth. Alda was the first Minister of Education at independence. Alberto, who had joined Unicef from the Ministry, had introduced me to her early on.

I thought back to the beginning days and how I had changed our Unicef office. We now had two national officers for programme. In my last weeks Fatima Silva had joined from VOA as our new operations officer. She had received excellent training there, so much so that her boss regretted that she now left with all knowledge she had acquired during her time there. Since more than a year we had had a decent operating system with email and Internet. I sent Noemia, Idalécio and Alberto to regional network meetings. In the process they became known in the region. Idalécio and Fatima made the transition to international staff. Alberto, who spoke excellent English, certainly had the profile, but preferred to remain in his own country.

Some of the last evenings I spent alone at *Campo do Milho*. Most of the expats had gone on leave. I listened to far away sounds such as Fernando's pole ticking on the pavement, music and voices of people at the Spanish residence; and the sound of the rolling waves, never far away. I had a satisfied but sad feeling. Perhaps this is how dying might be, I thought, when one listens to sounds far away for the last time. I thought I had done it all. I even had arranged jobs for my *empregados* so they were safe. Zé and Fernando were to continue with Barbosa; and Jorgina would cook for Dieudonné Itegali from Rwanda, who had come to train our new Operations officer in Unicef procedures, rules and regulations.

Manfred offered the conference room for my official farewell with government counterparts, the diplomatic community, NGOs and friends. The place was packed. Prime Minister Posser da Costa came, along with Alda Bandeira; Minister of Planning Maria das Neves, Dr António Lima and Alda do Espirito Santo. São Tomé is in many ways a very informal place; and so I had no qualms inviting my *empregados* Fernando, Jorgina and Zé. Zé's friend Leila came along for the ride. They were totally at ease with the other guests, some of whom even knew them.

When most had left I took off my inseparable blue linen jacket on the spur of the moment and gave it as a present to Fernando. Putting it on he declared: *"agora eu sou Mohr preto[141]"*. Mr Treasurer of the Association for the Handicapped simply looked splendid in it. One month after witnessing the attack on the World Trade Towers, I received a letter from him in Aix-en-Provence. It moved me much to see the address on that envelope that I have kept all these years: *"De Mohr preto para Mohr branco"*.[142]

> *Senhor Mohr, escrevou esta curta linha só para ouvires os meus maiores cumprimentos; eu vou normalmente bem de saude cá em São Tomé graça à Deus, mais fiquei muito triste quando ouvio que aconteceu lá no Estados Unidos de America porque fiquei pensar em meu grande patrão e sua esposa, porque dissera-me que senhor estava lá no local do acontecimento, mais depois fiquei-me um poco aliviado quando o Alex disse-me que ele viu o Nadim e ele disse que o senhor ja tinha dislocado do sitio antes do acontecimento. Recebe um abraço de Mohr preto.*
>
> *Fernando, S. Tomé 15/10/01*

Turning over in the comfortable bed of the presidential suite that Manfred had given me for my last days, I turned off the lights. The next day I flew back to our farm. It was there that I learned that Carol Bellamy had approved my appointment to be officer-in-charge for Gabon and São Tomé and Principe. I would be based in Libreville for six months. Equatorial Guinea would join us on the 1st of January 2002. I could not wait to pick up the challenge to put into practice what I had in mind.

---

[141] "Now I am black Mohr".
[142] "From black Mohr" to white Mohr".

Chapter 12: Towards an African Movement for Children

In 1999 Regional Director Rima Salah appointed a regional *Task Force on Small Country Offices* for the West and Central Africa Region. Small was an office based in a country with a population of less than 1.5 million, and a general resources ceiling at 850,000 dollars. I was the task force's coordinator of the task force. My first assignment was to go on a fact-finding mission to the six Unicef offices in small countries.[143]

Small offices had much in common. Although they could generally implement faster with more immediate impact, they were vulnerable in staffing and available resources. A colleague struck down by malaria could paralyse the office for several weeks. To fill in for absentees, staff had to be polyvalent. Multi-tasking added to work pressure and affected quality of output. Frequent turnover of government staff and the brain drain hit small countries harder. Government capacities were taxed by international agencies hiring away their staff at much higher pay, which we called the *internal* brain drain. Unicef itself had limited human resource capacities. In landlocked or island nations the cost of delivering services is abnormally high. The question came down to this: how should these small offices reorganise to achieve optimum impact for children.

The task force convened in Libreville in February 2000 under the leadership of Christian Voumard. Its members tended to favour autonomous structures with a representative. But that was in contradiction to what I had proposed to Carol Bellamy. Such a structure would significantly add to programme delivery cost. I felt that it did not meet the norms of an *"optimum"* management structure

---

[143] Cape Verde, Gambia and Guinea Bissau in West Africa; and Equatorial Guinea, Gabon and São Tomé and Principe in Central Africa.

that the group was striving for. A *core* programme tailored to specific country context that left out certain global priorities was a good idea but the spectrum of excessive delivery cost would simply not go away. In hindsight I feel that I did not make my innermost convictions sufficiently clear to the group. There was simply an avalanche of consensus building coming my way. I thought it would be awkward if there were one dissenting voice. In the end I joined the vote by acclamation. The Regional Management Meeting subsequently endorsed our recommendations.

That was at the same time my last RMT before retirement. Rima made a little speech heaping praise on me for what I had done for the region for so many years. I felt sincerely embarrassed. I could only reply: *"je tiens cette région à coeur"*. Then Carol Bellamy approached where I was sitting, her thin frame covered by a huge bouquet of tropical flowers. I weighed with much anxiety whether to shake her hand or kiss her. Having adopted several French habits over time, I opted for the kiss.

After the RMT Rima called me in her office and broke the news: She was going to ask the Executive Director to extend me for six months to relocate me to Libreville to prepare the ground for a link between São Tomé with Gabon. The assignment would be from the first of October, which would have been the first day of my retirement. As her Deputy Ndolamb Ngokwey walked in, Rima asked him what he thought of it all: *"Il n'y a pas de meilleure solution"*, was his simple and so full-of-meaning endorsement. [144] I had known Ndolamb for a long time and had a great respect for him. He was an academic by nature, practical by application. He slept little at night, was as fit as anything and became intellectually active when the sun had set.

---

[144] After retiring two years later, Unicef called me regularly out of retirement to assist country offices in Africa with situation analysis, country programme preparation, mid-term reviews and review of management and operations. In all, the period of my life with Unicef would last some 28 years.

CHAPTER 12: TOWARDS AN AFRICAN MOVEMENT FOR CHILDREN

I was convinced that one of the Libreville recommendations would be not tenable with Headquarters. With donor funds falling there was simple no room for tiny independent offices. Perhaps the answers would lie in making SCO's interdependent, while safeguarding a certain equality and autonomy at least in programming. A grouping of small country offices with an integrated programme management supported by an operations centre at an area office (with better definitions of autonomy and accountability for each office) – did eventually win the day. Although I did not know it then, it turned out that my proposal to the Executive Director to regroup SCO's was still very much on the table.

Ndolamb Ngokwey came to explain to the governments of Gabon and São Tomé the linking of the two countries in the Unicef sub-regional set-up. He did this with great diplomatic skill. He was fluent in Portuguese and that created goodwill in São Tomé. The Gabonese government was elated that the Unicef office was elevated to area office. Equatorial Guinea was more complicated. Its government had for years pressed Unicef to upgrade the office. And now that it had itself become an oil-producing nation –whereas Gabon was reportedly running out of oil – Equatorial Guinea felt itself becoming more powerful in the sub-region and beyond.

Three-countries consultation

One of my first moves in Libreville was to hire a former Unicef staff member to help strengthen the operations section in Unicef procedures. Dieudonné Itegeli, a Tutsi from Rwanda, was focused on our outstanding cash advances to government that were unaccounted for since many months. If these advances were not justified soon, Unicef aid to Gabon would be suspended. That was my first challenge. Dieudonné got a handle on it and the problem was gradually solved. Now we could move on to what I had actually come here for: linking three country offices into one integrated programme and management team. I now needed to consult with staff from the three offices and get their take on this.

Dieudonné and I worked hand in hand in preparing the content and modules of the Three-Countries Consultation. In the process we became good friends. On Sundays we often kept each other company at a beach restaurant. The new Unicef representative in Mozambique, Marie-Pierre Poirier, released Gabriel Pereira to assist as a resource person for intergovernmental affairs. I convinced her by making the point that Gabriel would be helpful in flagging potentially sensitive issues that could arise among the three respective governments.

Herbert Schembri came from Malabo with three colleagues; from São Tomé Fatima Silva and Alberto Neto joined; from Gabon we had with us Denisa Ionete, the programme coordinator and Louise Mvono from education. Irene Ndimal held the secretariat. Irene spent her weekends on working for the cause of the Pygmies. I learned much from her about the plight of this neglected ethnic group of hunters and forest dwellers who straddle five countries in Central Africa.[145] With the pressures of an evolving society around them their traditions were at risk of disappearing. They were generally marginalised in social services, such as health and hygiene; and or simply did not have access to education. Denisa, who grew up as a pioneer under the Ceausescu regime was effectively the number two of the office. Louise covered her sector with great promise.

The venue was a small hotel with pleasant surroundings and good service. It confirmed to me that Libreville had it all together in logistics as well as culinary terms. In the opening session I sketched the principles of an integrated programme management and operations set-up the way I saw it: *equality:* no office would dominate the other two – and that included the area office; *accountability:* each head of office would remain fully accountable; *solidarity:* support other offices with financial and human resources as required; and last but not least, the added value of integration: the opportunity to respect and benefit from *cultural diversity*. The SCO study had revealed that the responsibilities of an area

---

[145] Democratic Republic of the Congo (DRC), Republic of Congo, Central African Republic, Cameroon, Equatorial Guinea, Gabon.

CHAPTER 12: TOWARDS AN AFRICAN MOVEMENT FOR CHILDREN

office were almost never clearly defined. Here was then an opportunity to re-define them based on these principles.

We reached consensus on how to apply these four principles. In terms of equality it would be up to the area representative to ensure it. Culturally diverse the Unicef team certainly was. French, Spanish, English, were intermittently used in our meeting without constraint. Gabriel spoke once in a while in Portuguese because he was convinced that it should become an official language of the United Nations. We agreed that multicultural acceptance among the three governments might be the hardest to achieve. It was only natural that the consultation requested a mission by Ngokwey to Malabo to prepare the ground, just as he had done so well in São Tomé and Gabon. I was thinking of his words expressed in regard to me barely a few months before: *"il n'y a pas de meilleure solution..."*

The challenge was to explain the benefits of such an arrangement to respective governments. We would have to prove that children in the end would be better off. Just like international staff, national officers should be fully accepted as programme advisers in another country. There would not automatically be a need to hire another expensive education specialist elsewhere in that case. As an example of equality, an education expert from São Tomé might well continue to reside in his own country. That was consistent with the spirit of staff exchange among offices in the Region that HR had begun to promote. The three-countries approach could more effectively address cross-border issues, for example control of epidemics, child trafficking and response to emergencies. Child trafficking between Equatorial Guinea and Gabon was an issue, violence and abuse were not uncommon. Irene pleaded that Pygmies represented an equally important issue that should be added to the list of cross-border collaboration.

A centralised operations hub would organise joint procurement, potentially resulting in important price reductions. Gabon was chosen for the hub as it was further advanced in logistics and services. We had already identified new and more appropriate office space, taking the premises of the embassy of Angola that was moving elsewhere. Unicef had just begun implementing an electronic programme management system that could be run from the hub with operational links to the other two offices. We saw the value of an "Integrated Management Team" (IMT) with national and international programme and operations colleagues from the three countries. We adopted an integrated management plan (IMP) based on individual country programme management plans. This way the IMP would offer at a glance if there was a duplication of posts.

Special Session of the UN General Assembly on Children
After my mission in the sub region, Rima Salah appointed me coordinator for Unicef in West and Central Africa for the upcoming UN Special Session on Children. Former PFO colleague Samir Sobhy, who was appointed at first, had dropped out at the beginning of his assignment. The reason was that the Organisation of African Unity[146] had unexpectedly shifted the preparatory meeting to prepare for the *African Common Position* on the future of Africa's children from Addis Ababa to Cairo under pressure from the Egyptian government. That did not please our Egyptian colleague who had serious misgivings about his own government.

That the choice fell on me was not strange in itself. Back in 1999 I had been part of a regional consultation with African NGOs, academics and other intellectuals on developing a joint *Vision for Africa's Children*. I was a resource person for the working group on *Government and Civil Society*. I had made passionate plea for a new, rolling *"social contract"* between the state and its people that would be updated at regular intervals as required. It might be a way of building mutual trust.

Unicef as the global lead agency for children was deeply involved with the organisation of the UN Special Session General Assembly

---

[146] The OAU was founded in 1963 in Addis Abeba. It was the brainchild of Emperor Haile Selassi. At the 2001 Lusaka Summit, the OAU transformed itself into the African Union, modelled after the EU. The change became effective at the following Summit.

CHAPTER 12: TOWARDS AN AFRICAN MOVEMENT FOR CHILDREN

Session on Children in September 2001. In fact Unicef was forging ever-stronger alliances with Africa's civil society that had the potential to become the driving force of a *Global Movement for Children*.[147] Another Children's Summit sounded all very lofty and well meant but this was not quite up my alley. I had come to prefer by far the concrete and practical side of development, conceiving and implementing projects for children in the field. But I had been at global meetings before, so I knew what I was accepting.

Towards the turn of the century, a new wind was blowing all over Africa. African leaders and intellectuals had begun to take initiatives towards promoting a more independent stance vis-à-vis the international donor community. The watchword in development was self-reliance. Thomas Sankara inspired his people to do more for themselves. Thousands of villages all over Burkina built simple, first aid health posts in a matter of months. Several countries in Africa began to experience double-digit growth. Young author Axelle Kabou from Cameroon posed hard questions in her 1991 bestselling book.[148] She pointed to stagnation and failures in development of Africa during 30 years of "independence", perpetuated by lack of courage, solidarity and vision of its leaders. She called for abolishing the OAU, because "the OAU does not promote African unity". China began to invest heavily on the continent, taking a new approach to empowering Africa economically. The drawback was that China cared less for human rights. Moreover, its investments failed to create many jobs for Africans.

The New African Initiative (NAI) merged the African economic recovery plans of Algeria, Nigeria, Senegal and South Africa, thus forging a strengthened, more equal partnership between Africa and the international donor community. NAI's preamble clearly set the stage: *"Social exclusion of the vast majority of its peoples*

---

[147] GMC was an initiative of UNICEF, Save the Children, World Vision, BRAC (Bangladesh Rural Advancement Committee), CARE International, Plan International and Netaid. The SAY YES TO CHILDREN campaign kicked off the Global Movement for Children.

[148] Axelle Kabou, *Et si l'Afrique refusait le Développement?*, 1991

constitute a serious threat to global stability. Changing the relationship that underpins it should reverse this abnormal situation. Africans are appealing neither for further entrenchment of dependency through aid nor for marginal concessions".

Several countries began to take timid steps towards adoption of a democratic model of government. That in turn led to a timidly greater acceptance of civil society organisations. All around there was a renewal going on that inspired some to start calling the new Millennium the "African century".[149] *L'Autre Afrique* claimed on its July 2001 cover: *"A nous le siècle: le temps d'être enfin maître de son destin"*. As far as I was concerned, that was to be the underlying point of the African position we were going to work out: *Africa for the Africans*.

Towards an African common position on the welfare of its children

I was part of an advance team to develop the agenda of the *Pan-African Forum on the Future of Children*, scheduled for end of May 2001. For the first time Africa's government leaders and civil society were to come together in jointly drafting an African Common Position on the future of Children. African thinking coming from common people would be considered and respected. The idea was that African people were now part of their own destiny, no more top down approach from the West.

The Unicef team worked hand in hand with Madame Nagwa Khallaf who was the National Director of the National Commission on Children. She was a former Minister of Health. A most gracious and elegant woman in her early fifties, Nagwa led the meetings with great skill. She was close to First Lady Suzan Mubarak. That helped with certain agenda items, such as the prepared statement by Nobel laureate, poet and novelist Naguib Mahfouz of *Cairo Trilogy* fame, who was not well enough to

---

[149] At the time of writing Chancellor Angela Merkel had invited nine African Heads of State and Government to a G20 Summit in Berlin to review Africa's investment potential through public-private partnership arrangements.

CHAPTER 12: TOWARDS AN AFRICAN MOVEMENT FOR CHILDREN

attend. An attacker in a Cairo street had blinded Mahfouz back in 1994.

Regional Director Urban Jonsson was the leader of our organising team. He brought his monitoring and evaluation officer along, a brilliant statistician from India. I remember that he had an astounding memory for figures and facts. Alex DeWaal[150] was a resource person for emergencies. Abdul Mohammed, liaison with the AU in Addis was there. Abdul had a delightful sense of humour. His jokes and anecdotes kept me glued. One was a story about our Executive Director. After the 1996 OAU Summit in Yaounde – Abdul had been part of the Unicef delegation – Carol Bellamy travelled unexpectedly through Libreville, Gabon on the way to Paris. While jogging on the beach at five in the morning, our Unicef resident programme officer from Benin, whose name was Ladjouant, was informed that Bellamy was about to land. With time running out, our man on the spot had no choice but to dash off in shorts and sneakers to the VIP lounge. Nervously presenting himself, he stammered, "Good morning Madame, I am Ladjouant". Bellamy, who got by in French, mistook that for "*l'adjoint*[151]". And she exclaimed, "What?? Get me the rep!!"

Most of us stayed at the Semiramis, a stunning hotel overlooking the Nile[152]. The day of my arrival I dined on my private terrace on *steak au poivre* and an excellent red *Fleur du Cap* watching the lit-up boats gliding to and fro, while the Mosque was calling the faithful to prayers, with blaring music all around drowning out the words of the Imam. The ambiance on and near the river was delightfully vibrant to say the least. One evening after work I went on a sunset camel ride with Abdul and Alex DeWaal to the Great

---

[150] Alex DeWaal made his mark with his book *Famine Crimes: Politics and the Disaster Relief Industry*, published in 1997; he is currently Executive Director of World Peace Foundation in Somerville, Massachussetts and a Research Professor at The Fletcher School of Tufts University.
[151] Deputy.
[152] The old Semiramis opened in 1907 and was the first hotel on the Nile. In 1974 the historic building was torn down and a new Semiramis built on the same spot.

Pyramid of Giza. A guide kept my camel on a leash. He joked that Libya was not far, so he could go on if we wanted. The ride was a wobbly affair. Unfortunately we stayed quite far from the Pyramids. The camel caravan stopped for a while to give us time to stare at these wonders until modern floodlights came on to replace the redness of a sinking sun.

A few weeks later the official Unicef delegation from West Africa led by Rima Salah arrived in Cairo. Former Regional Director Stan Adotevi was part of the group. Jacques Adande, then representative in Burkina Faso and a few other Unicef representatives were also of the party. The Forum was held at the Cairo International Convention Centre, not far from the spot where President Sadat was assassinated in October 1981. Security was extremely tight all around. Some delegates had been refused entry and missed the opening speeches. Jacques Adande was one of them. Rima had arranged for a pass for A., so that she could at least attend the opening day. First Lady Susan Mubarak delivered the keynote speech in the place of her husband. Many country delegations spoke about their concerns for children living in poverty and out of school. Two children from countries in war, Burundi and Sierra Leone, made an emotional appeal to the leaders to stop all wars. The moving speech of the Burundian girl seemed to come straight from her heart.

Jerry Rowlings made a rather rambling speech, mostly about himself and his time as President of Ghana. In the pressroom A. chatted briefly with Amadou Toumani Toure (ATT), who was the coup leader when Moussa Traore was overthrown. When A. mentioned Tuaregs, ATT was pulled away to his interview with the BBC. ATT later addressed the plenary. I remember him saying jokingly what a mistake he had made by not running for President in 1992, as he had now been unemployed for some time! But he was soon to become Mali's second democratically elected President.

On the last day I was one of five rapporteurs who recorded the conclusions and recommendations for the *"Cairo Declaration"*. Concerns of children and youth of Africa had to be at the core of

CHAPTER 12: TOWARDS AN AFRICAN MOVEMENT FOR CHILDREN

the global movement's agenda. Hence the Forum's striving for a common position that would make Africa speak with one strong voice in the final outcome document of the special session called *"A World Fit For Children"*. Cairo committed to putting in place national plans for children with realistic goals. The OAU agreed to monitor progress and issue a report on the State of the African Child every other year.[153] The common position would put more emphasis on new models of education, emphasising learning related to local culture and teaching in the local language, at least in the early years. Information technology, seen as an important step in stimulating economies, would be increasingly linked to education. A breakthrough was the recognition that child trafficking – a hitherto often denied but rapidly growing phenomenon in Africa – should be punishable by law. Child protection was this time more clearly defined in terms of vulnerable target groups. Member states admitted that reduction of military expenditures would free up substantial funding for children in Africa. In general, youth participation was seen as the catalyst of an African movement for children.

One evening Rima invited all of us on a boat trip on the Nile. It is full-blown tourism with a belly dancer to boot. The dressed in red, ready-to-kill woman comes uncomfortably close to the edge of the long table where A. and I are sitting. I remember shifting inwards as best I could. When we run into good friend Dominique Buff of ICRC, I tell him A. and I plan to move out of the horrible place we are staying to go to Semiramis. He at once packs his bags and comes along. So does Regional HIV/AIDS adviser Eric Mercier, usually rather reserved, but loosening up by the delightful dinner atmosphere at the pool. We listen to sentimental Egyptian music with Egyptian men and some Arabs smoking long water pipes all around us.

---

[153] In 2004 I wrote the State of the Child in West and Central Africa, which was subsequently incorporated in the first State of the Child in Africa reported under the aegis of the African Union.

Before leaving for Abidjan, A. took me on a tour of the splendid Coptic churches and the old mosques. After two days of sightseeing with a taxi driver, she already knew her way around. In the evening we had dinner in the souk, and who did we run into: Unicef colleagues of course.

The second milestone meeting leading up to UNGASS was the OAU Summit of Heads of State in Lusaka, Zambia in July. Carol Bellamy led the Unicef delegation assisted by Rima Salah, Jacques Adande, Abdul Mohammed, Unicef Lusaka representative Stella Goings and myself. The OAU would become the Africa Union in 2002.

As is usual, every Head of State made a long address to the gathering. I remember Yasser Arafat. I had forgotten to get earphones, so I listened to his speech in Arabic. The tone had a surprisingly soft, singing sound to it. Then it was Khadaffi's turn. His was a predictable attack on the UN, the US and its Western allies. Suddenly there was a power cut. With some 40 African Heads of State in the room, that was not a good omen. Khadaffi was immediately surrounded by his security detail, some 50 good-looking Berber women. Somebody whispered, "sabotage". The Mozambican delegation in the row in front of me improvised some silly jokes to relieve tension. I planned a silent retreat to the exit, giving the power cut half an hour or so to resolve itself. When it did not, I slowly got up and headed inconspicuously to the door. When I was half way, the lights came back on. Soon thereafter the session broke up. Now I lingered on, watching the presidents filing by. Those I knew I greeted; Chissano from Mozambique and Omar Bongo from Gabon. Deep down I wondered about the fate of the Zambian president, who had to bear the ultimate responsibility for such a serious security lapse. The African common position was adopted and would now be negotiated to be taken into account in the outcome document of the special summit.

Mission accomplished, our little West African group flew back to Abidjan with a stopover in Nairobi. Representative Nick Alipui

CHAPTER 12: TOWARDS AN AFRICAN MOVEMENT FOR CHILDREN

had invited us to dinner at the Norfolk hotel. Before boarding there was some time to stop at one of the many roadside nurseries in Nairobi. I bought a Jacaranda tree for Rima's garden in Abidjan. When I saw it three years later, it was doing surprisingly well and that in a totally different climate. Jacques Adande got one for his farm outside Cotonou. At last count that Jacaranda was still going strong too.

The last milestone gathering before New York in which I participated was the UN World Youth Forum in Dakar. Some 400 youth delegates came from all over the world, many at their own expense. Young people presented programmes they were involved in such as HIV/AIDS and peace education. A young Dutch participant made a presentation on the marginalisation of Moroccan immigrants in Holland. It turned out that she herself was born from Moroccan immigrants, and had gone to school in Maastricht. She delivered her presentation professionally. She spoke a perfect and indeed a beautiful Dutch. Although she was only 21, it was not difficult to see a future leader in her. For a while I kept up a correspondence with her. I was convinced that she would have been a fabulous candidate for Unicef when she was ready for it.

The UN agencies recalled their collaboration with young people. UNFPA spoke about its support to HIV/AIDS peer-to-peer education. Regional Director Rima Salah made a pitch for the global movement's *Say Yes to Children* campaign. Millions of *SAY YES* votes would serve as a pressure group on world leaders to commit to a *"World fit For Children"*. I was not so crazy about the idea and wondered seriously about its value and impact in the long run. It felt to me like a New York inspired, "boy-scoutish" idea. The French said it all so much better; the simple goal was simply to create *"un monde digne des enfants"*. Just sticking to that purpose would be sufficient so that then no state was allowed to fail the world.

The youth meeting lacked broad vision, Discussions ranged from support in life skills to rural youth to training of marginalised youth in IT so that they could begin to organise themselves as an independent, economically sustainable group. There was much discussion on HIV/AIDS. In the "Culture of Peace" working group, we had a heated debate about what in the world this expression meant. Houphouet-Boigny used to say, *"la paix, ce n'est pas un mot, c'est un comportement."* In any event, slavery was certainly was not a culture of peace, as someone challenged; suddenly the issue of monetary reparations for slavery to Africa dominated the discussions in plenary.

Then, coming as a total surprise to participants, the chair suspended an afternoon session to allow hundreds of participants to set out on a pilgrimage to the former slave island of Gorée. The Chair's proposal was met with thundering applause. Several Unicef colleagues joined on the ferry ride across. The Unicef editor in the GMC Newsletter writes: *"Quaint houses with flower pots hanging from balconies, patios and narrow alleyways make the passing tourist think he is visiting a small village in the Provence rather than a place where world history took a turn for the worse"*.[154] In the courtyard of the slave prison house the curator tells the story of the slaves' last day on the island before walking us through a narrow tunnel to the ocean. Jacques Adande tells me he has taken visitors here many times. He says the tunnel is called the "doorway of no return". The surrounding waters are very deep. Permanently tied to a 5 kg metal ball, this ensured slaves who tried to escape would drown. Everyone is silent and suddenly in a pensive mood. The walk gives me a most eerie feeling to realise what went on here. The debate about reparations continued long afterwards.[155]

---

[154] Unicef Dakar Newsletter on the Global Movement for Children, August 2001.
[155] At the 2001 Durban World Conference against Racism, it was concluded that the principle of "crimes against humanity" could not be applied against descendants of colonisers (as that principle did not exist at the time) and could thus not establish clear responsibilities for reparations on the part of former colonial states.

CHAPTER 12: TOWARDS AN AFRICAN MOVEMENT FOR CHILDREN

The UN General Assembly Special Session on Children
Barely back on home base Abidjan, I was already packing my bags for a long stay in New York. I was part of an African advance team that included the Nairobi team with whom we shared a small conference room in programme division. There was Ayalew Abai, deputy regional director and a couple of representatives, including Jesper Morch. Rima Salah and Jacques Adande were held back at a conference with African Parliamentarians in Ouagadougou and would join later. One of our tasks was to identify delegates to participate in this or that side session, for example the session on public-private partnerships or one of the sectoral sessions such as HIV/AIDS or education. Another was to promote this or that African Head of State to address the plenary sessions. Saad Houry was my most useful link to the front office. There were daily early morning briefings in the Labouisse Conference Room of Unicef House. Potential problems were flagged and follow-up actions to solve them assigned.

On one such morning in Labouisse, it was Tuesday the 11th of September, the meeting got under way at around eight o'clock. There was much talk about the assassination of Afghan Tajik warlord Ahmad Massoud that had happened just two days before. Two suicide bombers posing as fake journalists from Belgium had been waiting for several weeks until they were finally allowed to interview Massoud. They claimed to be Belgians, but were apparently Tunisians. This was a serious blow to the Americans and its allies who were supporting Massoud in the fight against Al Quaeda and the Taliban.

Suddenly the door opens without a knock. Media relations colleague Lizzie rushes up to our executive director. Lizzie whispers something in Bellamy's ear. That takes less than two minutes. Then Lizzie gets up and rushes out the door. It is about five minutes to nine. What in the world was happening?

The executive director pauses briefly and then says, "a plane has hit the World Trade Centre and one Tower is on fire"; and she immediately suspends the meeting until the following day. We all get up fast. "Come with me, from my office I have a very clear view of the World Trade Towers", says Philippe Duhamel, executive assistant to Bellamy. I run with Saad and Philippe and other people to the front office, which is on the 13th floor, same as Labouisse. We see an immense cloud of black smoke coming out of the tower on the right; we are in a North to South viewing position. A few minutes later, at three minutes past nine, we witness a huge flame coming out of the second WT tower covering several floors near the top. "That's sabotage", I say out loud to myself. We are about five km away from the WTC. The sky is crystal clear at our end but fills up quickly up with smoke in the far distance. We are stunned.

Someone suggests going down to the situation room, where Unicef connects by radio to field offices in emergency situations. There's a big TV screen and we follow the live broadcast. Confusion everywhere. An announcement: Unicef House and the rest of the UN around us will be evacuated immediately. Some of us go downstairs and to the Unicef terrace outside, now named "James P. Grant Plaza". Saad decides to stay on for a while longer with the executive director. I want to stay with him, but he tells me to go to his home to care for Hoda and A., who had just arrived from France a few hours before. We are staying with the Hourys at their Waterside Plaza apartment on the 35th floor 25th Street and the East River, a sort of closed community formed by four red brick towers and a grand plaza where one can sit and have some peace and quiet. I go home and find both Hoda and A. up and about, watching TV. Hoda's mother had called them out of their sleep from Beirut to give them the news that was happening right on their doorstep.

In the beginning we did not much venture outside other than on the inner square at the Waterside Plaza. Manhattan was sealed off. Fighter jets continued swooping over town and ambulances never let go of their sirens. Watching the FDR Drive from Saad's windows, traffic slowed to a trickle until only fire trucks and

CHAPTER 12: TOWARDS AN AFRICAN MOVEMENT FOR CHILDREN

ambulances were left. Watching the second explosion, strangely enough I simply did not realise then that hundreds of people must have died that very instant. But that ignorance did not last long.

One image I will never forget are long lines of people waiting in line at Lenox Hill Hospital hoping to get news about their loved ones. I had gone out with A. for a stroll towards Union Square where people had laid lots of photos, messages and flowers for lost relatives and friends. There were no cars around anywhere. Another image to stay with me forever was the cloud cover in the area of Ground Zero that we could see from far away, whereas uptown the sky was still relatively clear. After a couple of days the wind turned south and then the particles began to reach us, carrying with them a strong smell of burned plastic.

Nadim called from São Tomé, where he was doing a consultancy for Bahnhof, the Swedish Internet Service Provider, giving IT training at the *Lyceu*. He was shocked why I had never called. I could not explain it. It had just not entered my mind to inform family and close friends that A. and I were safe. My brother Peter and friend Christopher also were able to get through to me somehow. Nadim had been sharing a flat with two friends downtown some 300 metres from the WTC. Just one month before he had left New York for good to take time off and go backpacking in Vietnam; serious job hunting could wait a little longer. Their apartment building was now covered with ash inside and had become a health hazard. It was closed for many months. I later got to see a photo of the inside of their flat taken by his flatmate Tommy, a friend from SOAS days in London. The ashes were inches deep. It was a colour photo, but the whole place looked grey.

The Special Session was of course cancelled. Planes already in the air carrying Heads of State and other participants were diverted to safer havens nearby or turned around. Staff from the field had no more task left to do. The UN secretariat and Unicef now had the daunting task of winding down its organisation. A memorial service was held in the General Assembly led by a very dignified

Kofi Annan. UN staff, the diplomatic community, NGOs and those from field locations already in New York attended an interfaith service at the Riverside Cathedral. Saad and I went there together.

It was Friday the 14th of September, and slowly traffic returned to the streets. Airports were beginning to reopen. I managed to rent a car. It was a strange feeling that evening to cross the George Washington Bridge, the "gateway" to our farm in upstate New York. After many summers of renovating the 200-year-old wooden farmhouse, it had now become a very comfortable place.

Up north the onset of autumn could already be felt. It was a cold and crystal clear night. The sound of sirens and low flying jet fighters had suddenly stopped. For the first time in five days all we heard was silence. And for the first time I found silence unsettling and strange.

Epilogue

The Special Session on Children was held in May 2002. But the glow of the event had faded for me. How times had changed. America was picking up the pieces of the World Trade Centre attack. "Ground Zero" had become a place of mourning and, at the same time, a tourist attraction. The US and the UK, its closest ally, had invaded Afghanistan to fight the Taliban and Al Qaeda on their home turf. There was more disturbing sabre rattling. Iraq was high on the list of America and the UK to be next. Was there ever going to be *un monde digne des enfants?* Would this world ever be worthy of its children?

During three days thousands participated. In plenary, member states reviewed progress for children and reaffirmed global commitments to children's rights. NGO's, academia, business and religious leaders took part in side events. I attended the session on public-private partnership. At the Youth Forum, where A. volunteered as a French translator for Anglophone Palestinian children, Nelson Mandela and Graça Machel announced the tally of the *Say Yes Campaign*. Millions had voted for *Say Yes*. When the famous couple, cheered on by the bystanders, performed a sort of *pirouette* in celebration, I wondered about it all.

A few days later, I left Unicef House for the last time, with an empty feeling and a pinch of sadness, with A. by my side. We were now suddenly alone.

Nobody expressed the feeling of parting better than Harold Nicolson in *"Journey to Java"*. After saying goodbye, together with wife and author Vita Sacksville-West, to his fellow passengers on the Dutch liner *"Willem Ruys"*, he wrote in his travel diary, "Time ceases to be a necklace when only two beads remain on a string".

A. and I had travelled the world, met hundreds of fascinating people, and most of them we would never see again. But the circle was round and closed.

For two months we remained at the farm, now for the last time, to ready this 200 year-old farmhouse for sale, and to retire to France.

Memories to lay to rest, but never to forget.

Goodbye to all that. Mission accomplished!

Boudewijn Mohr
13100 Aix-en-Provence

21230 Culêtre
Côte d'Or

19 January 2018

Annex: References of sources

- Bakker, Vincent: *De Krach van het Kapitaal*, Uitgeverij *De Achterkant*, Leiden 1985
- Black, Maggie: *The Children and the Nations: the Story of Unicef*, 1986
- Black, Maggie: *Children First, The Story of Unicef Past and Present*, Oxford University Press, 1996
- Brisset, Claire and Mohr, Boudewijn: *Quand le tiers-monde subventionne le développement des pays riches*, Le Monde Diplomatique, 8th December 1987
- Chambers, Robert: *Rural Development: putting the last first*, Harlow: Prentice Hall, 1983
- Community of Sant'Egidio: *War, mother of all poverty* – Mozambique
- Cross, Michael: *An unfilled promise: transforming schools in Mozambique*, 2011
- Fifield, Adam: *A mighty purpose: how Jim Grant sold the world on saving its children*, 2015
- Gorbachev, Mikhail: Address at the 43rd UN General Assembly, 7th December 1988
- Griffith-Jones, Stephany: Debt Reduction with a Human Face: The Inter American Development Bank and Unicef Initiative
- Hodges, Anthony: Common Country Analysis São Tomé and Principe
- Innocenti Research Centre, Florence, Italy, 2001: *Jim Grant: Unicef Visionary*
- Interpress Service (IPS): *Mozambique economy, climbing out of the rut*, January 1996
- Jolly, Richard, Andrea Cornia, Giovanni and Stewart, Frances: *The impact of world recession on children*, Oxford University Press, 1987
- Kabou, Axelle: *Et si l'Afrique refusait le Développement?*
- Kronfol, Fouad: *How Jim Grant put Africa on the map*, contribution to *Remembering Jim Grant: Champion for Children*, Savio, Roberto and European Centre for Peace and Development, Belgrade, 2016
- Machel, Graça, 1996: *Impact of armed conflict on children*, United Nations, New York
- Mohr, Boudewijn: Sovereign Debt: Towards a new world order, letter to the Editor, *The Economist*, July 1983
- Mohr, Boudewijn: "Towards an *African* Movement for Children", *RMT Abidjan* November 2001

- Mohr, Boudewijn: Feature articles on sovereign debt of developing countries, *NRC-Handelsblad* 1983–87
- Mohr, Nadim: Notes on UNDP briefing on landmines in Mozambique, March 1996
- Nouvel Observateur: *"Comment sont tombés les Willot"*, Paris, 1st August 1981
- Savio, Roberto and the European Centre for Peace and Development: *Remembering Jim Grant: Champion for Children,* Belgrade 2016
- Stern, Vita: Dutch educational radio programme on Mozambique steet children, *BBC Radio 4,* 1995
- Touré, Abdou: *Petits métiers d'Abidjan* , Editions Karthala, Paris, 1985
- UNESCO: *Governance, Civil Society and NGOs in Mozambique,* Stefano Bellucci, 2002
- Unicef: *Report of the Information/Development Education and Fundraising Workshop*, 11th–14th September 1989
- Unicef: *Annual report Programme Funding Section, Geneva* 1987–88
- Unicef and Basta, Samir, Director, Evaluation Office, Unicef New York: *"The Evaluation and Analysis of Unicef's External Relations Policies and Functions",* 1989
- Unicef: Peace Education in Unicef, Programme Division 1999
- Unicef: 1983 State of the World's Children Report
- Unicef: 1989 State of the World's Children Report
- University of Nairobi and African Studies Centre, Leiden University: *Urban agriculture, Food Security and Nutrition in low income areas of Nairobi,* 1996
- University Eduardo Mondlane, Wageningen University and International Institute for Environment and Development, London: *Trade Liberalisation, Gender and Livelihoods: the Mozambique Cashew Nut Case*
- UPI, *Geldof announces Sport Aid*, 5th March 1986
- Vianello-Chiodo, Marco: *Under-Soldier*, AuthorHouse, Bloomington, IN

About the Author

Prior to joining Unicef in 1985, Boudewijn Mohr was a senior international corporate banker in New York, first with Chase Manhattan Bank in Wall Street, and later at Société Générale's branch in midtown Manhattan. During that time he served on the Board of the First All Children's Theatre (First ACT) in Manhattan, was an active member of the US INSEAD Alumni Association, as well as the Dutch Financial Club.

Joining Unicef in Geneva, his brief was to support its National Committees to diversify their sources of income, more specifically through designing strategies for building partnerships and raising funds with corporations in Europe.

It was not until he reached Africa that Boudewijn Mohr began to feel professional satisfaction and fulfilment of a life's objective: public service in an international organisation "in the field". In the process he acquired more than 25 years of working experience in Africa. His role of a Unicef country programme and operational management specialist took him to some 36 countries on the African continent. Moreover he wrote extensively for Unicef, including Situation Analysis on children and women, mid-term reviews and official documents for Unicef's Executive Board.

He wrote a series of feature articles in the Dutch daily *NRC-Handelsblad* on the sovereign debt crisis as it unfolded in the developing world in the 1980s. He is the author of "The Language of International Trade", published by Regents Publishing Co of New York (Hachette) in 1978.

A national of the Netherlands, Boudewijn Mohr holds a Master degree in Law from Leiden University in the Netherlands and an MBA from INSEAD, Fontainebleau, France.

www.ingramcontent.com/pod-product-compliance
Lightning Source LLC
Chambersburg PA
CBHW020829160426
43192CB00007B/575